INVESTING ON A SHOESTRING

Barbara O'Neill, Ph.D., CFP

DEARBORN™
A **Kaplan Professional** Company

Dedication

This book is dedicated to the two people in my life who provide untiring love, encouragement, and support: my mother, Mary O'Neill, and my husband, Gene Bronson. Both of you are truly "the wind beneath my wings" and I thank you.

Editorial Director: Cynthia A. Zigmund
Managing Editor: Jack Kiburz
Interior Design: the dotted i
Cover Design: DePinto Studios
Typesetting: the dotted i

Library of Congress Cataloging-in-Publication Data

O'Neill, Barbara M.
  Investing on a shoestring / Barbara O'Neill.
    p.   cm.
  Includes index.
  ISBN 0-7931-3016-6 (pbk.)
    1. Investments.   2. Finance, Personal.   3. Retirement—Planning.
  I. Title.
  HG4521.0516 1999
  332.6—dc21   98-53433
                                                                  CIP

Dearborn books are available at special quantity discounts to use as premiums and sales promotions, or for use in corporate training programs. For more information, please call the Special Sales Manager at 800-621-9621, ext. 4514, or write to Dearborn Financial Publishing, Inc., 155 North Wacker Drive, Chicago, IL 60606-1719.

Contents

Foreword

Never before has investing successfully been more important for the average American. The days of lavish employer-paid pensions are diminishing for many employees and gone for the vast majority of Americans. The promise of government-financed retirement through generous Social Security payments was always overstated and is becoming more illusory than ever in light of the coming crisis in funding baby boomers' retirements. With companies and the government increasingly turning over the responsibility of funding people's retirements to the people themselves, it is crucial that they understand how to maximize their investment opportunities on their own. At the same time, investors in the 1990s have experienced the most prolonged and powerful bull market in history, and more and more people have wanted to learn about the sometimes arcane world of stock, bond, and mutual fund investing.

Barbara O'Neill's *Investing on a Shoestring* will teach you what you need to know to get started on a successful investment program, especially if you have a small amount of money to invest. She helps you set investment goals, figure out how much risk you can afford to take, and even helps you find the money you need to get started. So much successful investing is getting into the right habits, and Barbara helps you establish those patterns by helping you reduce your debt and invest automatically in low-cost mutual funds and individual stocks. She offers simple, practical tips that allow you to avoid the most common mistakes that investors make, while setting up procedures that increase your odds of earning substantial returns over time.

Investing on a Shoestring is loaded with specific resources to help you put general investing principles into action. There are names and phone numbers of mutual funds with low minimum initial and subsequent investments, trade associations to inform you about investing, software programs and Web sites that help you analyze your choices, and much more. Put this book and these resources to work and you can assemble a sizable portfolio!

—Jordan Elliot Goodman, Author, *Everyone's Money Book*, Financial Analyst on *NBC News*, and former Wall Street Correspondent for *Money* Magazine

Preface

In 1995, I wrote *Saving on a Shoestring*, a book that extols the advantages of saving money and describes dozens of tips for "finding" small amounts of money to save. Assuming you've gotten the savings "religion" (and I hope you have!), you'll find *Investing on a Shoestring* a logical sequel. Why? Because, while saving is an important—and necessary—first step toward financial security, history tells us that investing, especially over long time frames in a diversified portfolio that includes equities such as stocks and growth mutual funds, is a tried and true way to accumulate wealth. Using a baseball analogy, saving money in a bank passbook account or certificate of deposit is like hitting a single or double. Investing in well-chosen investments with good historical performance is the financial equivalent of a home run.

The two enemies of anyone trying to set money aside for future financial goals are taxes and inflation. Savers generally get clobbered when these two factors work in tandem against them. Take a saver earning 3.5 percent on a bank savings account. After paying federal income tax at the 28 percent rate, they're left with a 2.52 percent after-tax return, and even less if state income taxes are owed. Inflation has averaged between 2 percent and 3 percent annually in recent years so the 3.5 percent rate saver ends up with a very low or even negative real rate of return. It's like our saver is trying to climb a steep mountain (goal) and for every three steps forward, he or she falls back at least two. The moral of the story: Savings accounts are a great place to get started but, after setting aside several months' worth of expenses for emergencies, it's time to put your money somewhere where it can grow at a faster rate.

History tells us that investments such as stocks and bonds have the potential to provide a higher return than low-risk, low-return savings products. Between 1926 and 1997, stocks as an asset class (as represented by the Standard and Poor's 500 index—not any one particular company's stock) earned an 11 percent average annual return. Treasury bills, as an indicator of the return earned from cash investments, barely exceeded the average annual inflation rate and actually lost value after factoring in the loss due to taxes. With an 11 percent return in stocks, however, a long-term investor paying taxes at the 20 percent long-term capital gains rate would have earned almost 9 percent after taxes and more than 5 percent after inflation. Instead of climbing the mountain and falling back almost to square one, long-term investors generally make steady progress toward their financial goals because they earn a positive real rate of return.

Sounds so simple, doesn't it? Just plop your bank account balance into a hot stock or two and watch the money roll in, right? Not so fast! There are several important preliminary steps that *Investing on a Shoestring* describes in detail. One important prerequisite is an "investor's mind-set." What does this mean? Very simply, being psychologically ready to accept the uncertainty that comes with the territory of investing. Instead of that predictable (albeit low) 3.5 percent bank account rate, investment returns can—and do—vary. Even worse, you could lose all or part of the amount originally invested (principal). A drop in the stock market could take your growth or index mutual funds down with it and a rise in interest rates will make your bonds worth less than their face value. Knowledgeable and experienced investors accept these risks and take investment price swings in stride. Clueless or less experienced investors, on the other hand, often panic and sell their investments at a loss.

Another common investment error is *analysis paralysis*. When faced with an overwhelming array of financial decisions (e.g., over 12,000 mutual funds to choose from), many people freeze and do nothing. Yet, *not* making a decision (e.g., keeping money in a low-interest bank account instead of transferring it to a higher-yielding investment product) is a decision in and of itself. Often, people lose as much (if not more!) money from these decisions that they *don't* make than from the decisions they do. *Investing on a Shoestring* will demystify the investing process and increase your level of knowledge. As you read about concepts such as asset allocation and tax deferral and descriptions of specific investment products such as index funds and zero-coupon bonds, your comfort level and sense of empowerment will increase. You'll become a more informed investor and will be less likely to make emotionally driven investment decisions or to become an easy mark for investment fraud.

Like its predecessor, *Saving on a Shoestring, Investing on a Shoestring* starts with the premise that investing is possible with small amounts of money. Three important prerequisites are necessary, however: a "can do" positive attitude (remember, *any* amount of investing is better than *no* investing), positive cash flow (you need to spend less than you earn), and clearly defined financial goals (i.e., something to invest for). Another related success factor is debt reduction. If you can lower the amount paid to creditors, for example, by switching your credit card balance to a low-rate card, you'll have "found" money available to invest (e.g., $50 a month to dollar-cost-average into a mutual fund).

Investing on a Shoestring was written with real American families in mind. After 20 years as an adult educator with Rutgers University, I've observed that people want easy-to-digest personal finance information that they can readily apply to their own lives. Perhaps you want to take a specific action, such as to purchase stock, or to simply confirm that you've made good choices and are on the right track. Many people also appreciate lists and questions and recommended resources to help them distill available information to a manageable level from which to make important decisions. This book contains all three in an effort to personalize its contents and help you adapt it to your life.

I hope that you'll find *Investing on a Shoestring* a valuable personal finance reference. Use it to define your investment goals and to develop and implement a plan of action to achieve them. Whatever you do, don't delay getting started. Many people make the mistake of waiting to make their first investment until "the market improves" or they get a raise or some other external event "happens." This is a mistake. Remember that compound interest is not retroactive: It needs time—preferably several decades—to work its magic. The best time to start investing on a shoestring is today.

Be healthy, wealthy, and happy.

—Barbara O'Neill, Ph.D., CFP

Acknowledgments

My sincere thanks to the following individuals and organizations that have helped to transform *Investing on a Shoestring* from a concept to reality:

- Cynthia Zigmund, editorial director at Dearborn Financial Publishing, for believing in the project and assisting with its completion

- Cook College, Rutgers University, a generous employer that has enabled me to develop my financial planning knowledge and skills

- The American Savings Education Council (ASEC) and its president, Don Blandin, for granting permission to reproduce the *Ballpark Estimate* retirement planning worksheet

- *The New Jersey Herald* (Newton, N.J.) for providing me the opportunity to improve my skills as a financial journalist for the past 20 years

Developing an Investor's Mind-Set

You may delay, but time will not.

—Benjamin Franklin

Four things can not come back: the spoken word, the spent arrow, the past, and the neglected opportunity.

—Omar Ibn Al-Halif

Do what you can, with what you have, where you are.

—Theodore Roosevelt

This book was designed to help people with limited investment experience make a successful transition from saver to investor and build wealth over time. Furthermore, it assumes that readers will be able to invest small sums of money at regular intervals (for example, per paycheck) rather than reposition a large amount of cash all at once. In short, it was written for most Americans whose largest financial "asset" isn't their assets—but their earning power. To get started, let's look at the fundamental differences between saving and investing.

Many people use the words *saving* and *investing* interchangeably to describe actions taken to position their money. They might say "I'm saving for retirement in a mutual fund" or "I just invested $5,000 in a bank CD." Although there has definitely been a blurring of the lines between financial products in recent years with deregulation of the banking industry, there are still distinct differences between saving and investing. Each type of cash management has its own purpose and characteristics and should not be confused with the other. Ideally, you'll have funds in both savings and investments because, together, they provide diversification and reduce financial risk.

The goal of savings is to provide funds for emergencies and near-term purchases, like the purchase of a new car in two years. Many financial experts recommend setting aside an emergency fund of three to six months' expenses (about $6,000 to $12,000 for a household with $2,000 of monthly expenses). Savings products provide a "parking place" for at least some of this money and keep it safe without fluctuation in the value of principal (the amount originally set aside). At least one to two months' worth of expenses should be placed in interest-bearing accounts insured by the federal government or in products known for their liquidity (that is, in the form of cash or easily converted to cash with minimal or no loss of value). Savings principal remains intact and earns a fixed or variable rate of return.

Examples of savings products include cash equivalents such as bank passbook and money market deposit accounts, short-term certificates of deposit (CDs), and money market mutual funds. The downside of savings products is their generally lower yields compared to longer-term investments. A saver's principal is safe but it earns a low rate of return, which is even lower (and sometimes even a loss) when inflation and taxes are considered.

The goal of investing is to increase net worth and accumulate funds for financial goals, such as retirement. Historical investment return data tell us that investing beats saving hands down as the way to build wealth over time. Between 1926 and 1997, U.S. large company stocks averaged an 11 percent annual return, compared to only 5.2 percent for government bonds and 3.8 percent for Treasury bills, according to the Chicago investment research firm Ibbotson Associates. Inflation during this period averaged 3.1 percent, virtually negating the after-tax return of cash assets (savings).

The downside of investing is that it involves more risk. Investment earnings are generally not guaranteed but, instead, fluctuate with changes in market conditions. In addition, you could lose all or part of your original investment (principal). Examples of investments include: stocks, bonds, real estate, growth or income mutual funds, futures contracts, and collectibles such as antiques and coins.

Why Be an Investor?

With more investment options today than ever before and the recent reduction of capital gains tax rates, now more than ever it pays to be an investor. Consider the following ten advantages.

1. Higher returns. Historically, the rate of return provided by stocks and bonds has exceeded that of cash equivalents. According to data compiled by Ibbotson Associates, over the past 72 years people with all of their money in cash assets barely would have kept up with inflation and probably had a negative return after taxes.

2. The magic of compounding. Over time, compounding magnifies the difference in the returns of asset classes. According to Ibbotson Associates, a dollar invested in stock in 1950 grew to $287 by 1996. That same dollar invested in five-year Treasury notes grew to only $17. Over 46 years, the difference in growth of the two asset classes differed by a 17:1 ratio, not a 3:1 or 2:1 ratio as many people would expect by looking at the average annual returns.

3. Long-term growth. Money grows faster over time in investment products than in savings. From 1926 to 1997, that 11 percent average annual return in stocks doubled investors' money approximately every seven years. To figure out how fast money doubles, use the rule of 72. Simply divide an investment's return into 72 (72 divided by 11 = 6.55) to determine the number of years it takes for a sum of money to double. Short-term savings products, as measured by the return on Treasury bills, averaged a 3.8 percent return over the past 70 years. At this rate, it would take almost 20 years (72 divided by 3.8 = 18.95) for a sum of money to double.

4. Time diversification. It is a proven fact that time decreases the volatility, that is, the ups and downs, of investment prices. This is especially true for stocks and mutual funds that invest in stocks. For this reason, investors should know the time frame for their financial goals and plan on investing for at least five years to reduce the risk of loss. Another key to success is simply not putting all your eggs in one basket. For example, it is wise to select stocks of companies that are affected differently by the same economic events. For instance, if oil prices rise, oil companies would profit but airlines that consume huge quantities of fuel would find their profit margins eroding.

5. Relative safety. Of the three major classes of assets—stocks, bonds, and cash equivalents—stocks provide the greatest potential reward and have the greatest amount of risk. Having said that, it also can be argued that the relative safety of stocks increases with time. A study by the New York brokerage firm J&W Seligman examined investment returns between 1950 and 1995 and found that the worst five-year return for big company stocks (a 2.36 percent loss) was almost identical to the worst returns for supposedly safer corporate and government bonds (losses of 2.22 percent and 2.14 percent, respectively). Over 10- and 20-year periods, stocks actually did a better job of protecting principal than bonds did.

6. Tax-free investing options. Except for low-return, tax-exempt municipal money market funds, interest earned on savings products, such as CDs and bank accounts, is fully taxable. A number of investments, on the other hand, provide tax-free income, which is especially beneficial to high marginal tax bracket investors. Available options include individual state or local municipal bonds, municipal bond unit trusts, and tax-exempt municipal bond mutual funds.

7. Affordability. You don't need the wealth of Donald Trump or Bill Gates to start investing. Many investments require only small dollar amounts to get started. Examples include stocks that offer direct purchase plans and mutual funds that open accounts for $1,000 or less. You can reduce the average cost of an investment over time by depositing a fixed amount at regular intervals, for example, $100 per month, a strategy called dollar cost averaging (DCA). DCA won't protect you from losses but it does fit the way most people receive money to invest: weekly, biweekly, or monthly, depending on how often they get paid.

8. Mix and match possibilities. Savings products pay a relatively low rate of return in exchange for their low level of risk. Period. Investments, on the other hand, provide the opportunity to combine assets to provide a return that investors desire at a level of risk they can live with. The more stock in the asset allocation mix, the greater the potential return with a higher probability of loss. For example, a 10.6 percent return was achieved between 1950 and 1997 with a 60 percent stock, 30 percent bonds, and 10 percent cash mix. The largest one-year loss was –22 percent. With a mix of 40 percent stock, 50 percent bonds, and 10 percent cash, however, the average annual return dropped to 9.2 percent, but the largest one-year loss also dropped (to –14 percent).

9. Upside market bias. Investing in equities (investments that provide ownership in a company or property) has its rewards amidst the challenges. In 20 of the 72 years between 1926 and 1997, stocks had negative returns. The worst single year, 1931, was –43.3 percent. Thus, in about two of every seven years, stocks performed poorly. Looking at the data more positively, however, note that there were 52 up years. Five-year Treasury notes had 65 up years and only seven down years during the past seven decades. Clearly, financial markets have an upward tendency. Of course, historical performance data doesn't provide any future guarantees . . . but it is a helpful guide for investment decisions.

10. Plentiful opportunity. A multitude of investment options abound including over 12,000 mutual funds, three types of individual retirement accounts (IRAs) (Roth, traditional deductible, and traditional nondeductible), and employer salary-reduction plans (for example, 401(k)s and 403(b)s). Their common denominator is that consumers must make their own investment decisions and review their performance periodically. Also plentiful are personal finance resources including books, magazines, and Web sites, many of which are described in the resources section at the end of the book.

Today, there is simply no excuse for *not* investing, assuming you can find the money to do so (see Chapter 4 for ideas). And don't worry, you won't be alone as an investment "newbie." According to the December 1996 *Journal of Financial Planning*, 70 percent of all money ever invested in mutual funds was invested during the previous four years. In short, investing has gone mainstream with millions of investors—new and experienced—taking charge of their financial future. You, too, can be one of them.

Staying Ahead of Taxes and Inflation

The two enemies of anyone trying to accumulate money for future goals are inflation and taxes. As noted previously, investing provides the best opportunity to beat inflation and taxes, especially over the long term. A simple formula to use to determine the investment return you need just to break even after taxes and inflation is to divide an assumed inflation rate by 100 minus your marginal tax bracket. You must exceed the result in order for your nest egg to grow.

Here's an example. If inflation is assumed to average 4 percent and you are in the 15 percent tax bracket, the rate of return needed to break even is 4.7 percent. In the 28 percent tax bracket, the breakeven rate with a 4 percent inflation assumption is now 5.5 percent. The math for these calculations is as follows:

Breakeven rate (15% bracket) = 4 ÷ (100% − 15%) or .85 = 4.7%
Breakeven rate (28% bracket) = 4 ÷ (100% − 28%) or .72 = 5.5%

Note that a 4 percent inflation rate is used for illustrative purposes. You can be as optimistic or as conservative as you wish with the assumption you make for the rate of inflation.

Can you break even with all of your money in savings products? Perhaps. You might be able to find some CDs or a money market fund that barely tops your breakeven figure. But if you want to build wealth without taking decades to do so (remember The Rule of 72!), aim for an average investment return of at least 2 percent to 4 percent above your breakeven rate. This doesn't mean, however, that *every* asset you own has to earn more than the breakeven rate: just their weighted average. Consider the following: an investor with 50 percent of his or her assets in 10 percent growth mutual funds, 40 percent in 7 percent government bonds, and 10 percent in a 4 percent money market mutual fund. The investor's weighted average return would be 8.2 percent, calculated as follows:

$$50\% \times .10 = 5.0\%$$
$$40\% \times .07 = 2.8$$
$$10\% \times .04 = \underline{.4}$$
$$\text{Total} \qquad 8.2\%$$

In this hypothetical example, the 8.2 percent average rate of return is 3.5 percent above the breakeven rate for taxpayers in the 15 percent bracket and 2.7 percent above the required rate for those in the 28 percent bracket. Compare this to perhaps a 5 percent return on CDs that just barely tops the breakeven rate for the 15 percent tax bracket investors and falls below the breakeven return for those with higher incomes. The moral of the story: Investments—not savings—will move you closest to your financial goals. It is important to accept, and plan for, taxes and inflation and earn enough to offset their negative effects.

What Is an "Investor's Mind-Set?"

As noted in the preface, an *investor's mind-set* is an important prerequisite for successful investing. Having one simply means feeling comfortable enough to accept the volatility and uncertainty that comes with the territory of investing. As noted previously, savers can expect no loss of principal and a predictable (albeit low) rate of return. Investors, on the other hand, can lose their original investment and often find their returns fluctuating widely. To state it another way, you can't expect a growth mutual fund to behave like a bank CD. It's not going to happen. When you cross the line from saving to investing, it's time to ditch the "CD mentality" (that is, expecting predictable returns and safety of principal) and, instead, become familiar with characteristics of your chosen investments. Not to do so is foolish and can result in undue stress, perhaps even health problems, in addition to financial losses.

To explain what can happen without an investor's mind-set, let me tell you two true stories. Every once in a while I attend a brokerage firm seminar when there is a topic of personal interest. One night, while leaving such an event, I was handed a piece of paper by "Clueless Investor A," who was distributing leaflets disparaging the major national brokerage firm that had sponsored the session. His face was beet red and he was seething with anger, so much so that I thought he'd have a heart attack. On his flyer, Clueless accused the brokerage firm of losing almost $18,000 of his money. I continued to read on, expecting to see mention of "churning" by a broker or some exotic investment like cattle futures, options, or penny stocks. To my surprise, it was none of the above. Instead, I realized that Clueless simply lacked an investor's mind-set. Worse yet, he also lacked an understanding of the characteristics of fixed-income investments.

It turned out that Clueless hadn't purchased anything speculative at all but, rather, U.S. Treasury notes, one of the safest and most conservative investments available. Market interest rates had simply been fluctuating (as they always do) since his purchase. Clueless was characterizing a paper loss, caused by fluctuating interest rates, as an "out of pocket cost" (his words) and blaming the brokerage firm because he panicked and didn't understand the concept of interest rate risk. This is the risk associated with the purchase of bonds or mutual funds that invest in bonds, such as income funds. The basic premise is this: When interest rates go up, bond prices go down. The reverse is also true: When interest rates go down, bond prices go up. Thus, there is an inverse relationship between interest rates and bond prices. If you hold bonds to maturity, interest rate risk is not an issue. Investors get their full principal back (although it will buy less because of inflation). Where interest rate risk is a concern is when investors need to sell a bond prior to maturity or when they panic like Clueless did after seeing a smaller number than their original investment on an account statement.

"Clueless Investor B," who I saw in a counseling session the very next day, caused me even more concern. Like many people I meet, she wanted a 20 percent return on her money with no risk of loss of principal. Once we cleared that up (read: lots of luck!), I looked at her portfolio. Clueless had over $500,000 of assets but absolutely no idea of what she owned or why or how her investments were performing. She also seemed too eager to have someone—anyone—do her financial decision making for her. What can we learn from my experiences with Clueless Investors A and B? Two things:

1. If you don't understand an investment, or you feel that it is beyond your risk tolerance level, don't buy it. Instead, make the time—through reading or seminars—to learn about characteristics, such as interest rate risk, of various investment options.

2. Seek professional assistance if you'd rather do anything else than manage money. Many certified financial planners, brokerage firms, and commercial bank trust departments provide asset management services, usually for a percentage of the assets being managed. Delegate, but don't abdicate, responsibility however.

Other Investing Prerequisites

In addition to an investor's mind-set, there are three more things you need to have before investing: an adequate emergency fund, comprehensive insurance coverage, and low consumer debt. The rationale for the first two is pretty obvious: You don't want to have to pull money out of an investment because you lose your job or suffer an uninsured loss (e.g., disability). As for low consumer debt, there is no better investment (guaranteed rate, risk free, tax free) than paying off an 18 percent credit card. As long as large amounts of consumer debt are hanging over your head, it's hard to move ahead financially. Below are additional details about each prerequisite.

Adequate Emergency Fund

As noted previously in the description of savings, cash equivalent assets are necessary to quickly provide funds for emergencies without loss of principal. Examples of financial emergencies include: unemployment, a broken car or appliances, and immediate travel to visit an ill loved one. To determine if your emergency reserve is adequate, divide the amount of your liquid assets (savings) by the total of monthly expenses. The result is your *liquidity ratio*. Here's an example: A family with $5,000 of liquid assets and monthly expenses of $1,700 have a liquidity ratio of 2.94 (5,000 divided by 1,700), just under the minimum recommended amount. In other words, their savings would provide 2.94 months of living expenses. Should they save more? It depends. The fewer safety nets (e.g., stable jobs, two employed spouses) a family has, the more emergency savings they should probably amass. Emergency funds in excess of 2 to 3 months' expenses should be put in CDs, a short-term bond fund, or a diversified stock fund to avoid the loss of purchasing power.

Comprehensive Insurance

Before investing, make sure that you have purchased the following types of coverage:

- At least a 100/300/50 liability and property damage limit on auto insurance

- Renters (HO-4) insurance equal to the replacement cost of personal property (if you are a tenant)

- Homeowners insurance with at least a $300,000 liability limit, replacement cost coverage on personal property, and dwelling coverage equal to at least 80 percent of the replacement value of your home (Ask your agent to help you calculate this.)

- Adequate life insurance if a spouse and/or children depend on your income (Ask your agent to do a needs analysis to determine the proper amount of coverage on family earners.)

- Adequate (at least $1 million per person) major medical health coverage for all family members, either as an employee benefit or through an individually purchased policy

- Disability income (DI) insurance, which protects wage earners unable to work because of illness or accident by replacing a portion of lost income. The best DI policies define disability as the inability to fulfill regular duties of your current occupation and will replace at least 60 percent of your income through retirement age.

Low Consumer Debt

According to a January 1998 article in *The Wall Street Journal*, typical U.S. households pay about $1,000 a year in interest and fees on $7,000 to $8,000 credit card balances. The longer consumer debt lingers, the more it costs and the longer it ties up future income. With the exception of tax-deferred retirement plans (especially those with employer matching) and emergency savings, there is probably no good reason to set aside money that will return less than the amount earned by accelerating debt repayment. Once debts are repaid, that $1,000 a year formerly spent on interest can be invested without affecting household cash flow (read: your lifestyle) one iota. With an average 9 percent return, $1,000 invested annually for 20 years will be worth about $51,000.

Tips to Get Started

A common financial practice for many American families is living paycheck to paycheck. A characteristic of this lifestyle is that there's barely enough money to pay bills and little or nothing to invest for the future. Yet, many other people are able to grow rich over time and retire in comfort. Do they have some secret or magic formula? Hardly. But, then again, they obviously did something right or they wouldn't have done so well. Experts often recommend the following ten strategies or cite them as reasons why investors are successful.

1. Set financial goals. It's much easier to invest for something specific than to just put money aside without a plan. Begin by writing down the things you want to do or purchase in the future and an approximate cost and time deadline for each financial goal. For added motivation, "get close" to your goals. Post pictures of them on your refrigerator or, in the case of a car, take it for a test drive. Then "Swiss cheese" your goal by poking it full of holes (small, doable steps). For example, disregarding both inflation and investment earnings to keep things simple, $30,000 for a child's college education will require an annual investment of $3,000 ($58 per week) for ten years.

2. Match investments to goals. The deadline for a financial goal should match the holding period of an investment. Never fund a long-term goal (e.g., retirement) with a short-term product (e.g., money market fund) or a short-term goal (e.g., closing costs for a house) with a long-term product (e.g., stock).

3. Live below your means. Find the leaks in your spending that hemorrhage money and then use this found income to invest. One example is snacks and soda at vending machines that can cost several hundred dollars a year. Invest that amount at just 5 percent interest and you'd have more than $2,200 in five years.

4. Start early. Time can be an investor's best friend. Not only can it reduce the long-term risk of certain investments but, combined with systematic deposits and products that earn more than the rate of inflation, it can produce spectacular growth. Funding long-term goals in early adulthood will mean a significantly greater accumulation of money.

5. Be realistic. Hillary Clinton's cattle futures story aside, few people—and especially neophyte investors—ever make a killing overnight on their investments. Instead, they grow rich slowly over time. The tradeoff for a higher return is generally more risk. Deals that sound too good to be true usually are.

6. Invest at work. Enroll in a tax-deferred employer retirement savings plan, such as a 401(k) or 403(b), and invest the maximum amount allowed. Your employer will deduct—and deposit—a predetermined amount of your salary. These plans are especially attractive if your employer matches your contribution (e.g., 50 cents on the dollar). Employees can usually choose to invest either a percentage of their pay (e.g., 5 %) or a fixed dollar amount (e.g., $20 per paycheck).

7. Invest automatically. Where possible, investments should be automated so you don't need to remember where and when to make deposits. A common example is authorizing a mutual fund to debit your bank account by a fixed amount each month to purchase additional shares.

8. Seek assistance. Periodicals such as *Money* and *The Wall Street Journal* contain a wealth of information, as do personal finance television programs, books, Web sites, and seminars. Financial professionals also can provide helpful information.

9. Keep good records. Good records are important for tax purposes to monitor and report capital gains and losses. They also are helpful to analyze the performance of investments over time.

10. Think positively. Some people never start investing because they say they'll never be able to accumulate enough money to fund big-ticket items, such as college or retirement. While this may or

PRIMERICA
Financial Services

Charles S. Marsh

(215) 654-1282
Fax: (215) 654-7889

800-232-8200

Piney Pine Elen

00596791

A Member of *TravelersGroup*

may not be true (depending on their definition of *enough*), it is a fact that *any* investing is better than no investing at all. Think positively about the accumulation that is possible and picture yourself achieving at least one financial goal. As with many things in life, when there's a will, there's a way.

Investment Fraud and How to Avoid It

Each year, thousands of consumers lose billions of dollars to investment fraud. Fraudulent marketers these days have a new weapon in their arsenal: computer technology. It is not uncommon for con artists to use a computer bulletin board to post "urgent" messages telling users to buy a particular stock. This fraud, called pump and dump, artificially inflates the price of shares and allows stock manipulators to make a huge profit by selling their shares before values fall.

Scam artists also continue to use the mail and telephones to take advantage of unsuspecting investors, often mimicking the sales techniques of legitimate investment firms. So-called *boiler rooms* remain a favorite way for swindlers to contact large numbers of potential victims. Even if a swindler has to make several hundred calls to find a *mooch* (one of the terms that swindlers use for their victims), the opportunity to pocket thousands of dollars of someone's life savings is still good pay for the time and expense involved.

So how do you know if an investment is legitimate? According to *Consumer Reports* magazine and the Federal Trade Commission (FTC), there are several red flags to help you spot an investment scam, no matter how it is presented:

- *Future predictions.* Beware of marketers that guarantee an investment's future return. Many fraudulent marketers call consumers several times: first to make a prediction and, next, to close a sale after they prove that their prediction came true.

- *Fast bucks.* Scam artists often promise fast, low-risk payoffs and compare their returns to low rates available on bank accounts or bonds. There is no such thing as a free lunch. Even with perfectly legal investments, the higher an investment's potential yield, the higher the potential risk of loss.

- *Obscure origins.* Background information about the origin and performance of fraudulent investments is misleading or not provided. This is because marketers do not want consumers to be able to assess their claims. Be wary, also, if you can't find information about a product in reputable investment publications (e.g., stock listings in newspapers).

- *Immediate response.* Requiring an immediate response and deposit of funds is another hallmark of investment fraud. Marketers might say that "you must buy before others find out about it" or request that you send money by courier or overnight delivery. Urgency is important to swindlers: so they get your money fast and so you don't have time to become suspicious or contact others for advice.

- *Recovery attempts.* Fraud victims' names are widely circulated. If you've fallen prey to a previous scam, you could get a call promising to recover the money you've already lost. Of course, this service comes at a price. Be suspicious if people call and already know where you've invested before.

Another type of fraud that's also becoming popular today is so-called identity fraud. This is where a caller, claiming to be offering a credit card or prize, asks people to reveal personal information such as their Social Security number or mother's maiden name. They then use this information to open fraudulent accounts in the victim's name. Victims of identity fraud may not feel the impact for months until they apply for a loan or start getting contacted by creditors.

The bottom line: Beware of callers you don't know and be very wary of disclosing personal or financial information over the phone. If you don't want a seller to call you back, say so. If they call back, hang up. If an investment deal sounds too good to be true, it probably is. The safest course when investing is to initiate the process yourself, deal only with well-established local or national financial services firms, and follow this advice from the FTC:

- Don't buy investments from unfamiliar companies.

- Ask for written information, such as a prospectus, about an offer.

- Check out unfamiliar companies or suspicious offers with government agencies.

- Don't be pressured into making an immediate decision.

- Don't give out bank or credit card numbers on calls you don't initiate.

As long as unwary investors fall prey to unscrupulous promoters, investment fraud will continue. Your best line of defense against investment fraud is to ask plenty of questions and—until you get the right answers—to just say no.

Common Investment Errors

Even when investors are able to steer clear of scams and fraud, they can—and do—make mistakes. Listed below are 20 common investment errors to avoid.

1. Unclear investment objectives. Investors need to understand both what they own and why they own it. In other words, what financial goal do you want to achieve with an investment and when do you want to achieve it?

2. Investing without understanding. I'll never forget the day that two clients tearfully told me about their venture into a West Virginia gas drilling limited partnership. All they knew was that the salesperson who had promised them a 20 percent return was in jail and that they had lost all their money. NEVER make an investment without understanding both its costs and characteristics. If you don't understand an investment or feel uncomfortable about the risk involved, don't buy it. Instead, keep learning about various investments and find a more suitable alternative.

3. Failure to adapt to changing conditions. Changes that affect investment decisions include economic indicators such as the consumer price index and Dow Jones Industrial Average, new tax laws, and changes in personal circumstances such as widowhood or a new job.

4. Investing today with yesterday's products. Investing is no longer always a "buy and hold" proposition. New investment products and services continue to be introduced and need to at least be considered. Three recent examples are Roth IRAs, online stock trading firms, and inflation-adjusted Treasury securities.

5. Analysis paralysis. With an overwhelming array of investment choices and information overload, some investors freeze and do nothing. In fear of making the wrong choice—or any choice—they stand pat financially which, although they may not realize it, is in and of itself a decision.

6. Fad investing. Gold . . . variable annuities . . . momentum funds . . . some people see an investment in the news a lot and automatically assume that it's the right place to put their money—until the next investment fad comes along.

7. Assuming cash assets are risk-free. As noted previously, the return on cash equivalents, such as CDs and money market funds, barely (if at all) keeps pace with inflation and taxes. While principal remains intact, the purchasing power of cash assets can become severely eroded.

8. Market timing. Basically, it's futile. Even the pros don't do it well. As the New York state lottery is fond of saying, "You have to be in it to win it." Investors who try to time the market invariably lose out on some of the biggest gains, because they have to be right twice: when to get in and when to get out.

9. Investing solely on reputation. An investment's reputation is usually based on past performance and, in some cases, hearsay or misinformation. Whatever the source of an investment's reputation, any prospectus will tell you that past performance should not be used as an indicator of future results.

10. Emotion-driven decisions. Not everyone has the stomach to invest in traditionally volatile long-term bonds, stocks, and stock mutual funds. Investors who are susceptible to sleepless nights or selling in a panic should avoid volatile investments.

11. Ignoring investment advice. This includes tips from financial professionals (such as the CPA who says you should start a simplified employee pension to shelter self-employment income) to consensus opinions among financial experts. If five or six financial publications, for example, recommend the same mutual fund, there is probably good cause to explore it.

12. Ignoring transaction costs. Expenses such as taxes, brokerage commissions, and mutual fund 12b-1 fees can take a big chunk out of investment performance. Look for ways to reduce transaction costs and purchase investments with below-average expenses.

13. Inconsistent investment selection. Investors should stick to their financial objectives and risk tolerance level when making investment decisions. To do otherwise is to risk buying assets that do not reflect your goals and emotions.

14. Overdiversification. Some investors seize virtually every opportunity that comes along and end up owning dozens of overlapping stocks and/or mutual funds. Don't buy more investments than you can handle—keep seven or eight *different* mutual funds, tops. Otherwise, you'll be drowning in paperwork, especially at tax time. You also could end up with a *closet index fund*, that is, owning virtually all of the stocks that comprise a market index, but with the expenses of individual actively managed accounts instead of a lower-cost index fund.

15. Underdiversification. It is also a mistake to spread your money among too few investments so that there is a disproportionate amount in any one type of asset or industry. A common example: workers who place the bulk of their retirement assets in employer stock. Not only is their livelihood tied to one company but so is their future financial security. Another example of underdiversification is neglecting the opportunity to profit through international investing.

16. Profits taken too soon. Some people move in and out of investments too quickly. They buy high and sell low. The mutual fund research firm Morningstar showed what happens by comparing fund returns versus actual investor returns of 219 growth funds for the five years ending May 31, 1994. The difference was startling: 12.5 percent for the funds themselves versus –2.5 percent for individual investors. Many people simply don't hang in there long enough to reap the rewards that the stock market offers over time.

17. Losses allowed to run. The exact opposite problem is to not sell investments that are on the decline. Investors either can't be bothered, are oblivious to their poor performance, or are waiting for a turnaround that may never happen. Another reason for not selling a loser is that it is psychologically difficult to admit we made a mistake. Nevertheless, if there has been a sustained drop in investment performance, a sale is probably in order.

18. Lack of understanding of tax laws. Tax avoidance is the use of available methods to reduce tax liability to its lowest legal amount. Taxes should always be a factor (although not the *only* factor) in investment decision making. Example: selecting between a taxable corporate bond or a tax-exempt municipal bond. Investors who ignore the tax consequences of their investments often earn less than they have to.

19. Ignorance of the time value of money. A dollar today is worth more in the future because it can be invested to earn dividends or interest. Many investors fail to recognize the awesome impact of compound interest that has sometimes been dubbed "the eighth wonder of the world." Instead, they procrastinate and take years to make their first investment. Remember that even small amounts of money, given some time, will grow to tidy sums. In addition, compound interest is at its best in a tax-free or tax-deferred investment.

20. Unrealistic expectations. This is a dangerous error, especially now as investors follow four successive years (1995–98) where the Standard and Poor's 500 stock index delivered gains greater than 20 percent. Many investors, especially "newbies," now think this is normal. Yet it is simply unrealistic to expect a consistent 20 percent return on common stocks or index funds (or any other investment, for that matter!) and investors would be unwise to do so. Instead, the Ibbotson data tell us that in any one year between 1926 and 1997, stocks lost as much as 43.3 percent and gained as much as 54 percent. As stocks are held longer, their volatility decreases. Investment expectations should be based on long-term historical returns and not recent short-term performance.

2

What Are You Investing For?

*Obstacles are those frightful things you see when
you take your eyes off your goals.*

—Sydney Smith

Do you have financial goals or are they financial dreams? What's the difference, you say? A financial dream, for example, to accumulate wealth, is often vague and ill-defined. Other examples include: "I/we want to retire comfortably" or "I/we want to send a child to a good college" or "In a few years, I/we want to buy a house." These are all dreams, not goals. Goals are specific plans or purposes that people have in life. A goal should be written down and have a beginning and ending date as well as a targeted amount needed to invest. Examples of financial goals include: "I/we will have $15,000 set aside in three years for the down payment on a house" or "By the time a child is 18, I/we will have $30,000 invested to partially pay college tuition" or "By the time I/we reach age 62, there will be enough invested to retire on 80 percent of preretirement income."

Financial goals are action-oriented. Ideally, they are the driving force behind investment decisions. Setting goals helps determine how much you need to set aside, and at what interest rate, in order to achieve what is important to you. Financial goals can be easily monitored when they are specific. They should be written with a dollar cost and a time frame (e.g., to save $2,000 by the year 2000). That way you'll know how you're progressing toward your goal. Once your financial goals are specified, they may need to be revised several times until they're affordable. This is normal and to be expected. For example, you might need to buy a less expensive car than planned or wait another year or two to accumulate funds for the car you really want. You could also look for ways to increase income or reduce expenses to "find" money to invest. One financial goal could wait until another is achieved or plans could be altered. An example is when a child has their heart set on a particular college and the cost of tuition, etc., is out of reach. As an alternative, your child could attend a less expensive community college for two years and then transfer their credits. Their bachelor's degree would still come from the four-year school but you could save thousands of dollars (assuming you plan your courses properly).

Financial goals should be SMART goals. SMART is an acronym that stands for the following key characteristics:

- *Specific*—SMART goals tell what will be done. They should include a dollar cost figure per year and per pay period (e.g., biweekly) and a time deadline (e.g., the year 2008). That way, you can divide the number of savings periods into the cost (e.g., $7,000 divided by [26 paydays × 5 years, or 130] = $53.85) to calculate how much you need to invest and track your progress over time.

- *Measurable*—Financial goals should state exactly what you will do and when (e.g., start dollar cost averaging $100 a month into XYZ mutual fund). Over time, it should be easy to compare where you are financially with where you started when you set the goal.

- *Achievable*—Achievable financial goals are doable. They should be within your ability to accomplish during a desired time frame, given current income and household expenses. In other words, there is a high probability of success if you start investing regularly. You are not setting yourself up to fail.

- *Relevant*—Financial goals should reflect your personal lifestyle, wants/needs, and values, not those of persons outside your household or a financial adviser. To reinforce this characteristic, begin your goal statements with the words "I/we."

- *Trackable*—Progress toward financial goals should be able to be monitored using paper and pencil or computer software. A goal costing $5,000 in three years, for example, would require an investment of $1,666 a year, or about $65 biweekly, amounts that can easily be recorded and tallied.

The Financial Goal-Setting Process

It's a whole lot easier to invest money for something specific than to put money aside for no particular purpose. Financial goals, such as a new car or a college education for children, are examples of specific things that people want to do with their money. They are objectives that reflect personal values and change over time with income, age, and other factors. It is not enough, however, to just think about your financial goals. It is important to write them down so you can see what you say you want.

How do you set financial goals? Like a well-written newspaper article, begin by answering the "Five Ws" (Who?, What?, When?, Where?, and Why?). Write down exactly what you want to do and what it will cost. Include specific dates in your goal statement. Keep rewriting your financial goals until they are specific and achievable. Next, list several ways to achieve each goal, such as by increased income, reduced expenses, or payroll deduction. The final step of the financial goal-setting process is to prioritize your financial goals. Few families have enough money to achieve all of their goals (at least, not all at once) so choices must be made at all income levels. Weigh your goals, not only by their price tag, but by what you will give up by making a particular choice. By choosing to invest for a particular goal, you lose the opportunity to do other things with your money. Start investing for the goals that you deem most important.

As noted in Chapter 1, the time frame of financial goals is a major factor in investment selection. Typically, investors can afford to invest more aggressively for long-term goals because time reduces the volatility of growth investments. The time frame of financial goals can be classified as follows:

- *Short-term*—Goals you'd like to accomplish in less than three years, such as establishing an emergency fund to cover three months of expenses or paying off existing credit card balances.

- *Intermediate-term*—Goals you'd like to accomplish in three to ten years, such as buying a new car or investing for a preteen child's college education.

- *Long-term*—Goals you'd like to accomplish in more than ten years, such as investing for retirement.

Just because a goal is long-term doesn't mean it should wait to be funded, however. Quite the contrary. Small investments, started early, can easily outpace larger sums invested later. Prioritize your financial goals according to their overall level of importance, not their projected time frame. Although short-term goals may seem more urgent, it is important to fund long-term goals as well to take advantage of the power of compound interest.

Once you set your financial goals, be sure to commit to them. The following quote about New Year's resolutions, obtained from the E-mail subscription service Inspire (www.infoadvn.com/inspire), stresses the importance of committing to goals this way:

> Suppose you're in a romantic relationship and your partner says "I love you." That would probably make you feel pretty good. Now suppose your partner says "I love you and I want to marry you." That would probably make you feel even better. But suppose your partner says "I love you and I want to marry you AND let's get married on February 14, 1999." How does that make you feel? All of the sudden, you are taken out of the world of romance and emotion and into the world of reality and commitment.

> It's sort of like when you say "Let's do lunch sometime." If your friend says "good idea," there's no commitment there. But if your friend takes out his or her datebook and offers "How about next Wednesday at 12:30 PM," that's entirely different. Now you're called upon to make a commitment.

> It's the same with New Year's resolutions. Are your resolutions nice "wandering generalities" like "I want to lose weight this year" OR are they "meaningful specifics" that demand a commitment like "I am going to lose a pound a week."

No matter what area of your life you want to change, "meaningful specifics" demand commitments while "wandering generalities" are usually just nice platitudes. So if you want to get results from your New Year's resolutions [and financial goals], don't just fall in love with them . . . marry them.

Another organization, the National Center for Financial Education in San Diego, published an article describing financial goal setting as follows:

- A person with a vision, minus a plan, minus action, has but a **dream,**

- A person with a vision, plus a plan, minus action, has **frustration,**

- A person with a vision, plus a plan, plus action, has **reality** and it leads to **fulfillment.**

To become a successful investor, avoid making the following ten common goal-setting errors:

1. Setting vague financial goals where the amount needed to invest, and for how long, are unclear.

2. Setting unrealistic goals (e.g., a 50-year-old with average earnings and meager savings who wants to retire at 55).

3. Refusing to write down financial goals or develop and implement a plan of action to achieve them (aka denial).

4. Allowing others to define your financial goals for you instead of determining them for yourself.

5. Not discussing individual financial goals with a spouse or significant other.

6. Not accounting for inflation by using the rule of 72 or a financial calculator to determine how fast the cost of financial goals will double.

7. Postponing investing for financial goals until the amount needed to invest is simply not feasible based on current cash flow.

8. Ignoring financial goals as a major factor in investment decisions (e.g., putting short-term goal money into stocks).

9. Refusing to make short-term sacrifices today, such as reducing expenses, to provide funds for future goals. Realizing this error 20 years too late can make some goals unattainable.

10. Inaction caused by procrastination or fear of failure.

Your Most Important Travel Itinerary: The Future

It is helpful to think of investment selection as analogous to making plans for a big trip. To successfully complete a travel itinerary and achieve financial goals, you need to consider your starting point, the destination where you are headed, cost constraints, and an expected time frame. For example, Traveler (Investor) A might be planning a trip (goal) costing $60,000 in 12 years, such as a college education, while Traveler (Investor) B needs $12,000 in four years for a new car. Just as travel options vary widely (e.g., advance purchase sale tickets versus full fares), so, too, do the options and products available to investors. Below is a detailed description of the four key components of investment decisions.

Starting Point

Like the airport or train station that a traveler departs from, an investor's starting point is where they stand financially today. One of the most commonly used indicators of financial standing is net worth (aka balance sheet). Net worth is the sum total of investors' assets minus the sum total of their liabilities (debts). If John and Sue Dough have assets worth $200,000 and $75,000 of debt, their net worth is $125,000. A net worth statement provides a snapshot of financial status at a particular time and a benchmark against which to measure progress. It also can be used to identify existing assets that can be repositioned to earn a higher rate of return. See Figure 2.1 for a typical net worth statement format.

Destination

Like that Caribbean Island that you've always wanted to visit, your financial destination is a clearly defined goal with an identified cost and deadline date. Examples include:

Figure 2.1 Net Worth Statement

Net Worth as of _____ (Date)

ASSETS	*LIABILITIES*
Savings	Credit cards
Cash	Family loans
Certificates of deposit	Home equity loans
Checking account(s)	Mortgage
Credit union share-draft account	Student loans
Money market funds and	Unpaid bills
deposit accounts	Unpaid taxes
Savings account(s)	Vehicle
Other	loan(s)/lease(s)
	Other

Investments
Bonds
Individual retirement accounts
Life insurance cash value
Mutual funds
Pensions and retirement assets (e.g., 401(k)s)
Real estate
Stocks
Other

Property
Automobile(s)
Boat, motorcycle, RV
Collectibles (e.g., coins)
Furniture and appliances
House or condominium
Personal property (e.g., clothing)
Rental property
Other

- Establish a $6,000 emergency fund within three years.

- Make a $10,000 down payment on a new car in five years.

- Pay off a $2,500 balance on credit cards within a year.

- Increase net worth by at least 5 percent per year.

- Have $50,000 invested by 50th birthday.
- Accumulate $30,000 in seven years to start a business.
- Set aside $40,000 for childrens' college education.

Cost Constraints

This is the amount of money you have to travel financially, that is, to invest. In other words, how much of your current income can be set aside to achieve future financial goals? Just as some travelers can afford first class tickets while others wait for airfare wars and buy coach tickets on sale, so, too, investors will vary in the amount of investment capital they have available. A second indicator of financial status, in addition to net worth, is cash flow (aka income and expense statement). Cash flow is the sum total of investors' income minus the sum total of their expenses. If John and Sue Dough earn $50,000 annually and spend $45,000, they have $5,000 of positive cash flow. If, on the other hand, they spend $60,000, their cash flow is a negative $10,000, which indicates the use of credit and/or depletion of savings to make ends meet. Cash flow statements are the starting point for developing a spending plan that includes a line item for investing. Often, spending leaks can be identified and income "found" to purchase new financial assets. Examples of expense categories that often can be reworked include variable costs such as meals eaten at and away from home, utilities, entertainment, clothing, debt repayment, gifts, and personal care. See Figure 2.2 for a typical cash flow statement format.

Time Frame

Just like business or vacation trips require a time frame (e.g., a week in the Bahamas or a two-week tour of Europe) to complete an itinerary, so, too, do financial goals. Investment time frames are often based on characteristics of specific products, such as stock, or personal considerations, such as the age of an investor or an investor's children and the amount of money available to invest with. The less time an investor has to reach a financial goal (e.g., three years instead of ten years), the higher the amount that needs to be invested periodically to achieve it. When additional funds are not available, investors may decide to extend their time frame or to invest more

Figure 2.2   Cash Flow Statement

Cash Flow for the Month of _____ (Date)	
INCOME	*EXPENSES*
Alimony	Charitable contributions
Child support	Child care
Dividends, interest, and	Debt repayment (e.g., loans)
capital gains	Food
Gifts and inheritances	Gifts
Public assistance	Housing (mortgage or rent)
Salaries and wages	Insurance
Social Security and pensions	Medical expenses
Other	Personal care
	Recreation and entertainment
	Saving and investing
	Taxes
	Transportation
	Utilities
	Other

aggressively in products (e.g., stock, growth mutual funds) that entail greater risk in exchange for the potential of a higher return.

Now that we've identified the four key components of investment decisions, Worksheet #1 combines them into a personalized plan.

The Advantages of Planning Ahead

Many Americans are making some effort to prepare financially for the future but a large majority are falling short of reaching their financial goals. What distinguishes those who succeed financially from those who don't? According to a national telephone survey sponsored by Nationsbank and the Consumer Federation of America and conducted by Princeton Research Associates in 1997, it's planning. Financial decision makers in 1,770 households were asked questions about their goals, strategies for saving and investing, and knowledge of financial topics. The survey found that, aside from

WORKSHEET 1 *Go for the Goal!*

Use this worksheet to identify your financial goals, list their cost and expected time frame, and identify resources with which to achieve them.

Starting Point

Beginning Date: _____

Amount of Assets: $_____

Amount of Debts: $_____

Net Worth: $_____

Destination and Time Frame

Short-term Goals:

Goal #1: _____

Goal #2: _____

Goal #3: _____

Example: To accumulate $2,000 within a year for a new computer.

Intermediate-term Goals:

Goal #1: _____

Goal #2: _____

Goal #3: _____

Example: To accumulate $8,000 for a car down payment in five years.

Long-term Goals:

Goal #1: _____

Goal #2: _____

Goal #3: _____

Example: To accumulate a $100,000 retirement nest egg by age 65.

WORKSHEET 1 *Continued*

Cost Constraints

Amount of Monthly Income: $_____

Amount of Monthly Expenses: $_____

Positive/Negative Cash Flow: $_____

Resources Available to Achieve Financial Goals:

_____

_____

_____

_____

_____

Examples: credit union, employer match 401(k) plan, inheritance

Picture Your Goal

Draw Your Goal
or
Attach a Photograph
Here

income, the one critical factor that distinguishes those who are successful is preparation of a comprehensive financial plan. No matter what their income, people with a plan save more money, save or invest in smarter ways, and feel better about their progress than those without a plan. By comparison, knowledge of saving and investment principles has a more modest effect on financial success.

The sponsors of the study concluded that many Americans are at risk of not being able to afford important life goals because they are saving too little and making poor saving and investment decisions. Individuals can dramatically improve their chances of financial success by developing an overall financial plan and following these four tips found on the Nationsbank Web site (www.nationsbank.com/info/html/saverssurvey.htm):

1. *Set specific financial goals with a projected cost and time frame.* Then break down the goal into smaller pieces so a seemingly impossible goal, such as saving $10,000, can be accomplished successfully with small dollar amounts over time.

2. *Start saving today.* Any amount of savings is better than none. Try to automate your savings and investments through direct deposit, electronic funds transfers, and/or payroll deduction.

3. *Match investment characteristics to financial goals* (e.g., time horizon), *family lifestyle* (e.g., age), *and available income.*

4. *Perform an annual "checkup" to determine progress toward financial goals and investment performance.* Calculate your net worth at around the same time each year as a measure of change.

Selecting Investments That Match Your Goals

According to the old saying used frequently by financial planners, "People don't plan to fail . . . they fail to plan." Setting financial goals is one of the best ways to avoid this common error. A corollary piece of advice is to make sure that financial goals and investments chosen to achieve them are in synch with one another. As noted in Chapter 1, a common investing mistake is not matching the cost or time frame of financial goals with the characteristics of investments selected to achieve them.

Start by defining your overall investing objective (safety of principal, income, or growth). Then eliminate all of the investment products that don't match your objective or the amount of money available to invest with (e.g., Ginnie Maes for an investor who seeks growth or has less than the required $25,000 minimum to invest). Soon the universe of investment options will be narrowed considerably. You then can concentrate on finding products with good historical performance and below-average expenses. More about this later.

Financial goals should always be considered before making investment decisions. Not to do so is analogous to hopping in your car and driving around aimlessly with no particular place to go. You might eventually get somewhere you've always wanted to visit but, then again, you might not. Yet, so often, investors purchase investments and assemble entire portfolios in a hodgepodge manner with no regard for their overall objectives. Don't make this mistake! Invest with a plan to achieve specific goals and stick to it. Financial goals identify where you want to travel financially and provide a detailed road map to get there.

Keep in mind that the route to achieving your financial goals is just like any other journey: It will have bumps and curves and detours. Midtrip adjustments, such as new investments or rebalancing your portfolio, are often necessary also. As Stephen Covey so appropriately states in *The Seven Habits of Highly Effective People*, "Begin with the end in mind." SMART goals will help you define the end results that you aspire to and to develop a plan of action to achieve them.

How to Calculate the Cost
of Your Financial Goals

When you're investing money to achieve financial goals, time is an important ally. The earlier you start setting money aside, the more you can take advantage of the effects of compounding or the time value of money. It is important to remember that compound interest is not retroactive. You cannot earn interest on your money if you fail to invest it. The time value of money can work for you and against you. On the positive side, it will increase the value of your assets. Conversely, the cost of goods and services also will increase through inflation.

Financial planners often use time value charts to calculate how much a goal will cost in the future, assuming a given rate of inflation, and how much money is needed to invest annually at a given rate of interest. Of course, any calculation is only as good as the assumptions that underlie it. It is usually best to err on the conservative side, when making future predictions, so you aren't caught short. If you want to be very conservative, assume a 5 percent annual inflation rate, which is close to the average rate during the past 20 years. In more recent years, however, inflation rates have been averaging around 2 or 3 percent, a less conservative—but currently more accurate—figure.

The first step in calculating the amount needed to invest to reach a future financial goal is to decide which inflation factor assumption to use. Time value of money factors for both 3 percent and 5 percent inflation rates are provided in Table A of Worksheet #2. To find the factor by which inflation will increase the cost of your goals over the years, select the appropriate time frame and find the corresponding time value factor. You also can calculate the cost of financial goals using both inflation factor assumptions in two separate calculations. This will provide a range of required savings amounts.

Multiplying the current cost of a financial goal by the appropriate inflation factor is the second step in the process. Doing so gives you a goal's estimated future cost. For example, if you want to purchase home office equipment that costs $10,000 today to start a business in five years, your goal will cost $11,600 ($10,000 × 1.16), assuming a 3 percent inflation rate.

Once you've determined the future cost of a financial goal, the third step is to use a future value of annuity factor (see Table B) to determine how much you need to save on an annual and monthly basis. The table includes values for an average annual return of 4, 6, 8, and 10 percent. Use the annuity factor that best represents the average rate of return that you are earning (or will be earning) on investments earmarked for a particular financial goal. A sample illustration is provided. As the example shows, you'll need to invest more money each month to reach a given goal as the yield on your investments decreases. Another factor that affects the amount required to invest is your time frame. The more time an investor has to accumulate a sum of money, the less they need to save each year.

WORKSHEET 2 *How Much Do I Need to Invest?*

	Your Financial Goal	John and Sue Dough
1. Financial goal	_____	A late model car
2. Number of years away	_____	Five years
3. Cost of goal today	$_____	$15,000
4. Assumed inflation rate	_____%	5 percent
5. Inflation factor based on time horizon and inflation rate (see Table A)	_____	1.27 (5 percent, 5 years)
6. Future cost of goal	_____	$19,050

Table A: Future Value of Money Factors

Inflation Rate	Years to Financial Goal								
	3	5	10	15	20	25	30	35	40
3%	1.09	1.16	1.34	1.56	1.81	2.10	2.43	2.81	3.26
5%	1.16	1.27	1.63	2.08	2.65	3.39	4.32	5.52	7.04

7. Investment needed assuming a 4 percent average yield:

   a) Time value factor for years left until goal (see Table B) _____ 5.42

   b) Annual amount to invest (divide step 7a into step 6) _____ $3,515

   c) Monthly investment (divide step 7b by 12) _____ $ 293

8. Investment needed assuming a 6 percent average yield:

   a) Time value factor for years left until goal _____ 5.64

   b) Annual amount to invest (divide step 8a into step 6) _____ $3,378

   c) Monthly investment (divide step 8b by 12) _____ $ 282

(continued)

WORKSHEET 2 *Continued*
....

---

9. Investment needed assuming an 8 percent average yield:

   a) Time value factor for years left
   until goal   _____   5.87

   b) Annual amount to invest
   (divide step 9a into step 6)   _____ $3,245

   c) Monthly investment
   (divide step 9b by 12)   _____ $ 270

10. Investment needed assuming a 10 percent average yield:

   a) Time value factor for years
   left until goal   _____   6.11

   b) Annual amount to invest
   (divide step 10a into step 6) _____ $3,118

   c) Monthly investment (divide
   step 10b by 12)   _____ $ 260

Table B: Future Value of Annuity Factors

Estimated Average Annual Return	Number of Years to Goal								
	3	5	10	15	20	25	30	35	40
4%	3.12	5.42	12.01	20.02	29.78	41.64	56.08	73.65	95.02
6%	3.18	5.64	13.18	23.28	36.79	54.86	79.06	111.43	154.76
8%	3.25	5.87	14.49	27.15	45.76	73.11	113.28	172.32	259.06
10%	3.31	6.11	15.94	31.77	57.27	98.35	164.49	271.02	442.59

Retirement: The Ultimate Financial Destination

According to the 1997 Retirement Confidence Survey, sponsored by the Employee Benefit Research Institute (EBRI), about three-quarters of American workers have no idea how much money they need to accumulate for retirement. A summary of the Retirement Confidence Survey (RCS) can be found at the EBRI Web site (www.ebri.org) under "Programs," and at the American Savings Education Council Web site (www.asec.org) under "Programs and Events." The most frequently cited reason for not attempting a retirement savings needs calculation was "It won't be helpful because I can't save any more," followed by "It is too far in the future," "It is difficult to find time," "I'm afraid of the answer," and "The process is too complicated." Ironically, about seven in ten workers report feeling very confident (25%) or somewhat confident (43%) that they will have enough money to live comfortably in retirement. Yet, among those who reported feeling very confident in their personal retirement preparation, only 55 percent had done a retirement savings needs analysis. About one-third of workers queried said they would like to retire at age 55 and younger.

EBRI concluded that the confidence of many American workers in their retirement prospects may be misplaced. The good news from the Retirement Confidence Survey is that more workers have begun to save for retirement and are seeking educational material to assist them with investing decisions. The bad news is that most Americans are not planning for retirement based on a specific goal. The vast majority have not calculated the amount needed to maintain their lifestyle in retirement or determined a target saving amount. The authors of the EBRI report conclude, "Without a goal and a plan in place to achieve that goal, how can Americans be truly confident about their retirement income prospects?"

The moral of the EBRI study contradictions is that, just like any other financial goal, retirement needs to be a SMART goal with an estimated cost and time frame. Only then can calculations be done to determine the amount required to invest during your remaining working years. How much money a person needs to save for retirement depends on five primary factors:

1. How much Social Security, employer benefits, and other retirement assets are already accumulated

2. The dollar amount of income desired as a percentage of current income

3. The number of years between now and retirement

4. The number of years of retirement (life expectancy)

5. The growth rate on new and existing investments

The first step in planning for retirement is to take a look at where you stand financially today. The best way to determine this is with a net worth statement and an estimate of future pension and Social Security benefits. The next step is to calculate your retirement income gap, that is, the difference between the income you need in retirement and what you expect to receive from Social Security, employee benefit plans, and current assets. Many financial planners recommend planning to replace at least 70 percent of preretirement income to maintain your standard of living. If you want more money for travel or to pass on to heirs, you can use a higher percentage. Using age 90 or higher as a planning time horizon in retirement savings computations is also recommended. This helps compensate for inflationary periods and helps ensure that you won't outlive your assets.

In 1997, the American Savings Education Council (ASEC) developed *Ballpark Estimate*, a worksheet designed to help individuals quickly identify approximately how much savings they need to live comfortably in retirement. A blank form and completed sample of *Ballpark Estimate* are reproduced in Figure 2.3 and are also available on the ASEC Web site at www.asec.org. *Ballpark Estimate* was commissioned specifically to fit on one page and can be completed with a calculator in a matter of minutes. While not as detailed as other retirement planning worksheets or software, it is also not as intimidating. By simplifying issues that seem complicated, such as the future value of current savings, *Ballpark Estimate* provides a rough estimate of the amount needed for retirement and the savings required to get there. The worksheet assumes that you'll need 70 percent of current income, live to age 87, and will realize an after-inflation return of 3 percent.

In the example, Jane is a 35-year-old working woman earning $30,000 per year. Seventy percent of Jane's current income is $21,000 ($30,000 × .70). Jane would then subtract the income she expects to receive from Social Security ($12,000 in the example), equaling $9,000. This is her gap, or the amount she needs to make up during each year of retirement. Jane expects to retire at age 65, so she multiplies $9,000 times 16.4 (the factor for retirement at age 65), which equals $147,600. She has already saved $2,000 in her 401(k) plan. Multiplied by 2.4 (the factor for retirement in 30 years), this equals $4,800, which is subtracted from $147,600, making her projected retirement need $142,800. Jane plans to retire in 30 years so she multiplies $142,800 by .02 (the factor for 30 years) for an annual savings amount of $2,856. This is a rough estimate of the amount Jane needs to invest each year to achieve her retirement savings goal.

Figure 2.3   Ballpark Estimate Retirement Worksheet

BALLPARK E$TIMATE™

Planning for retirement is not a one-size-fits-all exercise. The purpose of Ballpark is simply to give you a basic idea of the savings you'll need when you retire. **So let's play ball!**

1. How much annual income will you want in retirement? (Figure 70% of your current annual gross income just to maintain your current standard of living. Really.)
   $ _____

2. Subtract the income you expect to receive annually from:
   - Social Security—If you make under $25,000, enter $8,000; between $25,000 - $40,000, enter $12,000; over $40,000, enter $14,500
     -$ _____
   - Traditional Employer Pension - a plan that pays a set dollar amount for life, where the dollar amount depends on salary and years of service (in today's dollars)
     -$ _____
   - Part-time income
     -$ _____
   - Other
     -$ _____

   This is how much you need to make up for each retirement year:
   =$ _____

   Now you want a ballpark estimate of how much money you'll need in the bank the day you retire. So the accountants went to work and devised this simple formula. For the record, they figure you'll realize a constant real rate of return of 3% after inflation, you'll live to age 87, and you'll begin to receive income from Social Security at age 65.

3. To determine the amount you'll need to save, multiply the amount you need to make up by the factor below.
   $ _____

Age you expect to retire:		Your factor is:	
55		21.0	
60		18.9	
65		16.4	
70		13.6	

4. If you expect to retire before age 65, multiply your Social Security benefit from line 2 by the factor below.
   +$ _____

Age you expect to retire:		Your factor is:	
55		8.8	
60		4.7	

5. Multiply your savings to date by the factor below (include money accumulated in a 401(k), IRA, or similar retirement plan).
   -$ _____

If you want to retire in:		Your factor is:	
10 years		1.3	
15 years		1.6	
20 years		1.8	
25 years		2.1	
30 years		2.4	
35 years		2.8	
40 years		3.3	

   Total additional savings needed at retirement:
   =$ _____

   Don't panic. Those same accountants devised another formula to show you how much to save each year in order to reach your goal amount. They factor in compounding. That's where your money not only makes interest, your interest starts making interest as well, creating a snowball effect.

6. To determine the ANNUAL amount you'll need to save, multiply the TOTAL amount by the factor below.
   =$ _____

If you want to retire in:		Your factor is:	
10 years		.085	
15 years		.052	
20 years		.036	
25 years		.027	
30 years		.020	
35 years		.016	
40 years		.013	

ASEC

AMERICAN
SAVINGS
EDUCATION
COUNCIL

ASEC/EBRI-ERF
Suite 600
2121 K Street NW
Washington, DC
20037-1896

202-775-9130 or
202-659-0670
Fax 202-775-6312
www.asec.org
www.ebri.org

See? It's not impossible or even particularly painful. It just takes planning. And the sooner you start, the better off you'll be.

This worksheet simplifies several retirement planning issues such as projected Social Security benefits and earnings assumptions on savings. It also reflects today's dollars; therefore you will need to re-calculate your retirement needs annually and as your salary and circumstances change. You may want to consider doing further analysis, either by yourself using a more detailed worksheet or computer software or with the assistance of a financial professional.   1/98

(continued)

Figure 2.3   Continued

BALLPARK E$TIMATE

Planning for retirement is not a one-size-fits-all exercise. The purpose of Ballpark is simply to give you a basic idea of the savings you'll need when you retire. *So let's play ball!*

1. How much annual income will you want in retirement? (Figure 70% of your current annual gross income just to maintain your current standard of living. Really.) $ *21,000*

2. Subtract the income you expect to receive annually from:
   - Social Security—If you make under $25,000, enter $8,000; between $25,000 - $40,000, enter $12,000; over $40,000, enter $14,500   -$ *12,000*
   - Traditional Employer Pension – a plan that pays a set dollar amount for life, where the dollar amount depends on salary and years of service (in today's dollars)   -$ _____
   - Part-time income   -$ _____
   - Other   -$ _____

   This is how much you need to make up for each retirement year: =$ *9,000*

   Now you want a ballpark estimate of how much money you'll need in the bank the day you retire. So the accountants went to work and devised this simple formula. For the record, they figure you'll realize a constant real rate of return of 3% after inflation, you'll live to age 87, and you'll begin to receive income from Social Security at age 65.

3. To determine the amount you'll need to save, multiply the amount you need to make up by the factor below. $ *147,600*

Age you expect to retire:		Your factor is:	
	55		21.0
	60		18.9
→65			16.4 ←
	70		13.6

4. If you expect to retire before age 65, multiply your Social Security benefit from line 2 by the factor below.   +$ _____

Age you expect to retire:		Your factor is:	
	55		8.8
	60		4.7

5. Multiply your savings to date by the factor below (include money accumulated in a 401(k), IRA, or similar retirement plan).   -$ *4,800*

If you want to retire in:		Your factor is:	
	10 years		1.3
	15 years		1.6
	20 years		1.8
	25 years		2.1
→30 years			2.4 ←
	35 years		2.8
	40 years		3.3

   Total savings needed at retirement: =$ *142,800*

   Don't panic. Those same accountants devised another formula to show you how much to save each year in order to reach your goal amount. They factor in compounding. That's where your money not only makes interest, your interest starts making interest as well, creating a snowball effect.

6. To determine the ANNUAL amount you'll need to save, multiply the TOTAL amount by the factor below.   =$ *2,856*

If you want to retire in:		Your factor is:	
	10 years		.085
	15 years		.052
	20 years		.036
	25 years		.027
→30 years			.020 ←
	35 years		.016
	40 years		.013

ASEC
AMERICAN SAVINGS EDUCATION COUNCIL®

ASEC/EBRI-ERF
Suite 600
2121 K Street NW
Washington, DC
20037-1896
202-775-9130 or
202-659-0670
Fax 202-775-6312
www.asec.org
www.ebri.org

See? It's not impossible or even particularly painful. It just takes planning. And the sooner you start, the better off you'll be.

This worksheet simplifies several retirement planning issues such as projected Social Security benefits and earnings assumptions on savings. It also reflects today's dollars; therefore you will need to re-calculate your retirement needs annually and as your salary and circumstances change. You may want to consider doing further analysis, either by yourself using a more detailed worksheet or computer software or with the assistance of a financial professional.   1/98

Other Retirement Pointers

It used to be that most people retired around age 65 and died in their early 70s. Their retirement lasted about seven years. Not anymore. Today, many people retire between age 55 and 60 and can look forward to 30 or more years of living. Retirement today can encompass a third of your life span. At some point in their lives, many retirees stop going to work. Instead, they shift their attention to hobbies or traveling or community activities or grandchildren. Retirement years also bring many new and sometimes difficult financial decisions. Below are a dozen tips for retirees or those planning to retire within the next few years.

1. Become familiar with retirement plan distribution options. Start reading retirement plan documents and find out when and how benefits will be paid. Consider whether you'll select a joint and survivor annuity, if married, or make alternative plans (e.g., purchase a life insurance policy) to protect your spouse.

2. Check on retirement health coverage. Find out from your employer if your health insurance is transferable to a retirement policy and, if so, at what cost. If this is not an option, begin investigating Medigap health policies as a supplement to Medicare (if over age 65) or COBRA, which entitles you to pay for continuing coverage under an employer's health plan (if under age 65).

3. Request a Social Security benefit estimate. Call 800-772-1213 or check the Web site www.ssa.gov to obtain a free estimate of benefits available at ages 62, 65, and 70. You'll also get a statement of your prior annual earnings, which can be checked for accuracy.

4. Set new financial goals. Retirement is not your last financial goal. Many people want to travel or spend money on hobbies and you'll most likely need money for cars and home improvements over the years. Plan ahead for these expenses.

5. Seek professional assistance with lump sum distributions. For many people, pension payouts are the largest sum of money they'll ever have at one time. Contact a certified financial planner

(CFP) and/or a certified public accountant (CPA) to invest this money wisely and pay the least amount of tax legally possible. After all, this money has to last a lifetime!

6. Practice leisure. Consider how you will spend your time in retirement. Investigate various options such as starting a small business, finding hobbies, or getting involved with community organizations.

7. Test out your options. If you think you may want to move to another area of the country, visit potential retirement sites at different times of the year. Subscribe to their local newspaper to get a feel for the area. If you decide to move, rent first. Many retirees find it hard to move back home once they've sold their house and bought another one elsewhere.

8. Prepare for widowhood. Nobody likes to talk about it, much less plan for it, but, more than 70 percent of the time, wives outlive their husbands. Make sure that both spouses are familiar with family finances and will have adequate income in the event of an untimely death. Your future security depends on it!

9. Keep pace with taxes and inflation. To make sure that your retirement nest egg doesn't lose purchasing power over time, consider keeping a portion of it in a growth investment, such as a stock mutual fund.

10. Consider long-term care insurance. Although still a relatively new product, better policies have become available in recent years. Ask plenty of questions about coverage and exclusions, and make sure that "inflation protection" is included to cover future nursing home price increases.

11. Consider postretirement employment. For many retirees, the "three-legged stool" of Social Security, employer benefits, and invested assets (as sources of retirement income) has become a "four-legged chair," adding employment as a fourth source of funds plus a source of identity and structure for daily living.

12. Be prepared for change. Retirement can last for decades. Your needs in your 80s will be different from those in your 60s. You'll need to adapt, not only to personal changes, such as the death of a spouse, but to changes in the economy, investment products, and tax laws. Keep learning about personal finance and stay informed.

Remember that your retirement lifestyle will almost certainly depend on how well you plan for it. Of course, it's fun to fantasize about winning the lottery or getting a visit from the prize patrol. However, for most of us, it's a dream that simply won't come true. What can come true (with some work, of course) is financial stability through successful investing. A critical prerequisite is a set of SMART goals that provide a framework for making decisions about where you want to travel financially and an appropriate itinerary, or action plan, to get there. Don't invest in a vacuum. Invest with a plan. If you haven't put anything aside for long-term goals like retirement, start today.

3

Investment Risk: How Much Is Enough?

Our basic nature is to act, and not be acted upon.

—Stephen R. Covey

Investment risk can be defined as the uncertainty that accompanies the performance of a specific security (e.g., stock). In other words, an investment may or may not perform as expected. When people say that an investment is risky, they usually mean that the yield received by investors can fluctuate widely from one year to the next, or that it is possible to lose your original investment (principal), or both. The greater an investment's level of risk, the more potential it generally has for higher returns. This potential to earn more on invested dollars than on bank deposits is what motivates many people to become investors.

History tells us that, over time periods of at least five to ten years, investors who take risks have been rewarded handsomely. Since 1926, the annual return on large company stocks was more than double that of government bonds and almost triple that of cash assets, according to Ibbotson Associates. But there also have been some very bumpy years in between 1926 and 1997 when stocks lost a great deal of value. This is why a diversified portfolio is recommended instead of putting all of your money in any one investment, even stock. Nobel laureate Merton Miller, when asked to describe the most important investment concept that investors should understand, once said, "Diversification is your buddy." What he meant is that if you own a variety of investments in different asset classes, for example, stocks or bonds, a decline in one investment will be balanced by others that are stable or increasing in value. Owning a variety of securities reduces investment risk, which is why diversification is perhaps the single most important rule that you can follow as an investor.

Numerous studies have shown that the investing public has a poor understanding of the relationship between risk and reward. In the minds of many people, the word *risk* is synonymous with gambling. They might as well be standing at a slot machine in Atlantic City. A word like *volatile,* which financial pros use routinely to describe characteristic price fluctuations, is often interpreted as a sure route to bankruptcy. Research also has shown that many investors don't have realistic expectations of investment performance or they put too much stock in words like low risk and guaranteed. To help combat the common misconception that investments purchased at banks are somehow safer than those purchased elsewhere, the Federal Reserve developed an educational program several years ago to teach consumers about the risks associated with purchasing investments. The key point emphasized in the campaign was that, unlike bank certificates of deposit (CDs) and deposit accounts, mutual funds, annuities, and other investments purchased at banks are not government (FDIC) insured.

Another common problem, with respect to risk, is unrealistic expectations. Expecting a 25 percent return just because it occurred recently is simply not reasonable. Yet, many investors extrapolate the past—especially the recent past—into the future. Small wonder that they sell in a panic when history doesn't repeat itself. Others simply want to earn a high return on a conservative portfolio even though it is historically unrealistic. It may not be desirable but what is often required is a reduction in the grandiosity of their goals or acceptance of greater risk (i.e., chance of loss).

What Type of Investor Are You?

Investors can be described as conservative or aggressive, with many stages of individual risk tolerance in between. Conservative investors prefer to take minimal risks with their money and are concerned primarily with safety. They accept the fact that leaving their money in low-risk investments will probably earn them a lower rate of return but they are willing to do it for the security of a predictable return and safety of principal. Aggressive investors, on the other hand, are willing to accept the greater risks that generally accompany higher potential returns. Their primary concern is maximizing their investment return and growing their money as quickly as possible. This is often accomplished by investing in small company stocks or aggressive growth mutual funds.

Many people say they don't want to take any investment risks but incur them anyway—often unwittingly. A common example: people with all of their money in CDs or money market funds. Yes, their principal is safe, but they are incurring the loss of purchasing power due to inflation. Behavioral finance experts, the folks who study human behavior as it relates to investing, tell us that people are much more sensitive to losses—especially their first loss—than they are to gains. It is often losses, more than risks, which drive investment decisions. A frequently cited example of loss aversion is the scenario where two people are on their way to a theater. The first person paid $50 for a show ticket and lost it while the second person lost $50 cash but still has plenty of money left with which to buy a ticket. Studies show that more people are willing to buy a ticket when they've lost the cash than they are if they've lost the ticket, even though they're out $50 either way. It is theorized that investors separate their money into different "mental accounts." Investing in a ticket from their "theater account," that is, buying a second ticket, feels like more of a loss than buying a ticket from "general funds." Similarly, investment losses often affect later decisions, depending on an individual investor's experiences and mental accounting techniques.

Types of Investment Risks

There is no risk-free investment. Repeat, there is no risk-free investment. All financial products, even seemingly safe CDs and bank deposit accounts, carry associated risks and tradeoffs. Risk is a part of everyday life, whether it's driving to work, or eating a meal, or selecting investments for your 401(k). We accept all kinds of risks in life because they sure beat the alternative. In investing, as in living, you can understand various risks and take steps to reduce them but you can't eliminate them entirely. Below are descriptions of ten common types of investment risk.

1. *Business (specific) risk*—The risk of events that affect only a specific company or industry, thereby influencing the value of an investment. Examples of such events include: legal actions such as a class action lawsuit, the death of a company owner or investment manager, FDA approval (e.g., for new drugs from pharmaceutical companies), and new technological breakthroughs.

2. *Call risk*—The risk of the issuer of a bond refinancing its debt by issuing replacement bonds that pay less interest. In other words, an investor might be counting on a certain stream of income (e.g., 8 percent interest) and now finds that it will be less (e.g., 6 percent) than they had planned.

3. *Credit (default) risk*—The risk of a corporation or government entity that has issued bonds being unable to make interest payments on its debt or repay investors' principal.

4. *Currency (exchange-rate) risk*—The risk of loss due to currency changes on international investments. When the U.S. dollar strengthens in relation to another currency, the value of an investor's assets in that country declines.

5. *Inflation (purchasing power) risk*—The risk of loss of purchasing power when the after-tax return on an investment fails to outpace inflation or barely keeps pace. Investments with this risk retain only a fraction of their purchasing power over time.

6. *Interest rate risk*—The risk that, as market interest rates rise, the value of previously issued fixed-income investments, such as bonds, will fall. Interest rate risk applies only to investments that are sold prior to maturity. When higher-yielding securities become available, investors earning a lower rate must sell at a discounted price in order to attract investors.

7. *Liquidity risk*—The risk of being unable to find a buyer for an investment or being forced to sell at a significant loss. Liquidity risk typically affects collectibles, such as antiques and art work, and real estate investments.

8. *Market risk*—The risk that the price of individual securities will be affected by the volatility of financial markets. In other words, a stock's price may fall simply because the overall stock market has experienced a downturn.

9. *Political risk*—The risk that political events (election results, citizen unrest, death of a leader, etc.) at home or abroad may affect the return on an investment.

10. *Reinvestment risk*—The risk of having to reinvest existing funds (for example, when a bond matures or is called) and earn a lower return than previously earned, resulting in a decline in income.

Systematic and Unsystematic Risk

The total risk of an investment can be divided into two categories: systematic (nondiversifiable) and unsystematic (diversifiable) risk (see Figure 3.1). Systematic risk is the risk associated with the economy as a whole and cannot be diversified away. Market risk is an example of systematic risk. Market risk is the risk of day-to-day fluctuations in security prices caused by a variety of factors including government policies, tax law changes, computerized program trading (for example, the day that options and futures contracts expire), investor expectations, and a "herd mentality." In other words, market risk is the risk of just being in the equity market rather than in any particular stock or fund.

Systematic risk is found in varying degrees in nearly all securities because prices of comparable investments, such as stocks and bonds, tend to move in the same direction. Companies with high systematic risk tend to be cyclical firms whose sales, profits, and stock prices follow movements in securities markets and the economy as a whole. Cyclical firms have above-average economic sensitivity and earnings variability. Airlines, resorts, casinos, and companies that supply raw materials (e.g., lumber for construction) and basic industrial goods often fall into this category.

Other types of risk that fall into the systematic risk category include: inflation risk, currency risk, interest rate risk, and reinvestment risk. All of these risks, in addition to market risk, share two common

Figure 3.1 Types of Investment Risk

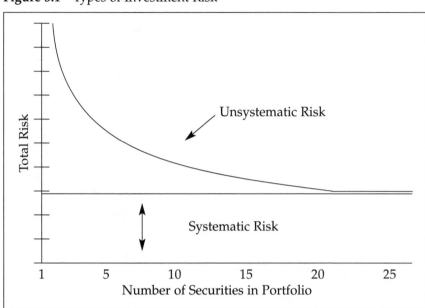

elements: They affect financial markets and all investments of one type (rather than individual securities) and they cannot be reduced or eliminated by diversification.

Unsystematic risk is the part of investment risk that *can* be reduced through diversification. It is estimated that investors can eliminate about 60 to 70 percent of their total investment risk by putting their eggs in several baskets. By selecting investments from different asset categories and industries, unsystematic risk is reduced. The adverse effect of any one investment on portfolio performance is less when it represents only a small percentage of the whole. It has been estimated that as little as 10 to 15 different securities in a portfolio can significantly reduce unsystematic risk (see Figure 3.1). Systematic risk, however, will always remain.

Stated another way, unsystematic risk is the risk associated with individual companies or investments rather than the economy or financial markets in general. Types of investment risk that fall into this category include: business risk, credit risk, liquidity risk, and political risk. Each of these risks is unique to a particular company,

Figure 3.2   Investment Risk of Common Securities

Investment Product	Primary Types of Investment Risk	
1. Treasury bills	Systematic:	inflation risk and interest rate risk
2. Certificates of deposit (CDs)	Systematic:	inflation risk and interest rate risk
3. Corporate bonds	Systematic:	inflation risk and interest rate risk
4. Municipal bonds	Systematic:	inflation risk and interest rate risk
5. Common stock	Systematic: Unsystematic:	market risk business risk
6. Speculative bonds (aka junk bonds)	Systematic: Unsystematic:	interest rate risk credit/default risk
7. Real estate	Systematic: Unsystematic:	market risk liquidity risk
8. Futures contracts	Systematic: Unsystematic:	market risk business risk

country, or type of investment. The chart in Figure 3.2 applies the concepts of systematic and unsystematic risk to eight common real-world investments.

Eight Ways to Reduce Investment Risk

1. Averaged purchases. Dollar cost averaging and value averaging allow investors to gradually set money aside as they earn it. Dollar cost averaging, the more well-known of the two, requires a regular investment amount (e.g., $100) at a regular interval (e.g., monthly). While no guarantee against investment losses, it does even out the prices paid for an investment (e.g., mutual fund shares). More shares are purchased at lower prices and fewer shares at higher prices. Dollar cost averaging can easily be set up through automated deposits.

Simply list your bank account number on a mutual fund application and the fund will automatically withdraw the amount of your monthly deposit. Value averaging entails buying more shares when an investment is low and buying less, or even selling, when an investment is high. The objective is to increase the value of an investment by a set dollar amount over a set period. For example, an investor may want to increase the value of their investment by $100 each month. The number of shares needed to obtain the amount of dollar increase is calculated and shares are purchased or sold accordingly. Like dollar cost averaging, more shares are purchased when a fund goes down. When prices go up, investors buy fewer shares or even sell some. The biggest disadvantage of value averaging is income taxes due when shares must be sold.

2. Ladder your portfolio. Laddering is a technique used to purchase fixed-income securities, such as Treasury notes, bonds, and CDs. Instead of purchasing just one investment with one maturity date, investment principal is divided among securities with varying maturities (one-year, two-year, five-year, etc.). Laddering provides liquidity at regular intervals and helps protect against the negative impact of interest rate fluctuations. If interest rates rise, some money can be reinvested periodically at a higher rate. If interest rates fall, money invested previously will continue to earn a higher return.

3. Rebalance periodically. Let's say you've decided to put 70 percent of your portfolio into stocks, 20 percent into bonds, and 10 percent into a money market fund. After a period (e.g., 1995 to 1998) of high stock market returns, the percentages could look more like 78 percent, 18 percent, and 4 percent. With a higher percentage of assets in stocks, investors inadvertently increase their level of investment risk. Rebalancing back to the original portfolio percentages can be accomplished by selling securities in the appreciated asset class (or not buying any more) or purchasing new securities in the underrepresented asset classes.

4. Time diversification. Time diversification means investing over a period of time, rather than investing a lump sum all at once, possibly at the low point in an economic cycle. Data compiled by Ibbotson Associates show that investment risk is reduced as an investor's time horizon increases because volatility (ups and downs in the price of a security) is reduced over time. In all of the "rolling one-year periods" between 1926 and 1997 (e.g., 1926–27, 1927–28 . . . 1996–97), stocks increased by as much as 54 percent and decreased by as much as 43 percent. In all of the rolling 20-year periods (e.g., 1926–45, etc.), however, the maximum price increase was 17 percent and the maximum "loss" was an average 3 percent gain. As an investor's time line increases, investment volatility declines.

5. Securities diversification. As noted previously, the unsystematic portion of investment risk can be reduced by investing in different assets and different industries so that no one investment comprises a significant portion of a total portfolio. Instead of having the portfolio return depend on the performance of just one or two securities, it is affected by the returns on many. Some people forget the principle of diversification when one asset class is particularly "hot" (such as large company stocks from 1995–1997). They wonder (in hindsight, of course) whether they should just put all of their money into the hot asset rather than dilute their overall return with other investments. The important thing to remember is that no one knows when financial market trends will change. Buying a variety of assets, including foreign stocks, provides effective portfolio insurance. According to John Bowen, Jr., a noted investment adviser and author, "You don't think you made a bad decision buying fire insurance on your home just because it didn't burn down last year. Investing internationally (and portfolio diversification in general) can be viewed in the same light."

6. Beware of beta. Beta is one of those fancy investment terms derived from statistics, along with R^2 and standard deviation. It simply means the volatility of an investment in relation to financial markets as a whole, which are assigned a beta coefficient of 1.0. The moral of the story: If you want an investment with less price volatility (or risk) than the overall market, choose investments with a beta of less than 1.0. A mutual fund with a beta of .50, for example, is half as volatile as market indices.

7. Use stop-loss limit orders. If you have stock that has performed well and you are afraid of losing all or part of your gain in a market downturn, place a stop-loss limit order with a broker. This tells the broker to sell your shares if they reach a certain price (for example, 10 to 20 percent less than their current level). If prices decline, the order will be executed, thereby shielding a designated portion of your gain.

8. Investment education. Take a course or read magazines about investments. Many people increase their investment risk because they are unaware of investment characteristics and sell at the first sign of a loss. This was evident in the early 1990s when many new bond fund investors with a "CD mentality" sold in a panic. Many undoubtedly thought they merely had bought higher-yielding versions of bank accounts or CDs. Then interest rates increased and bond prices fell (a classic interest rate risk scenario), causing a predictable decline in the value of their investments. A similar case of investor ignorance probably exists with stock mutual funds today. Many clueless investors have collectively poured billions of dollars into stock index funds that mirror the performance of market indices like the Standard and Poor's 500. Many, undoubtedly, falsely believe them to be safe. It is only a matter of time until the market cools again and index funds follow suit. Education is the key to preventing unnecessary losses caused by panic selling.

Personal Risk Tolerance

The myth that investment decisions are made rationally is just that—a myth. Many investors bring a lot of emotional baggage to the table. Nowhere is this more evident than in the area of risk tolerance. Financial risk tolerance reflects a person's values, beliefs, and goals and is largely determined by two factors: confidence and control. Generally, people are less fearful in situations where they have had some experience and more confident with decisions they have made before. They are also willing to accept more risk in proportion to the amount of control they have in a situation. In other words, people make decisions based not on what they know, but on how they feel about what they know.

Other factors that can affect an investor's tolerance for risk are their age, income, net worth, and time deadline for achieving financial goals. Generally speaking, younger investors, those with longer time horizons and those with substantial assets and incomes, can afford to take more risk (investing $5,000 of an $80,000 portfolio is a lot different than investing your only $5,000). Nevertheless, this is not always the way investors *feel*. Younger people and those well off may actually feel less confident about their finances or fear that they have more to lose. People base their decisions not on reality, but on their perception of reality.

A 1989 study by Kansas business professor Robert Masters shed some additional light on investor risk tolerance. It found that a relationship exists between risk-taking propensity and investment risk tolerance. People who are less inclined to take risks in their daily life tend to choose conservative or moderate investments, while those inclined to take risks tend to invest in more aggressive and growth-oriented products. The study also showed that an investor's knowledge of investments, rather than their general educational background, increased their willingness to take risks.

A variety of quizzes have been developed over the years for investors to determine how much investment risk they feel comfortable with. The higher the score, the more resources (for example, time, money, experience) an investor has with which to handle investment risk. Worksheet #3 summarizes 12 key factors commonly contained within risk-tolerance surveys. Use these factors as a guide to determine your own investment personality.

WORKSHEET 3 *Personal Risk-Tolerance Checklist*

Below is a list of 12 factors that affect financial risk tolerance. Review each one and consider those that affect you personally and determine the way you view investment risk.

1. *Emergency reserves*—Investors with six or more months of household expenses in reserve can handle more investment risk than those with more meager emergency savings.

2. *Income stability*—Investors with a chance of unemployment or a large financial burden in the next year or two may choose to invest more conservatively.

(continued)

WORKSHEET 3 *Continued*

3. *Investment experience*—Conservative investors often have little or no investment experience or have limited themselves to low-risk savings products.

4. *Investment objective*—Persons with a goal of capital appreciation often invest more aggressively than those whose major priority is safety of principal.

5. *Investment preferences*—Investors with assets currently invested in stocks and growth funds have already provided evidence of their willingness to incur risks in search of potential reward.

6. *Investment time horizon*—Investors with ten or more years until a financial goal have time to recoup a loss and can afford to invest more aggressively. Ditto for younger investors.

7. *Market drop reaction*—Conservative investors say they'll sell if an investment loses 10 percent or more of its value in a market correction. Moderate-risk investors say they will sit tight and wait for prices to rebound, and aggressive investors say they will buy additional shares.

8. *Net worth*—An investor can afford to take more risk with a six-figure net worth than a net worth of less than $10,000.

9. *Prize decisions (hypothetical)*—Conservative investors say they would take a prize (e.g., $1,000) in cash. More aggressive investors would take a chance (e.g., 20 percent odds) at winning a larger dollar amount.

10. *Role models*—According to a study by the Investment Company Institute, a trade association for the mutual fund industry, more high-risk tolerant shareholders grew up in households that were involved in investing than were low- and moderate-risk investors.

11. *The Hindsight Test*—Conservative investors say they feel better about not losing their principal in a low-yield money market fund than doubling their money in a higher-risk equity investment.

12. *The Sleep Test*—Conservative investors cannot stand as much anxiety related to the performance of their investments as aggressive investors and still be able to sleep at night.

Heuristics and Other Money Distortions

Our minds and memories sometimes play tricks on us when we make financial decisions. They distort reality and it costs us money. *Heuristic* is a fancy word used by behavioral finance experts to describe rules of thumb that investors use to simplify financial decisions. Heuristics are mental shortcuts that influence perceptions of investment risk and can be helpful or lead to dangerously misleading conclusions. Why do investors rely on heuristics? Because it is easier and faster to make decisions based on what we think we know about something than to take the time to research and analyze an issue. Some common financial heuristics include

- investing in the latest "hot" stocks or mutual funds,
- extrapolating the past into the future,
- equating a good company with a good investment irrespective of price,
- overemphasizing recent price information and market trends, and
- drawing illogical conclusions through fuzzy logic that links dissimilar items through common—but faulty—patterns.

According to Barbara Bristow, a personal finance educator at Cornell University, a second common money distortion is automatic behavior. People tend to make judgments about products based on how similar they are to typical images or stereotypes of that product. This often turns into automatic purchasing habits like buying the same brand of toothpaste or the same kind of car without thinking about or evaluating other possible alternatives. Automatic behavior saves us time (especially for routine purchases such as groceries) but can be costly. Before making an investment automatically, ask yourself two questions:

1. Is its objective incompatible with your personal financial goals? and

2. Is there a better-performing and/or less costly alternative available?

If the answer to either or both questions is yes, shop around.

Mental accounting is a third money mind game. As noted in the $50 theater ticket story, people tend to separate their money into various pots and make spending and investing decisions accordingly. Mental accounts are especially sensitive to where money is located. Cash in our pockets is more tempting than money in a savings account, while money in an IRA or 401(k) is less tempting than a savings account. Each account may have the same dollar amount but our mind tricks us into thinking they are different.

Bristow notes that mental accounting can work in an investor's favor. Instead of waiting to see "what's left" at the end of a month to invest, reframe the situation by paying your investing account first. Then spend what's left over. If you're very concerned about investment risk, purchase stock or growth funds with a small portion of personal assets (i.e., your risk account) and put the rest of your money where you feel secure. This form of mental accounting is analogous to bringing $10 to a bingo game or casino and leaving the rest of your cash at home to avoid losing more than your limit.

The best place to start an investment account is an employer's 401(k). Your contribution will be tax-deductible and employer matching provides a cushion against losses (i.e., you're losing your boss's money also; not just your own). Another suggestion to reduce investment risk: Invest small amounts gradually rather than building up a large sum and having to decide where to invest it all at once.

The Four-Year-Old Test

Investor: Know thyself. Never make investments that you don't understand or feel comfortable with. To gauge your investment knowledge, try the *four-year-old test*. In the 1994 hit movie *Philadelphia*, Denzel Washington played an attorney who asked clients to "Tell it to me like I was a four-year-old" when explaining their situation (that is, in simple words and terms). If you can't do the same and explain an investment simply to a friend (its characteristics, cost, risks, and pros and cons), it probably means that you don't understand it well yourself. Hold off making the investment until you ask a few more questions and learn some more. Then, once you fully understand an investment, consider whether it's an appropriate choice to achieve a financial goal and whether it fits your personal comfort level.

4

How to Find the Money to Invest

Think you can . . . think you can't . . .
Either way . . . you'll be right!

—Henry Ford

To improve *physical* fitness, one needs to increase exercise and reduce dietary fat. To improve *fiscal* fitness, increased savings and reduced spending and debt are often recommended. Making behavior changes necessary to establish habits to improve physical or fiscal fitness is easier said than done, however. Dr. James Prochaska describes self-change as a process that occurs in stages, based on an individual's readiness to change. In the book *Changing for Good,* he and his coauthors present a model for understanding how individuals change their behavior. According to the model, there are six stages of behavioral change: precontemplation, contemplation, preparation, action, maintenance, and termination.

Precontemplation is the stage of the change process where individuals are oblivious to a problem and have no intention to change behavior. At the contemplation stage, there is awareness of a problem but no commitment yet to making a change. During the preparation stage, individuals plan to establish new behaviors and get ready to take action. By the action stage, there is a commitment to begin a new habit and observable behavior changes. At the maintenance stage, individuals work to maintain progress and prevent a relapse. By termination, the final stage, a new behavior is fully integrated into an individual's lifestyle.

This chapter is about making behavioral changes to free up money to invest or, using the Prochaska model, moving from precontemplation (not investing) to action (e.g., opening a mutual fund account) to termination (e.g., making automatic $100 monthly deposits). The key to successful money management is to change current spending habits. According to Paul Richard of the National Center for Financial Education (NCFE), "Everyday spending decisions, especially credit-based ones, will have a far greater negative effect on one's financial future than any investment decision one might ever make." To illustrate the relationship between spending and asset accumulation, the NCFE estimates that the *real* difference in price between a full-size car and a compact car is not about $10,000 (as most people would guess) but rather over a half million dollars. Say what? Cars are expensive but not that bad, you say. Read on. The NCFE does the math as follows: Borrowing $25,000 for a new full-size car over 7 years will cost about $634 a month. Borrowing just $15,000 for a compact car will cost only $381 a month. At age 30, begin saving the difference—$253 a month—for 35 years. Earning an 8 percent average rate of return, the $253 a month will grow to $580,352. Just for spending less on a car. It is quite possible that a person could accumulate several million dollars if the same mathematical logic was applied to other spending decisions such as a house, vacations, clothing, and restaurant meals.

Which brings us back to the importance of spending habits. The best way to change spending habits is to find out where your money is going now. Fixed expenses are items that cost the same each time you pay them: rent/mortgage, car payment, various insurance premiums, etc. Flexible expenses are not the same each time you pay them. They change from week to week and month to month, depending on your use of products and services. Flexible expenses include: food, utilities, clothing, gifts, toiletries, recreation, and auto expenses (such as gas, oil, tolls, parking, etc.) and are where *nibblers* can be found. These are items that nibble dollars out of your budget and can add up to a chunk of change over time.

To find the nibblers that eat away your income, begin tracking your expenses. Get a pocket-size notebook and keep it handy. Write down what you buy (both the dollar amount and the item purchased) for a full month and get all family members to cooperate. If you withdraw money from an automatic teller machine (ATM), use the back of the withdrawal slip to record how you spend the money. Expenses should include everything: magazines, snacks from a vending machine, lottery tickets, lunches, parking, donations for office gifts, etc. When you put your hand into your pocket or purse to get money out, write it down. At the end of the month, review the list and the total for each expense category. Then ask yourself the following questions: Am I spending money the way I want to? and Can I make any changes?

Developing a Spending Plan That Works

Once you've reviewed current spending patterns, it's time to develop a plan for future spending and investing; that is, a budget. Many people consider preparing a budget a dull and dreary chore. On an excitement scale of one to ten, it ranks somewhere around a minus three. Therefore, the first thing that is needed is a change of vocabulary. Unlike the word budget, which is often perceived negatively (for example, as a deprivation and a financial straitjacket), the phrase *spending plan* indicates that people are in charge of their finances rather than the other way around. Each word is also much more positive: Most people enjoy spending money and the word plan emphasizes an element of control.

A successful spending plan should have positive cash flow (income greater than expenses) and money available to invest for future financial goals. Anything less is a prescription for trouble because it means that you are borrowing from somewhere (e.g., savings, credit cards) to make ends meet. No matter what your annual income—$10,000, $100,000, or any amount in between—if you spend more than you earn, you will eventually go broke. Perhaps the best illustration of this is the story of Woolworth heiress Barbara Hutton who inherited about $50 million back in the 1920s and died practically penniless after decades of extravagant spending.

To revisit the physical and fiscal fitness theme again, weight control and spending plans have a lot in common. Successful weight control requires fewer calories, increased exercise, or a combination of both. A successful spending plan (and positive cash flow) requires increased income, reduced expenses, or a combination of both. Increased income can be obtained in a number of ways in addition to a second job or overtime. Other methods include: adjusting tax withholding, increasing investment yields, obtaining public benefits, getting increased child support payments, selling assets, bartering services, and charging adult children room and board. Upgrading employment skills to obtain a better-paying job is another way to increase future income. There are probably thousands of ways to reduce expenses and hundreds of books written on this topic. Dozens of ideas will be explored in this chapter. The key point to remember is that investing on a shoestring is possible by increasing income and/or reducing expenses. Simply rework your spending plan until the income figure equals total expenses plus money to invest for future financial goals. Adjust your goals, if necessary, to fit available cash flow. Add a fudge factor to your spending plan, that is, a specific amount allotted for an unplanned expense, such as a flat tire. When bills are large and paid at infrequent intervals (e.g., car insurance and college tuition), divide the annual expense into 12 monthly installments. Divide as many expenses as possible into equal payments to avoid unpleasant surprises (e.g., a $300 fuel oil bill).

Reducing Grocery Bills

How would you like to save $1,000 a year at the supermarket and use this money for investing? To save $1,000 a year requires weekly savings of about $20. Consider the following suggestions to get started:

- Use fewer convenience foods by cooking main dishes (e.g., pasta dishes and casseroles) in batches and freezing them.

- Serve smaller portions, especially meat, high-fat foods, and desserts.

- Prepare nonmeat dishes for some meals or use meat in combination with other foods such as stir fry dishes and casseroles.

- Buy nonfood items (e.g., toothpaste, film) at a discount drugstore, warehouse, or other low-cost retailer.

- Stock up on items when they are on sale (e.g., canned goods) or in season (e.g., produce).

- Shop with a list with a "bottom line" figure (e.g., $60 per week) and items that total to this amount. To avoid impulse buying, include a certain amount (e.g., $10) on your list for unplanned items.

- Score a double play or triple play. A double play is a sale price plus the use of a coupon on the same item and a triple play is a sale price, plus a coupon, plus a cash or product rebate.

- Make greater use of store brand and generic food and nonfood items.

- Take advantage of special store promotions such as two-for-the-price-of-one deals and double (or even triple) coupons.

Reducing Housing and Utility Expenses

For many families, housing costs consume the largest share of household income. According to the Statistical Abstract of the United States, American households spent $32,277, on average, in 1995 and $10,465 (32.4%) of this amount was for housing, including a rent or mortgage payment, home maintenance and furnishings, and utilities. One of the best ways to reduce housing costs is to refinance an existing home mortgage. According to Andrew Feinberg, author of *Downsize Your Debt*, refinancing can "on an hourly basis, be the most profitable legal act people can perform." Yet, because of outdated rules of thumb (e.g., "It doesn't pay to refinance unless your new mortgage is 2 percent lower than an existing mortgage and you plan to stay put at least two years."), many people who could benefit from refinancing fail to do so.

Today, with no- and low-point loans, refinancing often can pay for itself in a year or less, making it attractive even for families that move frequently. The rule of thumb today is simply "If it saves money, do it." If you plan to stay in a home longer than the time necessary to recoup up-front costs, there is a strong case for refinancing.

To calculate the savings that can result from refinancing, you need to know the total of up-front costs, such as the application fee and points, and the monthly savings. Let's assume that refinancing will cost $1,300 and would save $100 per month. This is your before-tax savings. Because mortgage interest is tax-deductible, you need to multiply before-tax savings by your tax bracket (e.g., 28 percent) and subtract the result to get your after-tax savings (100 × .28 = $28 and $100 − $28 = $72). Next divide the after-tax savings into up-front expenses for the number of months to break even ($1,300 divided by $72 = 18.1 months). In this example, it would take about a year and a half to break even.

Once you've lowered your mortgage payment, it's time to look at utilities and home repairs. Below are five more money-saving tips to consider:

1. When making home improvements, select from among well-established, licensed contractors who have submitted written, fixed-price bids for the work. Do not sign any contract that requires full payment before satisfactory completion of a job.

2. To save as much as hundreds of dollars a year on electricity, purchase energy-efficient appliances, especially air conditioners and furnaces. Energy efficiency information is found on Energy Guide labels required by federal law.

3. Contact your utility company for discounts for running major appliances (e.g., a clothes washer) during off-peak hours, generally nights and weekends.

4. In the summer, dry clothing outdoors to save on energy or laundromat charges and use fans, instead of air conditioners, to cool your home. Also, have your oil tank filled during the summer, instead of the fall, to save 10 to 20 percent on the cost of your first delivery.

5. In the winter, close off unused rooms to conserve heat. Caulk or weatherstrip windows and doors and install storm windows. Install sweeps at the bottom of doors and use insulated window treatments, shades, or drapes to block cold air.

Reducing Transportation Expenses

If you're looking for ways to trim transportation costs, consider these five suggestions from the Consumer Literacy Consortium publication *66 Ways to Save Money:*

1. You can lower the cost of a round-trip airfare by as much as two-thirds by including a Saturday night stayover and purchasing a ticket in advance. Keep an eye out for fare wars and be prepared to act quickly.

2. Save money on the cost of gasoline by using the lowest octane called for in your owner's manual and pumping your own gas. Keeping your engine tuned and tires inflated to their proper pressure can save up to $100 a year.

3. Avoid wasting money on unneeded or poorly done car repairs by finding an honest, skilled mechanic. Look for a technician who is certified and well-established, recommended by satisfied customers, and communicates clearly about repair options and costs.

4. Talk to your auto insurance agent about raising deductibles on collision and comprehensive coverages to at least $500 or, if you have an old car, dropping these coverages altogether. Also ask about discounts, for example, for alarms or air bags.

5. If you are in the market for a car, you can save thousands of dollars over the life of your car by consulting buying guides at a library. Use this information to select a model that combines a low purchase price with low financing, insurance, maintenance, and repair costs and gets good gas mileage. Once you select a make and model, compare prices at three or more dealers.

Reducing Costly Fees

Many people spend more than necessary for goods and services, thereby reducing the amount of money available to invest. Below are five examples and a cheaper alternative for each.

1. *Credit insurance*—Many lenders require credit life or disability insurance to protect them if a borrower dies or becomes disabled before repaying a loan. If a lender suggests this insurance, explain that other assets or insurance will cover the loan.

2. *Extended warranties*—Consumers are often encouraged to buy extended warranties on autos, appliances, or electronic items.

Yet they rarely benefit from these warranties, which usually last no more than three to five years, the period you're least likely to need them. The best alternative is to just say no.

3. *Credit check services*—Several credit bureaus offer plans that provide a copy of your credit file as often as you want and notification when someone receives a copy. Again, just say no. Federal law already lets you see your credit file as often as you want and, in most cases, you already know who is requesting your file because it's your application that triggers a request.

4. *Biweekly mortgage companies*—Some companies charge a fee to convert monthly mortgage payments to a biweekly schedule. You can do this yourself, however, by dividing your monthly principal and interest payment (e.g., $800) by 12 and adding this amount (e.g., $67) to your regular payment.

5. *Costly bank accounts*—To avoid being nicked with fees, shop around and find the best match between personal banking habits and account features (e.g., minimum balance requirements).

Two More Spending Traps: Gambling and Holiday Shopping

Whether it's a $1 lottery ticket, a $10 night at bingo, or a $100 weekend in Atlantic City, gambling is an expense in many households. People exhibit a wide range of behaviors when it comes to gambling, from nongamblers who are disinterested or opposed to it for moral or religious reasons to compulsive gamblers who have a chronic impulse to gamble that disrupts their work and family life, not to mention their finances.

The decision to gamble is a personal choice. If it's done regularly, it should be anticipated in a household spending plan. Just like any other expense, money needs to be found for it, which means increasing income or reducing expenses elsewhere. Funds for gambling shouldn't come at the expense of savings plans, such as a 401(k) or individual retirement account (IRA). This puts your future at risk. The odds of winning the lottery to fund retirement are about 12 million to 1. Money in investments, while not guaranteed, is a much surer bet. Acceptable loss limits (for example, "no more than $50") also need to be established before starting to gamble. The unfortunate reality is that most people lose more than they win.

The holiday season is another time when many people overspend instead of investing. Five holiday money-saving tips include:

1. Create a written holiday spending plan and set a spending limit for everyone on your list.

2. Be aware of store policies (e.g., refunds for items that go on sale within 7 to 14 days of a purchase) and save receipts.

3. Shop early to avoid rush charges on gift mailings and catalog orders.

4. If you've had a tough year financially, talk with those you exchange gifts with and suggest fewer or less costly gifts.

5. Consider inexpensive gifts such as baked goods or coupons for services such as lawn care, pet care, or babysitting.

Tax Withholding:
Another Source of Money to Invest

Many people deliberately have extra federal and state income tax withheld from their pay. Two advantages of overwithholding are that there's no access to this money and, therefore, it can't be spent, and the refund check makes a nice windfall once a year. Two disadvantages are that taxpayers must wait over a year for their money and that the government pays no interest. A better alternative to overwithholding is to invest the money right away. A small refund, say $500, is fine but, if you're getting back more, you're losing money (that is, the foregone earnings on investments) by giving the government an interest-free loan.

If you want to have less tax withheld, ask your employer for a new W-4 form. Then check how many withholding allowances you are currently taking. To figure out how many additional allowances you can take, add one allowance for every $396 of refund in the 15 percent marginal tax bracket and $744, $828, $960, and $1,044 (1997 figures) of refund, respectively, in the 28, 31, 36, and 39.6 percent brackets. Drop any decimal numbers and round down. For example, a 28 percent tax bracket investor with a $1,600 tax refund can add two more allowances (1,600 divided by 744 = 2.15). If you want to be on the safe side, add only one. Then add the number of new allowances to those you already claim and return the revised W-4 to your employer.

Five More Ways to Find Money to Invest

1. Use a holiday or vacation club to start an IRA. A 50-week, $40 a week club plan will provide the annual $2,000 contribution.

2. Whenever you receive unexpected money (an inheritance, overtime, bingo winnings, retroactive pay, etc.), invest it.

3. Save your extra paychecks: twice a year if you're paid bi-weekly and four times a year if you get paid every week.

4. Reinvest dividends and capital gains from investments into additional shares rather than taking cash and spending it.

5. Save loose change in a can or jar. Saving a dollar a day, plus coins, should produce at least $500 annually to invest.

Not convinced that small dollar amounts make a difference? Worksheet #4 shows that by setting aside $10 a month or multiples thereof and investing it, it is possible to accumulate hundreds, even thousands, of dollars over time. Worksheet #4 shows how $10 a month will grow at various interest rates and time frames. For example, setting aside $10 a month for 15 years at 6 percent interest will give you $2,923—the figure at the intersection of 15 years and 6 percent interest. If you invest $50 a month (for 15 years at 6 percent), multiply $2,923 by 5 (5 × $10 = $50) and you will have $14,615 ($2,923 × 5).

Need some suggestions for ways to find the money to invest? Try completing Worksheet #5 to identify possible monthly and annual savings.

WORKSHEET 4 *How $10 a Month Will Grow*

Number of Years				Interest Rate Earned			
	4%	5%	6%	7%	8%	9%	10%
1	$ 122	$ 123	$ 124	$ 125	$ 125	$ 126	$ 127
2	249	253	256	258	261	264	267
3	382	389	395	402	408	415	421
4	520	532	544	555	567	580	592
5	663	683	701	720	740	760	781
6	812	841	868	897	926	957	989
7	968	1,008	1,046	1,086	1,129	1,173	1,220
8	1,129	1,182	1,234	1,289	1,348	1,409	1,474
9	1,297	1,366	1,435	1,507	1,585	1,667	1,755
10	1,472	1,559	1,647	1,741	1,842	1,950	2,066
15	2,461	2,684	2,923	3,188	3,483	3,812	4,179
20	3,668	4,128	4,644	5,240	5,929	6,729	7,657
25	5,152	5,980	6,965	8,148	9,574	11,295	13,379
30	6,940	8,357	10,095	12,271	15,003	18,445	22,793

Source: Matejic, D. and Pankow, D. (1995) adapted from "How $10 Per Month Will Grow—Dollar Sign Realism in Goal-Setting," *Changing Times, The Kiplinger Magazine,* 1990.

Once you have studied the table above, use it to answer the following questions:

1. How much can I set aside each month? $_____

2. What is my investment time frame?   _____

3. What rate of return do I expect to earn?   _____%

4. How much will I have in the future? $_____

WORKSHEET 5 *My Personal Plan to "Find" Investment Dollars*

Use the space below to list things you're willing to try to find the money to invest. List specific actions you plan to take and the amount of savings that can reasonably be expected per month and per year. Five examples are listed.

Action Planned	Monthly Savings	Annual Savings
• Use more coupons and store brands at the supermarket	$ 20	$ 240
• Raise insurance deductibles	$ 10	$ 120
• Bring lunch to work	$ 70	$ 800
• Buy fewer lottery tickets	$ 20	$ 240
• Change tax withholding	$ 50	$ 600
1. _____	$ _____	$ _____
2. _____	$ _____	$ _____
3. _____	$ _____	$ _____
4. _____	$ _____	$ _____
5. _____	$ _____	$ _____
6. _____	$ _____	$ _____
7. _____	$ _____	$ _____
8. _____	$ _____	$ _____
9. _____	$ _____	$ _____
10. _____	$ _____	$ _____

5

Dealing with Debt

There is no independence quite as important
as living within your means.

—Calvin Coolidge

Many people fail to invest because they owe hundreds of dollars monthly on thousands of dollars of debt. It is not unusual for household debts to consume 20 percent of take-home pay, which is considered an extremely high level. A 20 percent debt-to-income ratio is analogous to working five days and getting paid for four because an entire day's pay is already spoken for. W.K. Brunette, in the book *Conquer Your Debt*, classifies debtors into one of four types:

1. Responsible debtors who keep obligations to reasonable levels and pay bills on time

2. Situational debtors who get into difficulty as a result of unpredictable circumstances

3. Chronic debtors who spend compulsively or impulsively

4. Hybrid debtors who exhibit both chronic and situational traits

A number of problems can result from excessive debt including high finance charges and emotional distress caused by loss of control over money. Credit issuers also are quick to impose penalties, such as higher interest rates, if borrowers' debt load increases, and fees if they are even just one day late with a payment.

Not all debt is bad, however. *Good debt* is borrowing for things you need but can't afford out-of-pocket (e.g., car, home) or to improve your income or net worth (e.g., education, home improvements). *Bad debt* is borrowing for consumption (e.g., vacations, clothing, meals). According to financial expert Eric Tyson, "the financially healthy amount of bad debt is zero." Unfortunately, this is rarely the case. Many people spend years paying off items that have long since broken or been consumed. A $2,500 vacation, for example, charged on an 18.5 percent credit card, would take 30 years to repay with 2 percent minimum payments.

Many people get into debt slowly over time and stay there. Andrew Feinberg, author of *Downsize Your Debt*, coined the word "perma-debt" to describe nonmortgage and nonvehicle debt that is carried on a permanent or semipermanent basis, that is, a debt balance that never goes away. In the early stages of debt, people begin paying late fees, pay only the minimum due, and may be a month or two behind on bills. In the middle stage, bills are months overdue, even minimum payments are difficult to repay, and creditors are demanding payment. By the final stage of debt, court proceedings are threatened or pending and secured items, such as a car or furniture, may be repossessed.

How Much Do You Owe?

The first step in addressing debt concerns is to know where you stand today. Making a master list of every debt will help you see at a glance who and how much you owe. Worksheet #6 provides spaces to list who you owe, how much you owe, and details about the monthly payment. Several examples are provided. Another way to analyze your debt load is to calculate your consumer debt ratio and annual debt ratio. To determine your consumer debt ratio, add up total monthly payments on consumer debts like credit cards and car loans. Next divide that by your take-home pay for the month.

WORKSHEET 6 *My Personal Debt Profile*

Name of Creditor	Outstanding Balance	Annual Percentage Rate (Interest)	Monthly Payment	Payments Left (Number)
XYZ Bank (car loan)	$ 1,200	8.9%	$ 400	3
MasterCard (ABC Bank)	968	19.8	50	Unknown
1.				
2.				
3.				
4.				
5.				
6.				
7.				
8.				
9.				
10.				
11.				
12.				

1. Total of monthly debt payments: $_____

2. Monthly take-home (net) pay: $_____

3. Monthly housing expenses: $_____

4. Consumer debt ratio (#1 divided by #2):   _____ %

5. Annual debt ratio (#1 + #3 divided by #2):   _____ %

For example, if the Smith family has a monthly disposable income of $1,800 and owes $200 monthly on credit cards, plus a $190 car payment, their consumer debt ratio is 21.7 percent (390 divided by 1,800), which is above the 10 to 15 percent ratio considered acceptable. The other test, the annual debt ratio, adds housing costs such as rent or mortgage payments to consumer debt and then divides by take-home pay. Ratios of 40 percent or less suggest manageable debt levels, while ratios of 50 percent or more indicate you're in dangerous territory. If the Smiths also had a $720 monthly mortgage payment, their annual debt ratio would be 61.7 percent (1,110 divided by 1,800), an indicator of financial difficulty.

Reducing Credit Card Costs

Although general interest rates have dropped significantly in recent years, credit card charges remain stubbornly high and have become even more so as a result of new industry trends. One is the so-called "GE Fee" (named for the GE Rewards credit card) where some credit card companies penalize customers who pay their bills in full. Other creditors are reviewing consumers' credit files periodically and raising finance charges when they see an increase in total debt. A third trend is creditors who are encouraging consumers to pay less each month. Obviously, the lower a consumer's monthly payment, the more interest creditors earn. It is no wonder that the average debt load of American households has increased significantly over the past decade.

Even persons who are not experiencing financial difficulty are probably paying more than is necessary for borrowed money. Two common financial errors are not obtaining the best credit terms available and carrying a permanent debt balance. In the 1970s, the conventional wisdom regarding credit was to "borrow as much as you can for as long as you can. You'll be paying it back with cheaper dollars." In the 1990s, it is advisable to "borrow as little as possible and pay it back as quickly as you can." The result will be more money to spend on other things (such as investing) instead of finance charges.

The first place to start reducing credit card costs is to select a credit card that best matches your debt repayment style. *Revolvers* always pay the minimum payment or an amount just slightly above it.

Alternators vary anywhere between making full payments to paying just the minimum. *Convenience users* always pay in full. If you're a revolver, look for a credit card with a low interest rate (preferably less than 10 percent) because you'll be paying interest every month. If you pay your bill in full, seek a grace period (a 20-25 day period where interest is not charged on new purchases if the entire balance is repaid) and no (or a low) annual fee. Cardholders who switch between making full payments and paying just the minimum should select cards with a low interest rate and a grace period. To obtain a list of low-interest and no-fee cards, call RAM Research at 800-344-7714 or visit their Web site at www.ramresearch.com. The larger a revolving balance, the more important a lower interest rate becomes. For example, $10,000 balances are not uncommon among cardholders with high credit lines. With a $10,000 balance, interest would cost $1,980 on a 19.8 percent card and $1,190 on an 11.9 percent card—a $790 a year difference.

For some people who can't qualify for credit cards because they lack a credit history or have a poor credit rating, secured cards may need to be explored. A secured card is a credit card backed by money in a bank account, which serves as collateral for the card. If a borrower doesn't pay a bill, money in the account can be used to cover the debt. The Winter 1998 issue of *Consumer Action News* presented the results of a survey of secured credit cards. It noted that secured cards usually have annual fees. For 17 of 21 surveyed cards, these fees were $25 or higher. Interest rates tended to be higher as well. About half of the 21 cards surveyed had annual percentage rates (APRs) of 18 percent or higher. The amount of deposit required of borrowers varied, with a typical minimum of $300 to $500. Most banks allow deposits—and credit lines—up to $5,000. Consumer Action noted that secured cards can be a good way to establish credit but they are costly and should be used only as a stepping stone to unsecured cards.

Let's assume that you've found the "right" credit card. In fact, you've found several . . . and that's the problem. You'd like to dig out from under a pile of debt and get the balances on these cards down to zero. One way to do this is with a *fold-down plan*. The first step is to repay an initial debt, perhaps by using a tax refund. Next, the monthly payment from the repaid debt is applied (folded down) to another debt. All other payments remain the same, as does the total amount spent monthly on debt repayment. By the time several debts are repaid, large monthly payments are being made toward remaining debts. To visualize this, let's suppose you have five outstanding debts: Macys, J.C. Penney, Sears, a Visa card, and a MasterCard. Macys has the lowest balance and gets paid off first. The money that had been paid to Macys, say $35 a month, then gets added on to the payment owed to another creditor. Let's suppose that Sears has the highest interest rate of the four remaining debts. You would then add Macys' former $35 payment to Sears' payment of, say, $25 for a total payment to Sears of $60. As other debts get repaid, their former monthly payments get added to payments for remaining debts until every balance is zero.

Together, folding down existing debt and selecting an appropriate credit card can save hundreds, possibly thousands, of dollars of interest over time. But this is just the beginning. Below are six additional ideas for reducing credit card costs.

1. *Know the fees associated with your credit card(s) and take steps to avoid them.* Typical fees include: annual fees, over-the-limit fees, late fees, and transaction fees. Annual fees are charged each year for using a particular card. Over-the-limit fees are assessed when borrowers exceed their credit line. Late fees can be assessed if a payment is even one day past due. Transaction fees are charged every time a credit card is used.

2. *Negotiate a discount from lenders.* Many credit card issuers will reduce annual fees and/or interest rates on request. The less interest you're charged, the faster you'll get out of debt. Before calling to negotiate better terms, role-play your request with a friend to sharpen your assertiveness skills. If you have other credit cards or preapproved card offers, drop hints that you'll switch to another issuer unless your request is honored. Try to negotiate a permanent change so that you don't have to make a similar request every year.

3. *Beware of bells and whistles.* Credit cards that offer cash rebates, merchandise discounts, or frequent flyer miles are best suited for convenience users who charge frequently. For the majority of credit card users who carry a balance, interest and fees usually exceed the value of any givebacks.

4. *Transfer existing balances to a new credit card to take advantage of short-term teaser rates that range from 4.9 to 12.9 percent.* Pay off the balance due by the time the teaser rate ends. If this is not possible, transfer again to another low-rate card. Pros call this practice credit card surfing and it can be beneficial if done in moderation, especially when there's a big difference between your current interest rate and the teaser.

5. *If you generally carry a balance, pay your bill as soon as it arrives.* Letting a credit card bill sit on your desk for weeks can be costly. How so? Most credit card issuers use the *average daily balance* method to determine what balance to charge interest on. The balance for each day in a billing cycle is totaled, usually including new purchases. Then the daily balances are added together and divided by the number of days in the billing cycle. Below is an example.

Date	Charges	Payments	Balance
April 1	—	—	$200
April 12	$135	—	335
April 25	—	$110	225

11 days @ $200 = $2,200
13 days @ $335 = $4,355
 6 days @ $225 = $1,350   Total = $7,905
Average daily balance = $7,905/30 days = $263.50

Paying promptly decreases the average daily balance on which lenders charge interest because there are fewer days with a higher balance. Unlike utility or insurance bills, where there is no incentive to pay before the due date, credit cards reward users for repaying their debts quickly. Paying credit card bills promptly also avoids the possibility of incurring a late charge.

6. *Pay more than the required minimum payment.* Otherwise, you'll pay more for everything you charge. The interest payment becomes part of the price of what you buy. If you have an 18.5 percent rate credit card, it will take about 11 years to pay off a $2,000 balance if you pay only the minimum amount due each month (usually the lesser of 2 or 3 percent of the balance or $10). During this time, you will pay interest charges of $1,934, almost doubling the cost of a purchase.

Principal Prepayment: Does It Pay?

Many homeowners wonder if they should prepay principal to re- duce borrowing costs. How much will it save and is it a better option than putting money in investments like mutual funds? The answer is "it depends." Prepayments on a mortgage should be compared with alternative strategies and take factors like your interest rate, loan term, and marginal tax bracket into account. Ignoring the ques- tion of alternative investments for a moment, prepaying mortgage principal always saves time and money. Even small principal pre- payments can add up to substantial savings. For example, on a 30- year, 8 percent, $100,000 mortgage, the monthly payment for principal and interest is about $734. If $25 is added to the monthly payment, for a total of $759 monthly, the mortgage will be paid three and a half years early with a reduction of $23,337 in interest costs. If $100 is added, for a total of $834 monthly, a 30-year mortgage will be repaid in about 20 years with interest savings of $62,456. Prepaying principal works because it prevents a lender from collecting interest on the prepaid amount. The more you prepay, the greater the savings.

Prepayments can start with your first mortgage payment or any time during the life of a loan. No special arrangements need to be made. Simply notify your lender that the extra amount should go toward repayment of principal. Then keep track of extra principal payments to double-check the accuracy of the lender's year-end tax statement. Two common prepayment strategies are to:

1. obtain a loan amortization chart and send the amount of the following month's principal, and

2. add a certain amount (e.g., $50) to each monthly mortgage pay- ment. The prepayment amount can vary monthly or be elimi- nated entirely during months with high expenses.

Despite the benefits of principal prepayment, you may be able to do better elsewhere. Certainly, if you owe money on credit cards charging 18 to 22 percent, pay them off before prepaying principal on a mortgage. Ditto for contributions to a tax-deferred employer plan, such as a 401(k), especially if there is employer matching. As- suming consumer debts are repaid and employer plans fully funded, the decision to prepay principal then comes down to a question of investment return. If the choice is between prepaying a 7 percent mortgage or investing the money in equities that have historically yielded 10 or 11 percent, choose the latter option. If the prepayment amount would earn less, for example, in certificates of deposit than the mortgage rate, the reverse is probably true. Compare the after-tax interest rate paid on a mortgage with the after-tax return earned on alternative investments. This is a key factor when deciding if prepayment makes sense.

Time Is Money

By now, you should be convinced of the impact that even small behavioral changes can have on borrowing costs over time. Hundreds, even thousands, of dollars can be freed up to invest. Worksheet #7 contains spaces to develop a personal debt reduction plan. Simply list what you plan to do, and when, and the estimated cost savings. Several examples are provided. As you ponder your own financial future, consider the following calculation prepared by Barbara Bristow of Cornell University. The example shows differences in debt reduction and the amount of interest paid by three fictional families, each with a different repayment schedule. It assumes that each family has a credit card balance of $4,800 with a 17 percent annual percentage rate (APR) and that they do not add any more charges to their existing debt or miss any payments.

The Palmers pay just the minimum due each month (creditors charge around 2 percent of the unpaid balance with a minimum floor of $10). They will make 405 monthly payments (33.75 years!) and pay a total of $10,399.78 in interest charges, in addition to the $4,800 they borrowed, for a grand total of $15,199.78.

The Browns decide to pay $120 per month. At this rate of repayment, their debt will be repaid in exactly five years (60 payments) and they will pay a total of $2,333.83 in interest charges for a total of $7,133.83.

The Smiths decide to pay $240 per month. They will finish paying off the principal in 2 years (24 payments) with a total interest cost of $884.11 for a total of $5,684.11. The Smiths then decide to continue making a $240 payment to themselves and invest it. They find a quality mutual fund and contribute $240 per month for 381 months. This length of time coincides with the date that the Palmers finish repaying their $4,800 balance. If the Smiths' mutual fund earns 8 percent over the 31.75 years that they invest, they will accumulate $390,362 toward a secure retirement.

WORKSHEET 7 *My Personal Debt Reduction Plan*

Action Planned	Date of Action
• Add $25/month to credit card minimum payment	March 1999
• Switch to a lower-rate credit card	ASAP
• Call to drop private mortgage insurance (PMI)	Next month
1. _____	_____
2. _____	_____
3. _____	_____
4. _____	_____
5. _____	_____
6. _____	_____
7. _____	_____
8. _____	_____
9. _____	_____
10. _____	_____
11. _____	_____
12. _____	_____

Estimated monthly savings from actions listed above: $ _____

Plans for the use of this money: _____

_____

_____

6

The Magic of
Compound Interest

*Time is at once the most valuable and the most
perishable of all our possessions.*

—John Randolph

In Part One, you were introduced to important investment prerequisites. Things like goal setting, expense reduction, and risk tolerance. You're now ready for the next step on your financial journey:
a serious discussion of investing itself. Three things are required for
successful investing. You need to: *want* to do it (be motivated to invest), know *how* to do it (learn various investment techniques), and
receive *periodic feedback* (i.e., an answer to the question "How am I
doing?"). Part Two will focus on the second key success factor—
learning the nuts and bolts of investing. You'll be introduced to new
terms such as time diversification, compounding, and asset allocation. The objective of Chapters 6 through 8 is to build awareness of
investment fundamentals in preparation for discussion of specific
investment products, such as mutual funds, in Part Three. There is
no better place to begin, perhaps, than a discussion of the power of
compound interest.

Compound interest has been called the eighth wonder of the world
in recognition of its dramatic effect on the growth of investments.
Even small shoestring amounts of money, given adequate time, can

grow to significant sums. Figure 6.1, taken from an advertisement for the mutual fund company T. Rowe Price, shows the growth of monthly investments ranging from $50 to $500 that earn an 8 percent return compounded monthly before taxes. Note how regular investments, especially higher amounts over a longer time horizon, can grow to a small fortune.

Compounding works because assets earn interest, dividends, and/or capital gains which, when reinvested, grow an investor's principal, resulting in even higher earnings (i.e., interest on interest) each subsequent period that earnings are credited. Four key factors affect the return provided by compound interest: the frequency of compounding, the availability of tax deferral, the return earned on an investment, and how long funds are left to grow. The first factor is easy to understand: The more frequently that interest compounds (e.g., daily as opposed to monthly, quarterly, semiannually, or annually), the faster a sum of money will grow. When investments are made in a tax-deferred vehicle, such as an individual retirement account (IRA), they also compound at a faster rate because you don't have to subtract the amount paid out annually in taxes.

The higher the return on an investment, the more earnings there will be to compound. This can produce dramatic growth over time. In their booklet, *Investing for Retirement,* the mutual fund company Scudder, Stevens, & Clark, Inc., notes that $10,000 invested in a savings product with a 4 percent average annual return would be worth $26,658 after 25 years. That same $10,000, invested to earn an average of 10 percent annually, would be worth $108,347 after 25 years, or more than four times more. The tradeoff, of course, is the greater

Figure 6.1   How Regular Investments Can Grow*

Time Horizon	Monthly Investment			
	$50	**$100**	**$250**	**$500**
2 Years	$ 1,306	$ 2,610	$ 6,530	$ 13,055
5 Years	3,700	7,400	18,495	36,900
10 Years	9,210	18,420	46,040	92,090
20 Years	29,650	59,295	148,240	296,475

*Assumes 8 percent annual return

risk that accompanies investments that have historically produced higher returns. For this reason, conservative investors often seek to benefit from the fourth key factor that affects compounding: time. The longer a sum of money is invested, even at a lower rate of return, the more compounding periods it will experience for interest to earn more interest. Each one of these four factors (compounding frequency, tax deferral, yield, and time) is influential, but together (i.e., a tax-deferred investment with a high rate of return credited frequently over a long time frame), the results are spectacular. Small wonder that mathematical genius Albert Einstein is reported to have once remarked that "the greatest power in the world is the power of compounding."

The Rule of 72 Revisited

To further illustrate the impact of compounding on investment performance, recall the rule of 72 from Chapter 1. To quickly calculate how long it will take for a sum of money to double, divide 72 by the expected interest rate. For example, $2,000 placed in a mutual fund earning 8 percent would grow to $4,000 in nine years (72 divided by 8). The rule of 72 assumes that the interest rate stays the same for the life of an investment and that all earnings are reinvested. Let's look at how $2,000 could grow over an investor's lifetime. If a $2,000 investment is made at age 22 and earns an average 8 percent return, an investor would have:

> $ 4,000 at age 31 (nine years later),
> $ 8,000 at age 40 (nine more years),
> $16,000 at age 49 (nine more years),
> $32,000 at age 58 (nine more years), and
> $64,000 at age 67 (nine more years).

If a second investor also sets aside $2,000 but doesn't get started until age 31, they'd have:

> $ 4,000 at age 40 (nine years later),
> $ 8,000 at age 49 (nine more years),
> $16,000 at age 58 (nine more years), and
> $32,000 at age 67 (nine more years).

This is just half of the first investor's stash. The second investor lost the last doubling period, where the real payoff occurs, by waiting an extra decade to start investing. In other words, procrastination is costly. Of course, there are ways (e.g., more aggressive investing) to make up for lost time (see Chapter 14 for details) but there is no substitute for compound interest which, unfortunately, is not retroactive.

You also can use the rule of 72 to estimate the interest rate required to double a sum of money. If you know your time deadline, divide that number into 72 to find the yield that will be needed to achieve a financial goal on time. For example, if you want to double your money in ten years, you'll need to earn 7.2 percent (72 divided by 10). If you want to double your money in five years, you'll need to earn 14.4 percent (72 divided by 5). Again, the higher the interest rate, the faster a sum of money will double.

The rule of 72 also can be used to illustrate the tremendous advantage of tax-deferred compounding, especially for late-blooming investors. Let's assume that Investor A earns 9 percent on an investment and is in a 33 percent (federal and state taxes combined) marginal tax bracket. After taxes, Investor A's net return is 6 percent (9% − (33% × 9)), where money will double every 12 years (72 ÷ 6). Investor B's money also earns 9 percent but it is placed in a tax-deferred investment. Money earning 9 percent will double every eight years (72 divided by 9). Assuming both investors are age 45 and start with a $50,000 lump sum, their investment growth over time would look like this:

Investor A Taxable Investment 72/6 = 12 years to double	Age	Investor B Tax-Deferred Investment 72/9 = 8 years to double
$ 50,000	45	$ 50,000
	53 (+ 8)	100,000
100,000	57 (+ 12)	
	61 (+ 8)	200,000
200,000	69 (+ 12)	
	69 (+ 8)	400,000

Both investors started with the same amount of money and let it grow for 24 years but the second investor earned twice as much because of tax-deferred compounding. By postponing taxes, earnings accumulate at a much faster rate. Of course, taxes will need to be paid on Investor B's account later, when withdrawals begin. In the meantime, however, money that would have been paid in taxes stays invested and earning interest.

A final use of the rule of 72 is to determine the effects of inflation on a sum of money. By dividing 72 by an assumed inflation rate, say 4 percent, you can see that the purchasing power of a dollar will be cut in half every 18 years (72 divided by 4). The rule of 72 proves that, even with a relatively low rate of inflation, investments will lose ground if their after-tax rate of return doesn't outpace inflation. The way to avoid this problem is to earn more than the breakeven rate of return, as explained in Chapter 1. In other words, make compound interest work *for* you rather than against you. The earlier one starts investing, the better. For an investment goal of $100,000 at age 65, it takes only $48.36 a month (assuming an 8 percent annual return) at age 30 but increases to $113.99 at age 40, $306.91 at age 50, and $1,420.47 at age 60. Notice that the amount required to invest monthly almost triples for every decade that you delay.

Don't despair, however, if you're pushing 50 and haven't saved anything for retirement. Compound interest still can be your friend. An investor's time horizon, after all, is his or her lifetime, not retirement date, which means perhaps 40 or 50 more years for a late bloomer's investment earnings to compound handsomely. Many people wrongly assume that all investment activity ceases once they retire. The reality, however, is that retirees often spend a quarter to a third of their lives in retirement and their money needs to work hard to support them.

You Have to Stay in It to Win It

The one thing that compound interest needs most to work its magic is time. Yet, some investors think there's a better way to grow rich: market timing. Instead of leaving their money in one place long enough to grow, market timers move it around, trying to catch the highs and lows of various asset classes, such as stocks and bonds. While this sounds like a good idea, a number of studies have shown that market timing is not an easy concept to put into practice. Research has shown that market upswings tend to take place during a relatively small number of days and, if investors miss the best trading days by moving their money out of the market, their return drops dramatically.

Researcher John Manley found that a relatively small number of days contribute a great deal to the stock market's long-term returns. Using the performance of the Standard and Poor's 500 (S&P 500) stock market index from August 6, 1982, to December 29, 1995, Manley found that an investor who remained in the market over this 14-year period would have earned a 14.1 percent average annual return. If investors missed the best single day in that period—just one day—their return would have been nearly two percentage points lower. Investment performance got even worse, as more of the best trading days were missed, as indicated in Figure 6.2.

The data in Figure 6.2 clearly indicate that, as the number of "best days" missed increases, the return to investors steadily decreases, right down to a 0.1 percent return for investors out of the market for the best 60 days. Data for the five years ending March 31, 1995 (Figure 6.3), compiled by the investment firm Salomon Smith Barney, also illustrate this phenomenon. By missing the best 20 trading days, investment performance drops from 11.38 percent to 1.38 percent and, by missing the best 30 days, an investor would have had a negative return.

There are two morals to this story. First, successful investing is a long-term proposition and, second, market timing is easier explained than done. Not only do market timers have to guess when to move their money into an asset class but they also have to decide when to take it out. Even well-paid "experts" can't do this successfully all the time because the best indicator of market trends is hindsight. Given

Figure 6.2   Investment Performance: 8/6/82–12/29/95

Investment Period	S&P 500 Annualized Return
Full Period	14.1%
Less the 10 biggest up days	10.0
Less the 20 biggest up days	7.5
Less the 30 biggest up days	5.4
Less the 40 biggest up days	3.5
Less the 50 biggest up days	1.7
Less the 60 biggest up days	0.1

Figure 6.3   Investment Performance: Five Years Ending 3/31/95

Investment Period	Average Annual Return (S&P 500)
Full 1,265 trading days	11.38%
Less the 10 best days	5.47
Less the 20 best days	1.38
Less the 30 best days	–1.97
Less the 40 best days	–4.92

SOURCE: Smith Barney Research

the long odds of correctly predicting market movements, most people are better off investing for the long term and avoiding market timing.

Time Diversification

As noted in Chapters 1 and 3, historical investment data tell us that time decreases the volatility, or the ups and downs in prices, of investments in all asset classes. In other words, the highs aren't as high and the lows aren't as low as an investor's time horizon increases. According to the Chicago research firm Ibbotson Associates, stock returns, as measured by the Standard and Poor's 500 index, ranged from +54 percent (1933) to –43.3 percent (1931) in one-year periods between 1926 and 1997. In rolling five-year periods (e.g., 1926–30, 1927–31, etc.), the maximum gain and loss was +23.92 (1950–54) and –12.47 (1928–32). In rolling ten-year periods, the maximum gain and loss for stocks was +20.06 (1949–58) and –.89 (1929–38) and, in rolling twenty-year periods, the best and worst figures were +16.86 (1942–61) and +3.11 (1929–48), respectively.

Volatility in other asset classes is reduced as well over time. Figure 6.4, based on data compiled by Ibbotson Associates, shows the highest (H) and lowest (L) values for long-term government bonds and U.S. Treasury bills during the same four holding periods and the corresponding rate of inflation.

Notice that the range of returns for all asset classes is very wide in short holding periods but narrows dramatically as an investor's time horizon increases to 10 and 20 years. The worst 20-year return for stocks, for example, is actually a 3 percent gain. The risk of loss drops considerably for all asset classes as an investor's time horizon increases. Finance professors call this concept *time diversification* because, historically, time has reduced the risk of investing in a way similar to holding a variety of investments. Time diversification particularly reduces the risk of investing in stocks. In fact, when the effects of inflation and taxes are considered, stocks are often less risky than other asset classes in 20-year holding periods because they produce a positive real rate of return.

An important lesson that can be learned from the concept of time diversification is to invest with a goal in mind and consider your time horizon so that it matches the characteristics of a particular asset class. In short time frames, stock market performance can be compared to a roller coaster. For this reason, stocks should generally be avoided for goals with a time frame of five to ten years or less. Over longer time frames, however, the stock market can be compared to a railroad train gathering steam. In addition, to continue the gambling analogy, the odds of winning are increasingly in your favor.

Figure 6.4   The Impact of Time on Investment Risk*

Asset Class	One-Year	Five-Year	Ten-Year	Twenty-Year
		Holding Period		
Large co. stocks	H: 53.99% L: −43.34	H: 23.92% L: −12.47	H: 20.06% L: −.89	H: 16.86% L: 3.11
Long-term government bonds	H: 40.36 L: −9.18	H: 21.62 L: −2.14	H: 15.56 L: −.07	H: 10.45 L: −.69
Treasury bills	H: 14.71 L: −.02	H: 11.12 L: −.07	H: 9.17 L: .15	H: 7.72 L: .42
Inflation rate	H: 18.16 L: −10.30	H: 10.06 L: −5.42	H: 8.67 L: −2.57	H: 6.36 L: .07

*Compound annual rates of return in percentages

Windfall Investment Opportunities

Windfalls are large, often unexpected lump-sum payments received only once or very infrequently. Contrary to popular myth (and fantasy!), most windfalls don't come from kindly strangers bearing gifts (e.g., a casino or the Prize Patrol). Instead, they usually arrive from more mundane sources such as retroactive pay or a lump-sum pension payout at a job, stressful life events (e.g., unemployment, death, divorce), or the sale of valuable assets (e.g., a home or business). Regardless of the source, large lump sums are often a double-edged sword. On the plus side, they provide a tremendous resource with which to achieve financial goals. On the downside, windfalls can cause as many problems as a drop in income if they are not handled properly. Two examples of financial distress are when recipients overextend themselves to live up to their changed financial status and when they become overwhelmed by decisions about how to handle a windfall.

Grady Cash, author of *Spend Yourself Rich*, describes people in the latter group as "hot potato spenders." Their windfall is analogous to being handed a hot potato that can't be held for very long. Unable to decide what to do with this money, hot potato spenders put off decision making, often for months, for fear of making a mistake. Eventually the pressure of having to make a decision—any decision—becomes greater than the consequences of making a mistake and the hot potato takes action. Needless to say, this is often done in haste and, when large sums of money are involved, the results can be catastrophic.

So what should you do if your ship comes in and you find yourself with unexpected funds to invest? Here are five suggestions:

1. *Allow a cooling-off period of up to several months after receipt of a windfall.* There is nothing wrong with putting the money in a certificate of deposit (CD) or Treasury bill while you consider alternative options.

2. *Avoid hasty moves such as quitting your job.* After all, it will take a substantial windfall to replace lost earnings. If a person earns $40,000 a year, they'd need a $500,000 lump sum earning an average of 8 percent to replace their salary, plus additional funds

to replace lost fringe benefits such as health insurance. Other examples of hasty moves are paying off a mortgage and purchasing lavish gifts for friends and family.

3. *Revisit financial goals and calculate how the windfall will affect the investment required to achieve them.* If windfall dollars were originally earmarked for retirement (e.g., a lump-sum pension distribution), roll the money over into another tax-deferred plan, such as an IRA.

4. *Reconsider your risk tolerance level.* Some people who receive windfalls feel comfortable investing more aggressively with additional wealth backing them up. If this is the case, consider placing a higher percentage of stocks or growth funds in your portfolio.

5. *Consider hiring a financial adviser.* Windfalls often result in tax consequences and/or complicated decisions regarding investment options or how long a sum of money will last. Money spent on professional fees will be well spent if it results in action that increases net worth by the fee multiplied several times over.

A final thought about windfalls: Invest your tax refund. Many people just fritter this money away. Instead, use it to bulk up your investment portfolio. In 1997, the American Council of Life Insurance (ACLI) calculated the potential growth of a tax refund over time. They used the average refund amount, then $1,200, and found that, in 30 years, it would be worth: $3,892 at 4 percent, $6,892 at 6 percent, $12,075 at 8 percent, and $20,939 at 10 percent. Not impressed? It gets better. A second calculation by the ACLI estimated the growth of $1,200 *invested annually* for 30 years ($36,000 total). The results were: $74,042 at 4 percent, $107,868 at 6 percent, $159,856 at 8 percent, and $240,165 at 10 percent.

These results were then used to calculate a monthly annuity payment for 25 years, say ages 65 to 90 in retirement: $107,865 provided $695 per month, $159,856 provided $1,234 per month, and $240,165 provided $2,182 per month. Are you impressed now? Small wonder the Commission on Saving and Investment in America began a campaign several years ago to encourage Americans to invest their tax refund.

Determining Your Portfolio's Total Return

The phrase *total return* refers to the combination of ways that investments make money. The first way is current income, such as interest paid on bonds or dividends paid to stockholders. The second revenue component is capital gains (or losses). This is the change in the price of an investment compared to its original purchase price. The combination of interest or dividends and changes in the value of an asset is its total return.

Total return can be used to measure the performance of an individual investment or an entire portfolio. The calculation is the same. In order to make a rough estimate of how investments are doing, three key pieces of data are needed: the account balance at the beginning of the year, the account balance at the end of the year, and the amount of money deposited throughout the year. All of these numbers can be found on the year-end summary statement provided by brokers and mutual fund companies.

Half of the amount deposited throughout the year is added to the beginning balance and the other half is subtracted from the ending balance. The adjusted ending balance is then divided by the adjusted beginning balance and converted into a percentage. Below is an example of an investor who dollar cost averaged $300 per month into a mutual fund, or $3,600 over the course of a year:

> January 1 account balance: $ 16,500
> December 31 account balance: $ 22,000
> $16,500 – Beginning balance
> Add   1,800 – Half of annual deposit
> $18,300
> $22,000 – Ending balance
> Subtract   1,800 – Half of annual deposit
> $20,200
> Divide $20,200 divided by $18,300 = 1.1038 = 10.38%

In this example, the mutual fund investor's total return for the year was a little more than 10 percent. The same computation can be used for an investor's entire portfolio. Simply add up the value of all assets on January 1 and the following December 31 and the total of all deposits. Just as it is advisable to calculate net worth once a year, so, too, should you regularly check on investment performance.

Otherwise, it's impossible to know for sure how you're doing and if you'll achieve your goals on time.

Ten Tips for Investment Success

1. Start with the basics. Remember that everyday spending habits can affect financial security as much as investment decisions. A dollar spent daily on a cup of coffee, invested at 5 percent for 30 years, will be worth $25,416. At a 10 percent rate of return, this coffee money would add up to $69,632. There are three keys to financial success: Make money, don't spend it all, and start investing today.

2. Invest painlessly. Investments should be automated so you don't need to remember where and when to make deposits. Arrange to have money deducted from your paycheck or bank account. Examples include tax-deferred employer savings plans, preauthorized mutual fund deposits that transfer funds from a bank account, and the purchase of U.S. savings bonds by payroll deduction.

3. Follow the market. Most mutual funds don't beat market averages so consider placing some money in an index fund that mirrors a market index such as the S&P 500. Two other advantages of index funds are low expenses and relatively low turnover (i.e., buying and selling of fund assets), which can mean lower taxes.

4. Don't get cocky. When investment performance is exceptional, as it was during 1995–98, there's a tendency to think that this is normal. Resist the urge. Data from Ibbotson Associates tell us that stocks have had a positive return only 52 (72%) of the past 72 years.

5. Use your computer. Popular software programs like *Quicken*® and *Microsoft Money*® can simplify recordkeeping. There are also Web sites where stocks can be screened against various criteria.

6. Get support from others. Consider taking a personal finance course or joining an investment club to learn more about products such as stocks in a supportive environment.

7. Start today. You may have to play catch-up if you haven't made your first investment. That's okay. The key point to remember is that the sooner you get started, the longer your money will have to grow and the greater the overall return.

8. Diversify your portfolio. Diversification can be achieved in two ways: within an investment product (e.g., buying a mutual fund that contains dozens of stocks) and by dividing investment dollars among different types of assets (e.g., stocks and bonds) and investment styles (e.g., growth and value).

9. Make retirement a priority. When you're investing for retirement, tap the growth potential of stocks. To minimize the risk of a poor selection, choose a stock mutual fund that includes a large portfolio of companies. Take advantage of tax-deferred opportunities such as an IRA or simplified employee pension (SEP).

10. Take your time with lump sums. A study of 1,000 baby boomers by Oppenheimer Funds found that 60 percent of those who lost their job and received a severance payout took less than a week to decide how to spend it. A quarter of those receiving inheritances also decided what to do with the money within a week. There are commonplace instances in life where people receive lump sums: divorce settlements, severance packages, retirement payouts, and inheritances, to name just a few. The larger the lump sum, the greater an investor's opportunity—and responsibility—to invest it wisely.

Using Asset Allocation to Build an Investment Portfolio

*We've been told, "don't put all your eggs
in one basket." Asset allocation takes diversification
a step further. It's not just "don't put all your
eggs in one basket" but "don't use all
the same kinds of baskets" as well.*

—Harold Evensky, CFP

In Chapter 3, you learned that diversification is a key ingredient in successful investing because it reduces unsystematic risk. One way to diversify is to purchase investments in different asset classes such as cash equivalents, bonds, and stocks. This strategy is known as asset allocation. The rationale for asset allocation is that asset classes have different characteristics and may perform differently in bull and bear markets. A bull, or up, market is a period where stock prices and market indicators, such as the widely quoted Dow Jones Industrial Average, are rising. A bear, or down, market is a period where prices fall before starting to climb back up again. According to the Securities Industry Association, the market generally must fall 15 percent before it is deemed a bear market.

The most common asset classes are cash, bonds, stocks, and real estate. Cash assets are short-term savings products such as bank certificates of deposit (CDs) and passbook accounts and money market mutual funds. They are very liquid but generally earn a low rate of return that may not protect against inflation. Bonds are loans to a corporation or government entity. They typically have maturities of more than one year and are sensitive to changes in interest rates. Examples include: Treasury bills, notes, and bonds, Ginnie Maes, and municipal bonds. Stocks represent an ownership interest in a company and an opportunity to benefit from its growth. As noted in Chapter 6, stocks have the greatest risk of short-term loss of any asset class, but also a better chance of beating inflation over the long term than cash or bonds.

Real estate assets are investments in land, residential homes, or commercial buildings, owned directly or through securities such as real estate investment trusts (REITs). Real estate is often illiquid, that is, it is difficult to quickly convert into cash, and it is subject to variability due to location. Like stock, real estate is considered an *ownership* asset because there is a potential for distribution of profits to investors who are owners (or part owners) of a property or company. Cash assets and bonds, on the other hand, are considered *loanership* assets because holders of these securities are simply lending their money to a bank, company, or government entity in exchange for a designated rate of return.

Asset Allocation Basics

Asset allocation is done for two main reasons: to reduce investment risk and to increase long-term results. By selecting investments in a variety of asset classes, an investor's portfolio is protected from the volatility of any one particular type of asset. In other words, losses in one asset class may be offset by gains in another. U.S. stocks might zig, for example, while bonds or international securities zag. A portfolio containing several different asset classes generally results in a lower return than one composed entirely of stocks. The tradeoff is less fluctuation in value, which often prevents investors from bailing out in a bear market and suffering a loss.

Consider the following example: Investor A has a portfolio that consists entirely of stocks and is subject to all of the volatility that "comes with the territory." If this investor's stocks earn an average rate of 12 percent over 20 years, their performance over time, when plotted on a graph, would probably look like the Coney Island Cyclone roller coaster. Investor B has a portfolio consisting of 60 percent stocks, 30 percent bonds, and 10 percent cash. These investments earn an average of 12, 8, and 4 percent, respectively. Investor B's portfolio return is 10 percent, the weighted average of the three asset classes, which is calculated as follows:

$$
\begin{aligned}
&60\% \text{ of the portfolio earns } 12\% \ (60 \times .12) = \ 7.2\% \\
&30\% \text{ of the portfolio earns } 8\% \ (30 \times .08) \ = \ 2.4 \\
&10\% \text{ of the portfolio earns } 4\% \ (10 \times .04) \ = \ \underline{.4} \\
&\text{Total portfolio return} \qquad\qquad\qquad\quad = 10.0\%
\end{aligned}
$$

Note that Investor B's return is lower than that of the 100 percent stock portfolio but higher than that of loanership assets. When plotted on a graph, its return over time will more likely look like a bumpy train ride, however, than the sharp peaks and valleys of the Cyclone.

In addition to reducing investment risk, asset allocation can dramatically increase long-term investment results, especially for investors who have previously restricted themselves to bonds and CDs. According to a hypothetical example provided by MetLife Securities, Inc., an investor who places $100,000 in an 8 percent, fixed-rate security will see it grow to $684,848 in 25 years. A second investor divides the same $100,000 equally among five investments with varying rates of return. Assuming one investment loses everything, a second earns nothing, and the other three earn average annualized returns of 5, 10, and 15 percent, respectively, that same $100,000 would grow to $962,800 in the diversified portfolio, or over $275,000 more than the fixed-rate account.

Like compound interest, asset allocation can have an awesome impact on investment performance over time. Small wonder that academic research has found that more than 90 percent of the return on a portfolio results from asset class selection (e.g., the percentage of funds in stock) rather than the choice of specific securities (e.g., Coke stock versus Pepsi stock). In a classic 1986 paper, Brinson, Hood, and Beebower reported the results of a study of 91 large U.S. pension plans and concluded that 93.6 percent of the variability in plan returns could be explained by asset class selection. A second study by Brinson, Beebower, and Singer, published in 1991 and based on the records of 82 pension plans, found similar results with asset allocation accounting for 91.5 percent of portfolio performance.

In both studies, neither the timing of investment purchases, nor the selection of specific stocks or bonds, was found to have a major impact on portfolio performance. Instead, the overriding factor was having an investment policy (i.e., a choice of asset classes and their percentages) that provides exposure to a variety of securities in varying proportions. For example, an investor with $3,000 might decide to put 10 percent in cash, 10 percent in bonds, and the remaining 80 percent in stocks, split three ways among large cap mutual funds (80%), a small cap fund (10%), and an international fund (10%). The word *cap* is short for capitalization, which is a company's current market price multiplied by the total number of outstanding shares.

Large cap stocks (or mutual funds composed of them) are issued by large companies—many with household names—with market capitalization over $5 billion. Mid cap companies are valued at $1 billion to $5 billion and small cap companies are worth less than $1 billion. Using the asset allocation strategy described above, the investor would divide their $3,000 as follows:

$300 (10% of $3,000) to a money market fund
$300 (10% of $3,000) to a bond mutual fund
$1,920 (80% of $2,400) to a large cap stock fund
$240 (10% of $2,400) to a small cap stock fund
$240 (10% of $2,400) to an international fund

Of course, the minimum deposit amounts required for various investments would also need to be considered. There is more about this in Chapter 13. Many investment companies require less for individual retirement accounts (IRAs), however, than they do for regular accounts.

In order to develop an effective asset allocation strategy, investors need to understand the concept of correlation. Correlation is a statistical term that indicates the degree to which the movement of two variables is related. When two assets share a positive correlation, they tend to move in tandem. When assets have a negative correlation, one increases in value while the other declines. Correlation coefficients range from +1.0 (perfect positive correlation) to −1.0 (perfect negative correlation). When constructing a portfolio, investment risk is reduced by combining assets with a low degree of positive correlation or a negative correlation. This way, assets move independently of one another and a total portfolio has less volatility than its individual components. If asset classes are highly correlated, on the other hand, they are like those proverbial eggs sharing the same basket.

Ibbotson Associates, the Chicago investment research firm that provided the historical investment data cited in Chapter 6, also tracks asset class correlations. Figure 7.1 shows the correlation coefficients of the historical (1926–1997) annual returns of six common asset classes.

Note the high correlation coefficients between large and small company stocks (.81) and long-term and intermediate-term bonds (correlations of .90 or higher). This shouldn't be surprising because these are correlations among asset classes with similar characteristics. Conversely, the lowest correlation coefficients (–.09 and –.03) are between large and small company stocks and short-term (Treasury bills) and intermediate-term fixed-income securities, asset classes that have little in common.

Figure 7.1   Correlation Coefficients of Asset Classes

Large company stocks and small company stocks	.81
Large company stocks and long-term corporate bonds	.26
Large company stocks and long-term government bonds	.19
Large company stocks and intermediate-term government bonds	.11
Large company stocks and U.S. Treasury bills	–.03
Small company stocks and long-term corporate bonds	.12
Small company stocks and long-term government bonds	.04
Small company stocks and intermediate-term government bonds	–.03
Small company stocks and U.S. Treasury bills	–.09
Long-term corporate bonds and long-term government bonds	.94
Long-term corporate bonds and intermediate-term government bonds	.90
Long-term corporate bonds and U.S. Treasury bills	.22
Long-term government bonds and intermediate-term government bonds	.90
Long-term government bonds and U.S. Treasury bills	.24
Intermediate-term government bonds and U.S. Treasury bills	.50

Undoubtedly, investors who divide their money among several asset classes with low correlations will earn less than if they owned only the best-performing asset during any given time period. This is the "opportunity cost" of asset allocation. However, the only true indicator of the best asset class is hindsight, which, of course, is too late. Investing in several asset classes with a low correlation is the next best thing because it shields you from being completely exposed to low-performing investments. In addition, asset allocation doesn't require a crystal ball and is guaranteed to stabilize portfolio returns, thereby reducing the risk needed to achieve a specific expected return.

Finding the Right Mix

Constructing an investment portfolio is as much an art as a science. Personal factors to consider include an investor's financial objectives (e.g., accumulate $20,000 for a child's education), age, marginal tax bracket, income, risk tolerance level, and time available to achieve financial goals. Young single professionals, for example, may decide to put 80 percent of their portfolio into stocks because they have time on their side and earn a sufficient income to pay household expenses. On the other hand, parents of a 14-year-old might choose to put college savings in cash or fixed-income securities because their time is limited.

A couple of 50-somethings, bearing down on retirement with little or nothing invested, might choose as aggressive a portfolio as the young professionals to make up for lost time. An older retired couple might keep 40 or 50 percent of their portfolio in stocks as an inflation hedge and invest the remainder in income-producing assets. Obviously, these examples are only a few of many possible ways to allocate assets within a portfolio. Just as there is no perfect investment, there is no one-size-fits-all asset allocation model. Investment portfolios need to be as individual as the people who develop them and have to live with the results.

Fortunately, data exist to help investors decide which combination of asset classes might provide them the return they need with an amount of risk that will let them sleep at night. Once again, Ibbotson Associates comes to the rescue with its data base of historical investment performance. Figure 7.2 shows the average annual return,

Figure 7.2   Asset Allocation Performance Figures, 1950–1997

Stock/Bond/Cash Percentages	Average Annual Return	Largest One-Year Loss	Largest One-Year Gain
90/0/10	12.9%	−34.3%	56.0%
80/10/0	12.2	−30.2	52.6
70/20/10	11.3	−26.2	49.2
60/30/10	10.6	−22.2	45.8
50/40/10	9.9	−18.2	42.4
40/50/10	9.2	−14.1	39.0
30/60/10	8.5	−10.1	35.5
20/70/10	7.6	−6.1	32.1
10/80/10	6.9	−3.9	28.9
0/90/10	6.2	−4.2	30.2

Used with permission. © 1998 Ibbotson Associates, Inc. All rights reserved. [Certain portions of the work were derived from copyrighted works of Roger G. Ibbotson and Rex Sinquefield.]

largest one-year loss, and largest one-year gain for the following combinations of stocks, bonds, and cash held between January 1950 and December 1997.

Note that the larger the percentage of stock in the asset mix (e.g., 80 percent versus 40 percent), the higher the average annual return and (except for the last two combinations) the larger the one-year gain and loss. The greater the range of returns for an investment, the larger its standard deviation and price volatility. Again, this is the risk/reward tradeoff in action and conservative investors will need to save more than investors who are comfortable with an aggressive (more stock) asset mix.

These data are based on historical returns of the three asset classes using the Standard and Poor's 500 index as a measure of stock performance, five-year Treasury note rates for bonds, and 90-day Treasury bill rates for cash. The average rates of return for the asset classes individually during this 48-year period were 13.2, 6.2, and 5.2 percent, respectively. Of course, past performance is no guarantee of future results, but it does provide a helpful frame of reference. This is especially true with long-term returns rather than recent performance figures.

Once an investor understands how various combinations of assets have performed over time, they can set about constructing an
investment portfolio that provides a desirable return with a level of
risk they can live with. A good place to start is to examine your current asset allocation strategy. Use your most recent net worth statement and Worksheet #8 to analyze the percentage of your portfolio
currently held in cash, bonds, stocks, and other asset classes.

Identifying current asset allocation percentages shows how far
you are from where you want to be. The next step is to develop a
personal investment policy that states the percentage of portfolio
funds to be allocated to various asset classes (i.e., a target portfolio).
This decision should be based on historical data and personal factors
such as age, net worth, income, risk tolerance, and optimism (or lack
thereof) about the economy. You may find, after completing Worksheet #8, that you already have an appropriate asset mix. More likely
than not, however, you'll need to reallocate assets to reach your target percentages. Remember that, at different times, asset classes will
always outperform (and underperform) others. This is to be expected.
Because it is impossible to predict winners in advance, asset allocation hedges your bets. By reducing exposure to any single asset
class, investment risk is reduced.

Worksheet #9, along with Ibbotson data on the performance of
combined asset classes, can be used to form a personal investment
policy. By answering questions about your reaction to risk and the
rate of return needed to achieve financial goals, you can select a suitable combination of assets. Conservative investors will want to limit
stocks and other growth investments to a small percentage of their
portfolio. Aggressive investors will want to incur a high level of risk
in exchange for the potential of higher returns. Moderate investors
fall somewhere in between.

Once you determine your target portfolio, it is time to realign
your current investments and "walk the walk." There are four common ways to do this:

1. Make a lump-sum deposit with new money (e.g., a bonus) to
   "deficit" asset classes to increase their percentage of portfolio
   assets (e.g., increasing stock percentage from 40 to 50 percent).

2. Exchange assets among mutual funds managed by a fund family (e.g., a transfer from the stock fund to the bond fund). A
   word of caution, however. Doing this is a taxable event, that is,

WORKSHEET 8   *My Current Asset Allocation Strategy*

List the type and amount invested in each asset class in the spaces below. An example of each is provided for illustration.

I Cash	II Bonds	III Stock	IV Other Assets
CD $2,000	Treasury Note $5,000	XYZ Growth Fund $2,000	REIT $1,000
_____	_____	_____	_____
_____	_____	_____	_____
_____	_____	_____	_____
_____	_____	_____	_____
_____	_____	_____	_____
_____	_____	_____	_____
_____	_____	_____	_____
_____	_____	_____	_____
_____	_____	_____	_____
_____	_____	_____	_____
_____	_____	_____	_____

Total _____   _____   _____   _____

V.   **Total Assets** (Add the total of columns I–IV): $10,000 _____

VI. **Percentage of Portfolio Assets in Each Asset Class:**
     Cash   (Divide column 1 total by line 5) $2,000/$10,000 = 20%
     Bonds (Divide column 2 total by line 5) $5,000/$10,000 = 50%
     Stocks (Divide column 3 total by line 5) $2,000/$10,000 = 20%
     Other (Divide column 4 total by line 5) $1,000/$10,000 = 10%

VII. **Pie Chart of Current Asset Allocation**

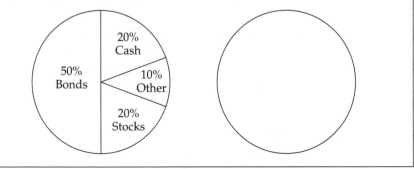

WORKSHEET 9 *My Personal Investment Policy*

1. What percentage of your portfolio are you willing to lose to achieve financial gain?   _____%

2. What average annual rate of return do you need to receive to achieve a financial goal?   _____%

3. Describe yourself as an investor: conservative, moderate, or aggressive?   _____

4. How long is your investment time horizon?   _____year(s)

5. What combination of asset classes will provide an adequate return with an acceptable level of investment risk? (stocks, bonds, cash)   ___%S ___%B ___%C

you will have a capital gain or loss, depending how the fund being sold has performed since your original purchase.

3. Set up an automatic investment program to gradually change asset class percentages by directing a mutual fund company to deduct the cost of share purchases monthly from a bank account.

4. Sell assets in a surplus area of your portfolio (e.g., cash) and reinvest the proceeds in a deficit area (e.g., stock). Again, income tax implications must be considered.

To summarize, the choice of asset classes and their designated percentages is called an investment policy. There are several schools of thought as to whether these percentages should remain fixed or be changed intentionally in response to economic conditions. What is not disputed is that investors need to proactively develop an investment policy rather than to just let it happen. Below are seven steps in the process as described in *The Prudent Investor's Guide to Beating the Market* by Reinhart, Werba, and Bowen:

1. Set clear and concise financial goals.

2. Define an acceptable level of risk.

3. Establish an expected time horizon.

4. Determine a rate of return objective.

5. Select asset classes to build a portfolio.

6. Establish an implementation plan (e.g., repositioning assets).

7. Make periodic adjustments to portfolio and measure progress.

Rebalancing to Stay on Track

In 1990, investments in stock accounted for 12 percent of American household assets. By 1997, this percentage had more than doubled to 28 percent. One reason for this change is undoubtedly that aging baby boomers are in their peak earning years and recognizing the need to invest for retirement. Another is that asset allocation percentages can shift significantly over time. This is especially the case after four years (1995–98) of double digit stock market returns. Thus, asset allocation percentages can be viewed as a moving target with constantly fluctuating values.

Pension fund giant TIAA-CREF recently noted that a plan participant who started making contributions with a 50/50 stock and fixed-income asset allocation in 1982 and stopped contributing in 1992 would have had a 64.5/35.5 percent ratio by December 1996 based on the relative performance of assets during this time period. Someone who made a single 50/50 contribution in January 1992 would have seen 57 percent of their portfolio drift into stock and 43 percent in fixed-income assets by December 1996. While this new asset allocation probably provided them a higher return (read: they were lucky) than their original target percentage, there is a downside. The higher the percentage of a portfolio in stock, the more risk an investor unwittingly incurs and the greater their chance of loss in a bear market.

So what can be done about asset allocation shifts due to the relative performance of investments? Investors need to reevaluate their portfolio at least once a year and rebalance to get back to their original target percentages. Unless this is done, a portfolio is likely to grow riskier over time. How rebalancing is done can vary. Some investors designate certain times of the year, for example, quarterly, to review and, if needed, rebalance their portfolio. This is called *calendar rebalancing*. Others rebalance only if target percentages have changed by a certain amount, say 5 to 10 percent above or below the original asset allocation model. This strategy is known as *contingent rebalancing*. It is important to note, however, that the trigger to rebalance can't be set too low or you'll be rebalancing every time the market shifts. Another reason to rebalance in moderation is tax implications. Unless assets are held inside a tax-deferred account, such as an IRA, capital gains realized on the sale of securities to rebalance a portfolio are subject to taxation. If assets are held at least 12 months, however, the 20 percent long-term capital gains rate applies.

The mechanics of rebalancing an out-of-kilter investment portfolio are similar to the steps listed earlier to develop a portfolio based on specific target percentages in the first place. Some investors simply transfer funds from a heavy asset class to a light one. The downside, of course, is the potential for capital gains taxes. Another option is to add new money to asset classes that have fallen below their targeted percentage. This avoids tax concerns and also enables one to buy investments "on sale" because they are being purchased in an underperforming asset class.

Rebalancing is often difficult for people to accept psychologically. Investors who are benefiting from growth in a particular asset class are naturally reluctant to part with their winners. It's like walking away from a poker game after a string of winning hands. The important thing to remember is that rebalancing is *not* done to increase investment performance. It is done to *reduce risk*. After all, if you weren't willing to put more than a certain percentage of your portfolio in stocks three years ago, why should you be any more willing to do so today? Investors who lack the stomach to rebalance may want to hire someone to do it for them. Two alternatives are financial planners who manage clients' portfolios for a fee based on a percentage of assets under management and free rebalancing services available to investors with large account balances at several major investment companies (e.g., T. Rowe Price).

Five Asset Allocation Tips

1. **Monitor target percentages.** Most mutual funds provide statements at least quarterly. Use them to calculate the total value of your portfolio and the amount of money in each asset class. For convenience sake (one statement instead of 10 or 20), consider transfer-

ring assets into a brokerage account or mutual fund *supermarket.* Supermarkets are a one-stop-shopping concept that allow investors to choose from among hundreds of mutual funds and receive one consolidated statement. Supermarkets were introduced in the early 1990s by several discount brokers. Fund companies pay supermarket sponsors a fee to be included so there's no direct cost to investors.

2. Avoid employer stock overload. In 1996, a study of 401(k) plans of 246 of the country's largest employers found that 42 percent of plan assets were invested in employer stock. Of a total of $318 billion in plans managed by surveyed employers, company stock accounted for $133 billion. In some cases, employees were found to have no choice: their employers matched 401(k) plan contributions exclusively with company stock. In other instances, however, the stock was selected by employees themselves. This can be a dangerous practice. Not only does your paycheck depend on the profitability of an employer but so does your future financial security. A much safer course of action is to limit employer stock to no more than 10 percent of your portfolio. If company regulations prohibit the transfer of funds while you're employed, sell surplus shares when you resign or retire and reinvest the proceeds into another tax-deferred plan.

3. Avoid simplistic rules of thumb. A commonly cited guideline is that the percentage of stocks in an investor's portfolio should equal 100 minus your age. Thus, a 30-year-old would have 70 (100 − 30) percent of their portfolio in stock and a 70-year-old would have 30 (100 − 70) percent. For many people, this guideline is dangerous. Asset allocation percentages should be based on an investor's personal risk tolerance and time horizon—not just their age. Even if a person is 60 or older, assets not needed for more than a decade should be invested aggressively to hedge inflation. The "subtract your age from 100" guideline is also too conservative for middle-aged persons trying to play financial catch-up. In order for them to accumulate an adequate nest egg, a healthy percentage of assets in stock is necessary both before and after retirement.

4. Watch for *style drift.* Just as asset class percentages change over time, style drift occurs when a mutual fund's stock-picking style strays from its intended strategy. A large cap U.S. fund starts to resemble a global or sector fund, for example, or a small cap fund starts buying large companies. The risk to investors is that their portfolio will perform worse than planned. In addition, with target percentages actually operating out of balance, a portfolio can be exposed to more risk than intended. Fortunately, a tool exists to help monitor style drift: The style box developed by Chicago mutual fund research firm Morningstar. Each Morningstar mutual fund report contains a box with nine squares, one of which is shaded to indicate a fund's investment style (value, growth, or blend) and the size of companies in which it invests (small, medium, or large cap). A fund might be categorized as large cap growth or small cap blend. Checking the Morningstar style box periodically will help to identify changes in investment style that can affect portfolio performance.

5. Consider an asset allocation mutual fund. As investor awareness of asset allocation has grown, mutual fund companies have begun offering all-in-one asset allocation funds that include varying combinations of stocks, bonds, and cash. Just like individual portfolios developed with an asset allocation investment policy, these funds are generally less volatile than those composed entirely of stocks. Some asset allocation funds offer a relatively consistent portfolio mix while others change the percentage of their portfolio in each asset class in response to market conditions. Examples of asset allocation funds include Fidelity Asset Manager and Vanguard Asset Allocation. A related fund category, known as life-cycle funds, allows investors to select from among three or four different portfolios. Each has a different combination of asset classes that matches a particular stage in life and/or investment objective (e.g., moderate growth, income). Examples include the Vanguard Life Strategy Funds and T. Rowe Price Personal Strategy Funds. Several life-cycle funds adjust automatically as an investor grows older by gradually decreasing the percentage of the portfolio in stocks and increasing the percentage in bonds and/or cash. These funds often have a date in their title (e.g., Fidelity Freedom 2030 and Wells Fargo Stagecoach LifePath 2040) that is designed to match an investor's planned retirement date. Look for asset allocation and life-cycle funds with a low expense ratio (more about this in Chapter 11) of 1 percent (.5 percent is better) or below and a portfolio mix that matches your financial goals and risk tolerance level.

8

Tax-Advantaged Investing

*I'm proud to be paying taxes in the United States.
The only thing is—I could be just as proud for
half the money.*

—Arthur Godfrey

Asset allocation and diversification are powerful investment strategies. Another is tax-advantaged investing. Tax-advantaged investments come in two varieties: tax-free and tax-deferred. The purchase of assets in either category helps investors keep more of their investment earnings and give less to Uncle Sam. Tax-advantaged investing is perfectly legal and is a key component of tax avoidance. Tax avoidance means paying the lowest required amount of tax possible to the IRS. Tax evasion, on the other hand, involves fraudulent underpayment of some sort and is what landed Al Capone and Leona Helmsley in jail.

Tax-free (aka tax-exempt) investing means that investment earnings are exempt from federal income taxes. Municipal bond earnings are tax-free as are earnings from the new Roth IRA (if specific rules are followed). In addition, most states and cities waive taxes on investment earnings from their own securities (e.g., municipal bonds). A resident of New Jersey, for example, would not have to pay state or federal tax on a New Jersey–issued bond and a New York City bond owned by a resident of one of the five city boroughs would be triple tax-free, that is, exempt from federal, state, and city income taxes.

With tax-free investing, no income is lost to taxes. Even before 1913, when the federal income tax was enacted, the federal government had agreed not to tax the debt of political subdivisions (e.g., states) and vice versa, a concept known as *reciprocal immunity*. Thus, interest earned on a federal debt, such as Treasury notes, is exempt from state and local income tax and earnings on state or city debt, such as municipal bonds, is exempt from federal taxation.

Unlike tax-free securities, investments that are *tax-deferred* don't escape income taxes forever, but they do buy an investor time. An example is the accumulation of funds in an individual retirement account (IRA). IRA earnings are free from taxation until withdrawals are made, usually at retirement. Until then, untaxed earnings get added to principal and earn additional interest. As noted in the discussion of compound interest in Chapter 6, investment earnings grow faster when they are added to principal on a tax-deferred basis.

To illustrate this point with dollar values, let's compare two people with a lump sum of $10,000 to invest. Both earn an 8 percent return over 20 years. The first investor selects a tax-deferred investment and elects to have all investment earnings reinvested. Two decades later, the original $10,000 will have grown to $46,610. The second investor, who is in the 28 percent marginal tax bracket, selects a taxable investment and reinvests all after-tax earnings. This account will be worth only $30,650 in 20 years, or $15,960 less than the tax-deferred investment.

Tax deferral works because it allows investors to postpone taxes due on investment earnings. Over time, its impact becomes readily apparent as the gap between the value of taxable and tax-deferred investments widens. For this reason, IRAs are attractive even if an investor doesn't qualify for a tax deduction on their contribution. An even better way to take advantage of tax deferral is to maximize contributions to an employer salary reduction retirement plan (e.g., 401(k), 403(b), and Section 457 plans). Not only do earnings grow tax-deferred, but the contribution limits (up to $10,000 a year for 401(k)s and 403(b)s and up to $8,000 for section 457s in 1998) are higher than the $2,000 a year maximum for IRAs. In addition, plan contributions are deductible from federal income tax, regardless of income.

In general, it pays to take maximum advantage of tax deferral opportunities, especially when investing for long-term goals, such as retirement. To put this advice into practice, consider the following investment hierarchy:

1. First, make a tax-deductible contribution to an employer 401(k) retirement plan that takes full advantage of employer matching (e.g., contributing the first 6 percent of pay). Employer matching is "free" money and is superior to any other alternative. A 25 percent match, for example, is equivalent to earning a guaranteed 25 percent return on an investment.

2. Contribute the next $2,000 a year to a traditional (only if tax-deductible) or Roth IRA. A Roth IRA is generally a better option than a 401(k) for the next $2,000 because, unlike employer plan earnings, which are taxed at ordinary income tax rates on withdrawal, earnings in a Roth IRA can be withdrawn tax-free if an investor reaches age 59½ and an account has been in place at least five years. This will result in a higher annual after-tax income than a taxable 401(k).

3. Next, contribute additional funds to an employer 401(k) up to the maximum contribution allowable (or that you can afford).

4. Next, consider other tax-deferred investments such as fixed or variable annuities. To maximize investment earnings, purchase only annuities with low operating expenses and good historical performance and hold variable annuities for at least a decade. Another tax-deferred investment option is a simplified employee pension (SEP) or Keogh for persons with self-employment income.

5. Save for retirement in other investments only after exhausting tax-deferred options. Then look for no- or low-tax products such as municipal bonds and index funds.

It also is important to maintain the tax-deferred status of retirement plan investments on leaving an employer. Two common ways to do this are transferring plan proceeds to a rollover IRA or to another employer-sponsored plan. Transfers must be made within 60 days of receiving a lump-sum distribution. Federal tax laws encourage investors to keep their retirement funds invested in tax-deferred accounts. A 10 percent penalty, plus regular income tax, is assessed on funds withdrawn before age 59½. There are several exceptions, however, but most (e.g., death, disability, high medical expenses, lack of health insurance) are not pleasant. Another exception is to *annuitize* withdrawals by making substantially equal payments over an investor's life expectancy or their joint life expectancy with a spouse.

What Is Your Marginal Tax Bracket?

Knowing how investments are taxed is an important factor when making portfolio decisions. Investors need to compare tax-free investment yields to returns on similar, taxable investments to determine which provides the greatest after-tax return. To quote the widely seen ads for Nuveen municipal bonds, "It's not what you earn, but what you keep." What you keep, of course, refers to an investment's return after subtracting federal and state taxes.

The place to begin is your marginal tax bracket. This is the rate of tax paid on the last dollar of income earned. A little over a decade ago, there were more than a dozen tax brackets. Today, there are just five: 15, 28, 31, 36, and 39.6 percent, with the latter two for affluent taxpayers. The 1999 income breakpoints for each of these tax brackets are shown in Figure 8.1.

Figure 8.1   Breakpoints for Determining Your Marginal Tax Bracket

	1999 Taxable Income	Tax Rate (Percent)
Married filing jointly		
	$ 0 to $ 43,050	15%
	43,051 to 104,050	28
	104,051 to 158,550	31
	158,551 to 283,150	36
	Over 283,150	39.6
Single		
	$ 0 to $ 25,750	15%
	25,751 to 62,450	28
	62,451 to 130,250	31
	130,251 to 283,150	36
	Over 283,150	39.6

Note that the amounts in Figure 8.1 refer to taxable income. This is the amount you look up in the tax table to determine what you owe after subtracting retirement plan contributions, deductions, and personal exemptions. In addition, the table only lists tax rates for federal income tax and does not include state income taxes. To account for overlapping levels of taxation (i.e., the ability to deduct state income taxes as an itemized deduction on a federal tax return), the following formula can be used to determine an investor's combined (federal and state) income tax bracket:

(100% − Federal tax rate) × State tax rate = Effective state rate

For example, if an investor is in a 6 percent state tax bracket and the 28 percent federal tax bracket, the effective state tax rate would be 4.32 percent, computed as follows:

(100% − 28%) × 6% = .72 × .06 = 4.32%

Next, add the effective state tax rate to an investor's federal tax bracket to determine the combined tax bracket, using the following formula:

Federal tax rate + Effective state tax rate = Combined tax rate

In the above example, using a 28 percent federal tax rate and a 6 percent state tax rate, the combined tax rate would be: 28% federal rate + 4.32% effective state rate = 32.32% combined rate.

Once you know your marginal tax bracket, you can use this information to determine whether a tax-exempt investment is better than a taxable one. To determine the equivalent taxable yield for a tax-exempt product, use the following formula:

Taxable equivalent rate = Tax-free yield
÷ (100% − Marginal tax bracket)

For example, assume you are in the 28 percent tax bracket and have an investment with a 4.5 percent tax-free yield. To get the equivalent taxable yield, divide 4.5 percent by .72 (100% − 28%). The taxable equivalent yield is 6.25 percent, which is the rate you would have to earn to keep the same amount of income earned by the tax-free investment. In this example, if you can earn a yield greater than 6.25 percent on a taxable investment, take it. Otherwise, the tax-exempt investment would provide the better after-tax return. To be even more precise, use your combined (state and federal) tax bracket when comparing equivalent rates.

Figure 8.2 shows a chart, derived from this formula, that indicates comparable tax-exempt and taxable investment yields for the three most common federal marginal tax brackets.

Again, the key to making the best investment choices is comparing tax equivalent yields and available market rates of return. In the 28 percent tax bracket, for example, the taxable equivalent yield for a 5 percent municipal bond is 6.94 percent. A taxable investment yielding more than 6.94 percent would obviously be more attractive while anything earning less would provide a lower after-tax rate of return. In the 15 percent tax bracket, however, the taxable equivalent for the 5 percent tax-free bond is just 5.88 percent. Assuming a choice between the 5 percent municipal bond and a 6.25 percent corporate bond, the latter would provide the superior return.

It should be noted that market conditions (i.e., the available rate of return on investments) can change, so the tax equivalency formula should be applied periodically to monitor the relative attractiveness of taxable versus tax-free investments. In addition, for the

---

Figure 8.2   Tax-Exempt and Taxable Investment Yields by
Marginal Tax Bracket

Tax-Exempt Yield	Taxable Equivalent Yield for Tax Bracket		
	15%	28%	31%
3.0%	3.53%	4.17%	4.35%
3.5	4.18	4.86	5.07
4.0	4.71	5.55	5.80
4.5	5.29	6.25	6.52
5.0	5.88	6.94	7.25
5.5	6.47	7.64	7.97
6.0	7.06	8.33	8.70
6.5	7.65	9.03	9.42
7.0	8.24	9.72	10.14
7.5	8.82	10.42	10.87
8.0	9.41	11.11	11.59

majority of investors who pay state income tax, in addition to federal tax, the yield advantage of tax-free investments generally increases when state-issued municipal securities are purchased. Like all investments, it is important to evaluate the risk involved with tax-free securities. The governing authority that issues a municipal bond can default just as any other debtor (remember Orange County, California?), and an investor risks losing all or a portion of his or her principal.

Now that you've learned the basics of tax-advantaged investing, it's time to apply them. Use Worksheet #10 to list your federal, state, and combined marginal tax rates and current and planned use of tax-advantaged investments. This worksheet also contains a section to calculate the taxable equivalent yield of tax-free investments. Use this section as a guide when comparing which type will provide the highest after-tax return.

Investment Tax Basics

When an investor sells securities—even municipal bonds—and makes a profit, capital gains tax is due. Assets held for a year or less are taxed at ordinary income tax rates ranging from 15 to 39.6 percent. Those held for more than a year are taxed at a maximum rate of 20 percent (10 percent for investors in the 15 percent marginal tax bracket). These rates will decrease further—to 18 and 8 percent, respectively—for assets acquired after December 31, 2000, and held more than five years. Prior to January 1, 1998, a holding period of 18 months was required to qualify for long-term capital gains tax rates.

To illustrate the effect of capital gains taxes, consider the following example: Assume an investor bought shares in XYZ growth fund for $20 and sold them for $70, a $50 profit, after five years. At a 20 percent capital gains tax rate, the tax due on the sale of this investment is $10 ($50 × .20) per share. Thus, the investor would earn an after-tax profit of $40 ($50 − $10).

Another capital gains tax that was reduced, in 1997, is the tax due on the sale of a home. Effective May 7, 1997, profits on the sale of a principal residence are exempt from taxation up to $500,000 for married couples filing jointly and $250,000 for singles. The exclusion is available every two years. To qualify, a homeowner must have lived in the house for two of the five years prior to the sale. The old

WORKSHEET 10 *My Personal After-Tax Return Analysis*

1. My federal marginal tax rate is: _____%

2. My state marginal tax rate is: _____%

3. My combined (federal and state) tax rate is: _____%

4. Tax-free investments that I currently own are:

   _____

   _____

   _____

   _____

5. Tax-deferred investments that I currently own are:

   _____

   _____

   _____

   _____

6. Tax-free investments that I plan to purchase are:

   _____

   _____

7. Tax-deferred investments that I plan to purchase are:

   _____

   _____

8. Comparison of market rates: taxable vs. tax-exempt:

   _____% tax-exempt rate = _____% taxable equivalent

   _____% tax-exempt rate = _____% taxable equivalent

   _____% tax-exempt rate = _____% taxable equivalent

rules about rolling over the proceeds into a new residence and the once-in-a-lifetime exemption for seniors who sell a home have been repealed.

A word to the wise to simplify investment-related taxes: Keep good records. For example, mutual funds record all of a shareholder's purchases and redemptions through periodic confirmation statements. They also send out an end-of-the-year summary of activity in a particular account. It is important to retain this annual summary to make tax calculations and as documentation to clarify a possible future dispute. If there is a capital loss from the sale of securities, it can be deducted from portfolio income up to $3,000 per year. Any unused loss can be carried forward to the following year's return. Another important tax form is IRS form 1099-DIV. This is the form that an investment company sends each year to shareholders (and to the IRS) to report taxable and nontaxable distributions. Read it carefully. From this form, investors can determine what they need to report to the IRS and add this amount to taxable income.

Investing in Tax-Deferred Employer Plans

Many Americans have a tremendous opportunity to invest in retirement plans offered by their employer. Employer plans are either qualified or nonqualified. Qualified plans (named because they qualify for special tax advantages) are more commonly used. They provide tax deductions and tax-deferred growth for employees and write-offs for employers. Relatively few plans are nonqualified, but they can be useful when companies want to attract star employees or fund benefits for a select group of workers.

The two types of qualified plans are defined-benefit and defined-contribution. In a *defined-benefit plan,* the amount of payment due an employee is predetermined by a formula based on income and/or years of service or both. Workers who have high salaries or long tenure with one employer do well with this type of plan. The other type of qualified plan is the more popular *defined-contribution plan.* There are over eight defined-contribution plans for every defined-benefit plan in existence today. Workers and/or employers contribute to these plans. The final benefit due an employee is not known in advance but, rather, depends on factors such as asset allocation decisions and investment earnings.

An example of a defined-contribution plan is the 401(k), which has become the most popular tax-deferred plan offered by employers today. 401(k)s, and salary reduction plans like it, make participants responsible for the funding and management of their own retirement account. Workers must decide if, how much, and where to invest and they bear all of the associated risk. In a typical tax-deferred plan, participants direct their employer to deduct a specific percentage of their salary to invest in choices available in the plan.

Following is a description of available plans including general characteristics, a description of who is qualified to participate, and annual contribution limits.

401(k) Plans

Named after a section of the tax code, 401(k)s are available to employees of private-sector companies that offer a plan. Participants must be at least 21 years old and complete a year of service. Part-time employees working less than 1,000 hours a year are usually ineligible. For 1999, the maximum annual 401(k) plan contribution is $10,000. Many employers cap contributions at a lower amount than the maximum, however, to comply with IRS rules that prevent plans from disproportionately favoring higher-paid workers. About 20 percent of 401(k)s allow voluntary after-tax contributions.

Major advantages of 401(k)s are a federal tax deduction (state regulations vary) for plan contributions and tax-deferred investment earnings. In addition, a majority of employers match employee contributions, typically 50 cents on the dollar up to 6 percent of pay. Thus, a person earning $50,000 and contributing 6 percent of pay would invest a total of $4,500: $3,000 from payroll deductions and $1,500 from the employer match. Taxes on the $4,500 that is invested are deferred until retirement.

Employer matches are the equivalent of receiving a 50 percent—in some cases, 100 percent—return on your money . . . risk free. Therefore, it's foolish (some would say stupid!) to contribute only 2 percent of pay when a match is available up to 6 percent. Over time, the effect of tax deferral, plus compound interest, plus employer matching is awesome. In his book, *401(k): Take Charge of Your Future,* Eric Schurenberg notes that after 30 years an $1,800 a year investment earning a 7 percent rate of return for an investor in the 28 and 5 percent federal and state tax brackets, respectively, would be worth

$75,988 in a taxable certificate of deposit (CD), $170,029 in a 401(k) without a match, and $255,044 in a 401(k) with a 50 percent match.

As with all tax-deferred retirement plans, 401(k) investors who withdraw money prior to 59½, or fail to begin mandatory withdrawals at age 70½, incur tax penalties. An exception for 401(k)s and other employer plans applies, however, as a result of 1996 tax law changes. If a participant continues to work past age 70½, he or she is allowed to delay making minimum withdrawals until retirement. Thus, money in their plan continues to grow tax-deferred. This exception does not apply to IRA withdrawals, however. Traditional IRA investors are required to begin taking minimum distributions at age 70½, even if they remain employed.

403(b) Plans

403(b) plans operate very much like 401(k)s except that they are available to nonprofit sector employees such as those who work for schools, universities, and charitable organizations. Like 401(k)s, an employee's salary is reduced by a designated amount and invested, tax-deferred, in available plan assets. Employer matching is less common (about 30 percent of plan sponsors) for 403(b)s than 401(k)s because many plan participants are paid with public (read: taxpayer-supported) funds. The same maximum annual limit ($10,000 in 1999) and withdrawal rules apply, however, as for 401(k)s.

A major disadvantage of 403(b) plans is that many offer poor investment choices. Specifically, a large percentage of available plan investments are high-cost variable annuities. Hence the acronym TSA (tax-sheltered annuity). Investments with high expenses often perform poorly as their earnings are eroded. A unique characteristic of 403(b)s is that, after 15 years of eligible service, catch-up rules allow many participants (especially late bloomers) to increase their maximum annual contribution by $3,000 (e.g., from $10,000 to $13,000 in 1998) with a lifetime limit of $15,000 of extra deferral. These rules are complex, however, so participants should check with their plan administrator before authorizing additional payroll deductions.

Section 457 Plans

Section 457 plans, available to state and local government workers, allow a maximum annual tax-deferred contribution (in 1999) of

$8,000. Employer matching is not available. A disadvantage of these plans is that money set aside by workers belongs to their employer until retirement. Thus, if a government entity experiences financial difficulty, a worker's nest egg is at risk. Another problem with Section 457 plans is that, like 403(b)s, many offer only high-cost annuities as an investment option. An investigative report in the December 1997 issue of *Money* noted that "the crucial process of evaluating a money manager for employees' assets is routinely muddied by political lobbying or by cold cash from vendors eager to drum up business." The best way for government and nonprofit workers to fight back is to lobby their employer—en masse—for lower-cost investment options, such as no-load mutual funds.

Getting Started

A tax-deferred employer plan is of little value unless you participate. If you've been thinking about enrolling, now is the time to take action by following these ten steps suggested by Karen Chan and Charlotte Crawford, financial educators at the University of Illinois:

1. Make a firm decision to participate and start making changes in spending to free up money to invest.

2. Call your employee benefits office to request a plan booklet and forms to authorize deductions from pay and the percentage allocation to available investments.

3. Determine your desired asset allocation. Asset categories often available in employer plans include large and small cap stocks, bonds, international funds, and cash equivalents such as money market funds and guaranteed investment contracts (GICs).

4. Investigate specific investments (e.g., growth mutual funds) within selected asset classes.

5. Do your homework. Order brochures, prospectuses, and other information about investments under consideration.

6. Study prospectuses carefully to determine an investment's goals, fees, management stability, and performance.

7. Read investment materials and attend seminars provided by your employer.

8. Make final choices of investments and the percentage you will invest in each. For example, let's say you decide to invest 8 percent of your salary in a tax-deferred employer plan. Within that amount, you might decide to place 20 percent in each of five mutual funds with different characteristics and objectives.

9. Complete the paperwork required to actually enroll.

10. Periodically evaluate asset allocation percentages and investment performance. Rebalance the portfolio as needed to maintain desired asset percentages.

Two final pieces of advice: Don't delay and leave the money alone. Start saving something, even 1 percent of pay, and increase this amount over time. Then give the money an opportunity to grow. Many tax-deferred plans allow participants to borrow up to half of their vested account balance up to a maximum of $50,000 (e.g., up to $5,000 in a 401(k) with $10,000). The downside is that funds withdrawn from a plan do not earn compound interest. This is the opportunity cost of borrowing. Worse yet, if additional contributions are suspended while a loan is repaid, an investor loses the opportunity to set aside more money tax-deferred, plus employer matching (if available). On leaving an employer, loans against plan assets must be repaid within 30 to 60 days. If a balance remains, it is treated as a premature distribution by the IRS and subject to a 10 percent penalty and regular taxes.

IRA Basics

Individual retirement accounts enable investors to set aside up to $2,000 per year tax-deferred. IRAs are not an investment per se but, rather, an account to hold assets until retirement. In 1986, the deductibility of IRA contributions for higher-income workers with access to a qualified employer retirement plan was eliminated. Between 1986 and 1987, IRA contributions fell by 62 percent. Recently, the pendulum has begun to swing back toward creating IRA incentives. As a result of 1996 tax law changes, married workers and their non-working spouses can contribute $4,000 annually (a maximum of $2,000 apiece), up from the previous limit of $2,250. In addition, the Roth IRA became available in 1998. The main advantage of Roth IRAs is that earnings can be withdrawn tax-free if an account is open at least five years and its owner is age 59½ or older. Roth IRAs are funded with after-tax dollar contributions, unlike traditional IRAs, which may or may not be tax-deductible.

Investing in an IRA offers several advantages. First, there is the opportunity for tax-deferred growth. Second, there is a tax deduction for owners of traditional IRAs who qualify. Those in the 28 percent marginal tax bracket, for example, who make a $2,000 contribution will save $560 in taxes ($2,000 × .28). A third advantage is the wide array of investments available to IRA owners, including conservative CDs and aggressive growth mutual funds.

IRAs also have several disadvantages. First, not everyone qualifies for a traditional IRA deduction. Hence the advice to invest first in employer plans, where there is a deduction regardless of income, employer matching, and the ability to contribute a higher annual amount. A second disadvantage is the extra recordkeeping (IRS form 8606) required of traditional IRA owners with nondeductible or partially deductible contributions. Lastly, as with all tax-deferred plans, IRA withdrawals before age 59½ are subject to a 10 percent penalty plus regular taxes.

Despite these drawbacks, IRAs are still a great tax shelter, especially for investors lacking an employer plan. Without an IRA, investment earnings would be eroded by taxes. One of the big decisions people face is which type of IRA (Roth or traditional) to establish. Below are five factors to consider.

1. Whether you have earned income. This is a salary, bonus, or self-employment income—not investment earnings such as dividends and capital gains. Anyone under age 70½ with earned income can contribute to a traditional IRA and anyone of any age with earned income can fund a Roth.

2. Household income. If an investor qualifies for a deductible IRA, that's often the best move because investing pretax is usually better than using after-tax dollars. If a couple has a 1999 adjusted gross income (AGI) less than $51,000 ($31,000 for singles), they can make a fully deductible contribution to a traditional IRA. Above

$61,000 ($41,000 for singles), traditional IRA contributions become nondeductible but can be made, no matter how high an income. With Roth IRAs, investors receive no up-front deduction for their contribution. Roth IRAs are available to couples and singles with AGIs under $160,000 and $110,000, respectively. Over the next decade, the income ranges where tax deductions for traditional IRAs are phased out are as follows:

Year	Joint Filers	Single Filers
2000	$52,000 to $ 62,000	$32,000 to $42,000
2001	53,000 to 63,000	33,000 to 43,000
2002	54,000 to 64,000	34,000 to 44,000
2003	60,000 to 70,000	40,000 to 50,000
2004	65,000 to 75,000	45,000 to 55,000
2005	70,000 to 80,000	50,000 to 60,000
2006	75,000 to 85,000	Same as 2005
2007	80,000 to 100,000	Same as 2005

3. Investment time horizon. The more years an investor has before retirement, the more attractive a Roth IRA becomes because contributions will have more time to compound tax-free.

4. The age when withdrawals are anticipated. Unlike traditional IRAs, which require mandatory withdrawals at age 70½, Roth IRAs have no mandatory age. This is an advantage for retirees with high incomes or those wishing to preserve assets for heirs.

5. Marginal tax bracket before and after retirement. If the same or a higher tax bracket is expected after withdrawals begin, a Roth IRA may save on taxes because distributions are tax-free. If a lower tax bracket is expected after retirement, a traditional IRA may provide a larger after-tax accumulation, assuming someone has the income level to qualify for a deductible contribution.

What type of IRA is better depends on all of the above factors. The best way to decide is to order software or check the Web sites of financial services firms and complete a personalized analysis. A good source of information is the Web site www.rothira.com, which provides links to a variety of interactive calculators. While you're deciding which IRA is best, also check out calculators that determine whether you should convert an existing traditional IRA to a Roth IRA. Taxpayers with an AGI below $100,000 are eligible to make this move without incurring a 10 percent early distribution penalty. The advantages of converting are future tax-free withdrawals from a Roth IRA at retirement and that traditional IRA minimum distribution rules at age 70½ don't apply. The downside of converting is that regular income taxes are due on the amount rolled over.

Tax-Deferred Plans for the Self-Employed

The widespread lack of participation in tax-deferred retirement plans by owners and employees of small businesses is an issue of concern. About 50 million Americans lack pension plans and, of this number, 33 million work for small businesses. In addition to IRAs, three types of tax-deferred plans—Keoghs, SEPs, and SIMPLEs—are available to owners of small businesses, sole proprietors, and persons who freelance in addition to their day job.

Keogh plans. Keoghs can be established as either a defined-benefit or defined-contribution plan, with the latter being the most common. Plans need to be established by December 31 of a calendar year and earnings accumulate tax-deferred until withdrawal. Withdrawals are penalized before age 59½ and must begin at 70½ for self-employed persons and 70½ or the year of retirement (whichever is later) for employees. Typical Keogh plans allow annual contributions of up to 20 percent of net self-employment income, up to a $30,000 annual maximum. The biggest disadvantage of Keoghs is a cumbersome tax form, 5500-C, that must be filed annually with the IRS.

SEPs. An acronym for simplified employee pension, SEPs require less paperwork than Keoghs to establish and administer. Another benefit for small business owners is flexibility in making contributions. Self-employed persons or business owners can choose to contribute nothing (e.g., in a year when business is poor) or make the maximum annual contribution of the lesser of 15 percent of net earnings or $24,000. This translates into 13.04 percent of net income before a contribution because the IRS defines net income as income after funding a SEP. SEPs must generally be opened and funded by

April 15. Thus, a self-employed taxpayer who wants to take a deduction on their 1999 tax return must establish a SEP by April 15, 2000. If an extension is requested, however, four additional months are available.

SIMPLE plans. An acronym for savings incentive match plan for employees, SIMPLE plans come in two varieties: a SIMPLE IRA and a SIMPLE 401(k). Both are available to employees of businesses with fewer than 100 workers and allow eligible workers to contribute up to $6,000 per year with a 2 or 3 percent employer match. In order to participate, workers must earn at least $5,000 during the current calendar year and any two preceding years. Money withdrawn less than two years from the date of initial plan participation is subject to a 25 percent early withdrawal penalty.

Tax-Deferred Annuities

An annuity is a contract between an investor and a life insurance company. An investor provides periodic deposits or a lump-sum payment in exchange for tax-deferred growth of principal and regular income for as long as they live or a designated time period. Although they are an insurance product, annuities can be purchased through a variety of sources including brokerage firms, financial planners, and banks. Unless part of a tax-deferred 403(b) or Section 457 plan, they are purchased with after-tax dollars. For this reason, annuities are generally recommended only after a person has contributed the maximum to an employer plan and IRA.

Annuities come in two basic types: fixed and variable. A fixed annuity provides a guaranteed rate of return for a specific period, similar to a CD (only tax-deferred). A variable annuity is similar to investing in a mutual fund family. Its return is not guaranteed but, rather, depends on the performance of the selected funds (e.g., bond fund, stock fund), called subaccounts. There are four parties to an annuity contract: the insurer issuing the contract, the contract owner (person investing in the annuity), the annuitant (person on whose life an annuity is based), and the beneficiary (person who receives annuity funds on the death of the annuitant). Often—but not always—the contract owner and the annuitant are the same person. Annuities also have two stages: an *accumulation period* that begins from the date of investment until a distribution is made and a *payout period* when an insurance company makes payments to an annuitant.

Advantages of annuities include tax-deferred growth of principal, professional portfolio management (variable annuities), guaranteed principal (fixed annuities), availability of tax-free Section 1035 exchanges that allow the swap of one insurance product for another, and—unlike IRAs and employer plans—no IRS limitation on the amount that can be invested annually. Disadvantages include a 10 percent penalty for early withdrawals, insurance company surrender charges, and high expenses, including an annual contract maintenance fee and a mortality charge (1.25% on average) to cover insurance company overhead and death claims. Combined with management fees for underlying mutual funds, the average expense ratio on variable annuities is about 2.09 percent—$209 on a $10,000 investment—versus 1.4 percent for an average stock mutual fund.

In an August 1997 article in the *Wall Street Journal,* returns on variable annuities and mutual funds taxed at the 20 percent capital gains rate were compared. The result? Because of high expenses, an investor would have to hold an annuity at least 20 years to earn as much money after taxes as the fund. It takes that long for an annuity's tax-deferral feature to offset the drag of high expenses and pull ahead of taxable investments.

Annuity withdrawal options include straight life and joint and survivor annuities, for those who wish to gamble that they'll outlive the amount they've invested, and period certain and refund annuity options for those that don't. With a straight life annuity, payments are made for the remainder of an annuitant's life and, with a joint and survivor annuity, for the lifetime of an annuitant and designated survivor. Straight life annuities are considered the most risky because an annuitant could die shortly after payments begin and their survivors would receive nothing. Any money left over reverts to the insurance company. The period certain payment option guarantees payment for a specific time period, usually 10 to 20 years. If an annuitant dies during this term, their beneficiary receives the remaining payments that are due. The fourth payout option is a refund annuity. If an annuitant dies before receiving payments equal to the premiums paid to an insurance company, their beneficiary receives payments until the entire amount is refunded.

Five Investment Tax Tips

1. Invest early each year. Doing so will maximize the magic of tax-deferred compound interest. If you put $2,000 in an IRA at the beginning of each year for 25 years and it grows at 9 percent, you will have about $184,650. However, if you make the same contribution at the end of each year, you would have only $169,400. Investing early produces over $15,000 more.

2. Rethink investment choices. It is foolish—and expensive—to put annuities in an IRA, which is already tax-deferred. It's like wearing two raincoats in a thunderstorm. Yet, almost a third of variable annuities sold in 1996 were placed in IRAs. Ditto for tax-free securities such as municipal bonds. Putting lower-yielding tax-free securities into a traditional IRA converts them from a tax-exempt investment to one in which taxes will someday have to be paid. Roth IRAs are tax-free already, so putting municipal bonds in them makes no sense either.

3. Stay invested. More than half of workers who leave a job take their lump-sum distribution and spend it, instead of rolling the money over into an IRA or other tax-deferred plan. This is a mistake, unless the money is genuinely needed for basic living expenses, and is referred to as "leakage" in the pension industry. According to the June 1998 National Summit on Retirement Savings, leakage from tax-deferred plans exceeds $150 billion annually.

4. Don't commingle assets. Place funds from a lump-sum distribution in a separate rollover IRA instead of a regular ($2,000 per year variety) IRA account. By doing so, you'll preserve the option of transferring this money later to a future employer's tax-deferred plan.

5. Position assets carefully. Income mutual funds and investments that generate significant capital gains are best placed in tax-deferred accounts. This way, taxes are delayed for decades on investment earnings. As for taxable accounts, if bonds are selected, less tax may be due on Treasury securities and municipal bonds. Index funds, which rarely sell portfolio holdings and hence have low capital gains, are another good choice for taxable accounts.

9

Ownership Investments: Going for Growth

The stock market is the only place where, when they announce a sale, most people run out of the store.

—Norman Boone, CFP

Thirty or 40 years ago, if someone said they were "in the market," they were probably talking about a grocery store. Most people routinely put their money in bank accounts and viewed the stock market as a giant casino. A lot has changed since then. Today, the average person has more money invested in the stock market than they do in their home. In 1997, stocks accounted for a record 43 percent of average household financial assets. More than four of every ten U.S. families own stock, directly or through mutual funds, according to the Federal Reserve Board.

This chapter is about *ownership* assets, including stock, real estate, and collectibles. Recall from Chapter 7 that ownership assets provide investors with an equity interest. As a partial owner of a company or piece of property, there is a potential for growth if the value of a financial asset increases. Stockholders also are entitled to dividends that a company decides to pay. There is a downside to ownership assets, however: more risk. Principal and a specific rate of return are not guaranteed as they are for loanership assets held to maturity.

Despite the risk, investors buy ownership assets with an expectation that they will benefit from the profits earned by the issuer (e.g., a company). Ownership assets also do a better job of outpacing inflation than other asset classes and have performed better than bonds and cash in periods of five to ten years or longer. In the 68 five-year time periods between 1926 and 1997, stocks were the optimal (read: highest-earning) asset class 84 percent of the time, according to Ibbotson Associates.

Common Stock: The Building Block of Equity Investing

Common stock is an ownership interest in a corporation and is sold in units called shares. As a result of high market returns in recent years, stocks (and mutual funds that invest in them) have become a popular investment choice. When companies need money to operate or grow, they may choose to sell shares of stock to investors, who then become part owners of the corporation. As owners, stockholders have the right to vote on policy decisions at annual meetings and share in a corporation's profits, if any. Unlike bonds, stocks do not have a specific maturity date or required periodic payment. It is up to a company's board of directors to determine what part of its earnings, if any, will be distributed to stockholders as dividends and what portion will be retained. Common stocks come in many varieties from well-known blue chips with stable earnings and a record of regular dividend payments to aggressive start-ups with no dividend payment history and great risk of loss of principal.

Neither a stock's future price nor the payment or amount of future dividends is guaranteed. If a company fails, its creditors (including bondholders) have a senior claim on assets. Holders of common stock, as owners of a company, must pay their creditors first and are therefore paid last. In return for assuming greater risk, stockholders have an opportunity for greater reward. If a company is successful in generating profits, stockholders are the ones who benefit when their stock becomes more valuable. Bondholders, on the other hand, give up the right to share in company profits in exchange for greater safety.

What makes stock prices go up and down? There are a lot of theories: the weather, sun spots, Super Bowl winners, skirt lengths, and presidential elections, to name just a few. And then there's market risk and investor psychology, both of which were discussed previously. The plain truth is that no one knows with absolute certainty what the stock market will do next. What we do know is that corporate earnings generally drive stock prices over the long term. In other words, it's a company itself that determines the success of its stock. Thus, the best piece of advice for investors is to "do your homework." Below are ten questions to ask about a company before you purchase its stock:

1. Does it have a record of long-term earnings growth?

2. Are its goods or services in demand?

3. Does it have a strong position in its industry?

4. Are the managers responsible for its success still in charge?

5. Does it have good future prospects (e.g., new products, patents, no pending lawsuits)?

6. Is its industry stable (e.g., food, utilities) or cyclical (e.g., entertainment, construction)?

7. Is it threatened by strong competition or a tough regulatory environment (e.g., utilities)?

8. Is it affected by politics (e.g., defense spending)?

9. Are earnings estimates rising or falling?

10. What price-earnings multiple (share price divided by earnings per share) is its stock trading at compared to competitors and industry averages?

A second piece of advice is to diversify by industry. Ownership of stock of at least 12 to 15 companies representing eight or more industry sectors is a commonly suggested guideline. If this is unaffordable, it is probably best to purchase mutual funds. Following is a list of 14 common industry sectors: capital goods (e.g., machinery, farm equipment), conglomerates (e.g., companies with divisions in a variety of industries), construction (e.g., building, forest products), consumer cyclicals (e.g., autos, appliances), consumer growth (e.g., health care, entertainment), consumer staples (e.g., food, tobacco), energy (e.g., oil, gas), financial (e.g., banks, brokers), materials (e.g., chemicals, paper), pharmaceuticals (e.g., prescription drugs, medicines), technology (e.g., electronics, computers), telecommunications (e.g., television, radio), transportation (e.g., airlines, trucking), and utilities (e.g., telephone, electric).

Stocks can be categorized in two ways. The first is by market capitalization (e.g., large cap, small cap), as discussed in Chapter 7. The second classification method is value versus growth. *Value* (aka cheap) stocks trade at prices that are low compared to their true worth or future prospects. They are issued by companies that have fallen out of favor, are unfairly affected by bad news, or have an uncertain future, like Chrysler in the 1970s. Investors make money if company earnings improve and share prices bounce back. In the meantime, they often have less to lose in declining markets because value stock prices are already depressed. When other investors take notice of an undervalued company's intrinsic value, its share prices rise accordingly. While value stock investing sounds so easy, in reality it is hard work. Buying stocks that no one wants requires courage, good timing, and careful research of company assets, earnings, and future prospects. The biggest risk of value stocks is uncertainty about future performance as many a hoped-for turnaround never materializes.

Growth stocks are another breed of animal entirely. They are issued by successful companies with above-average earnings. These companies are often well-known with a higher price relative to earnings than stocks on average. Another characteristic of growth companies is superior technology or unique products and services. The major risk of growth stocks is that price declines are inevitable. One reason is company earnings lower than investors' expectations. How can you tell a value stock from a growth stock? One way is to check a library reference like *Value Line* that describes characteristics of individual companies. Value stocks also tend to have lower price-earnings ratios (PEs) and higher dividends than growth stocks.

Buying Stock: Four Different Ways

The traditional way to buy stock has been through full-service or discount brokers who have access to stocks through stock exchanges and the over-the-counter market. Investors place a buy order that authorizes a broker to purchase shares at the best price available at the time of execution or, in the case of limit orders, at a price at or below the maximum amount that an investor is willing to pay. Commissions are sometimes negotiable and vary from broker to broker. It is generally more expensive to purchase less than a round lot (100 shares) because of the minimum commissions that are charged to execute a trade.

A relatively new, but rapidly increasing way to buy stock is through more than 80 online brokerage firms such as Accutrade, Ameritrade, Brown & Co., Bull & Bear, Datek Online, Discover Brokerage, DLJ Direct, E*Trade, Fidelity, NDB, Quick & Reilly, Schwab, Suretrade, Waterhouse, and Web Street. The big advantage of trading stock via the Internet is low commissions. The cost to trade up to 5,000 shares of stock generally ranges from $9.95 to $29.95 (a few firms charge less), compared to $100 or more through traditional brokerage firms. With low trading costs, even small investment amounts and stock price changes can produce capital gains.

A third way to purchase stock is through a dividend reinvestment plan (DRIP) or direct purchase plan (DPP, aka no-load stocks). Advantages are no brokerage commissions (although there may be a maintenance fee, enrollment fee, and/or transaction fees) and the ability to make inexpensive purchases for as little as $10 at a time. The downside to DRIPs and DPPs is that there is no broker hand-holding. Like online trading, investors must do their own research and decide which companies to buy or sell. Another disadvantage is a time lag between the time stock is ordered and the date of sale. The major difference between DRIPs and DPPs is that DRIPs require investors to buy their first share from a broker or other service (e.g., the National Association of Investors Corporation). DPPs, on the other hand, allow investors to buy their first share, as well as subsequent shares, directly through the company.

A fourth way to buy stock is through an investment club. Reasons to join include an opportunity to learn about investing in a supportive environment, and fun and socialization with people with a common interest. Most investment clubs align themselves with the National Association of Investors Corporation (NAIC), a nonprofit organization that provides information to new clubs and guides and software for investment selection. The NAIC can be reached at 248-583-6242 or www.better-investing.org.

The NAIC uses a fundamental analysis approach to picking stocks, which means it analyzes the performance of individual companies as the primary criteria for stock selection. It also recommends the following four principles:

1. Invest regularly for the long term (e.g., $100 per month).
2. Reinvest all earnings (i.e., dividends and capital gains).
3. Diversify by company size and industry.
4. Invest in growth companies averaging a 15 percent annual return.

Such lofty returns, of course, require time and effort. There's no free lunch when it comes to investing. Reference materials like *Value Line* must be studied for clues to company performance. The NAIC provides worksheets for investors to make sense of all the data. Club members typically pay dues of $25 to $100 a month, which are pooled to make investment purchases.

Other Ownership Investments

Stock and variable annuities (see Chapter 8) are two common ownership investments. Next is a description of four more products—collectibles, preferred stock, real estate, and real estate investment trusts—that are suitable for beginning investors and often don't require large amounts of cash.

Collectibles

This investment category includes everything from antiques, gems, cars, and fine art to Barbie dolls, rare books, and Beanie Babies. The keys to investment success are owning a sought after (read: scarce) item in mint condition and knowledge of a specialized market. Investing in collectibles often requires the services of a professional appraiser, dealer, or auction house, who charges a fee—often a percentage of an item's selling price—to market it to other collectors.

A disadvantage of collectibles is their lack of liquidity. This makes them inappropriate for short-term financial goals. Despite these shortcomings, it is possible to earn a handsome return on collectibles—if they are held long enough to become valuable and kept in good condition (save the original box or packaging). The cardinal rule of investing in collectibles is "condition matters."

Preferred Stock

Despite its name, preferred stock is actually a bond-like cross between common stock and bonds. Unlike common stock, preferred shares emphasize income over growth and generally pay a fixed dividend. The dividend is not guaranteed, however, and can be suspended by company directors. Preferred shareholders have no voting rights and are next in line after bondholders to get repaid in the event that a company is liquidated. For this reason, preferred shares are more risky than bonds and pay a slightly higher (e.g., one-half of 1 percent) rate of return.

Preferred stock investors are more interested in current income than the future growth of a company. Unlike bonds, however, there is no maturity date and no guarantee that principal will be repaid. Preferred stock pays interest more frequently: monthly or quarterly versus twice a year for bonds. It trades on major stock exchanges and conservative investors should look for an investment grade issuer with a credit rating of BBB or higher. The price per share for preferreds tends to stay near $25 par value so a round lot can be purchased for about $2,500 ($25 × 1,000 shares).

Real Estate

Real estate investments provide an opportunity for capital appreciation and, in some instances, periodic income. If the key to success for investing in collectibles is condition, the corollary word for real estate is *location*. One method of investing is to simply purchase raw land in the hope that, over time, it will increase in value. The downside is that land is illiquid and the owner must pay property taxes and insurance until it is sold. A second way to invest in real estate is to buy a rental property and collect income from tenants. Advantages of rental real estate include tax deductions for depreciation and the potential for capital gains if a property appreciates in value. Disadvantages include potential hassles with tenants, maintenance and repair costs, and the possibility of negative cash flow if rental income is less than operating and financing expenses.

Real estate limited partnerships are another investment option. In a limited partnership, the general partner invests in land, office buildings, apartment complexes, and/or shopping centers and assumes unlimited liability for the venture. Limited partners (investors), on the other hand, risk only the amount of their investment (e.g., $500 per unit) in exchange for periodic distributions from income (e.g., rent) earned on partnership assets. When a partnership dissolves after a specified time period, its assets are liquidated and any profits are distributed to limited partners as a capital gain.

Disadvantages of limited partnerships include high up-front sales charges and illiquidity. Investors who want to sell their units often find it difficult or must accept fire sale prices. The performance of the general partner also is a big unknown. Other drawbacks are the inability (since 1986) to deduct partnership losses from ordinary income and income tax complexity with the use of a K-1 partnership tax form.

Real Estate Investment Trusts (REITs)

Like limited partnerships, REITs provide an indirect investment in real estate through the purchase of shares in a diversified closed-end fund. Unlike most real estate investments, REITs are very liquid because their shares trade like stock on national exchanges. REITs also pay quarterly dividends and are professionally managed. In 1997, there were more than 300 REITs in operation, two-thirds of which were publicly traded. REITs come in three varieties: equity REITs that own real estate and receive revenue from rent (these comprise about 90 percent of the industry), mortgage REITs that loan money to real estate owners and earn interest on mortgage loans, and hybrid REITs that combine both investment strategies.

Two advantages of REITs are their excellent dividend yield of 6 to 12 percent and the potential for capital appreciation. Another advantage is that REITs have a low correlation with the stock market over periods of five years or longer. Thus, adding REITs to a portfolio can reduce its volatility and provide additional diversification. The biggest disadvantage of REITs is the difficulty of finding a good one. The quality of REITs varies significantly and the name of the game is research. Another drawback is that REITs must pass on virtually all of their earnings to shareholders. Thus, a REIT, not an individual investor, controls the amount and timing of taxable income.

REITs can be purchased as individual securities or indirectly through real estate mutual funds. Some examples of the latter include Cohen & Steers Realty Shares, Longleaf Partners Realty, and CGM Realty. By 1998, there were 45 real estate mutual funds, up from about ten five years earlier. The minimum investment amount varies from fund to fund.

Five Tips for Ownership Asset Investing

1. Know when to sell. Good reasons to sell an investment include: a significant loss in value, adverse changes in company management, when direct or indirect competition is affecting the prosperity of a company, and when a company, which has had great dependence on a single product, is losing its edge. Other reasons to sell are when money is needed to fund a financial goal, when investment parameters (e.g., time frame) change, to rebalance asset allocation percentages, and when a personal definition of loss (e.g., "no more than 10 percent of principal") or target price (e.g., $20 per share above the purchase price) are reached.

2. Go on the defensive. Defensive investing strategies that can hedge uncertainty about future market returns include: purchasing stocks and mutual funds with a good performance record during bear markets, cashing in assets when you're within three to five years of needing money for a financial goal, rebalancing asset classes within a portfolio to reduce its risk level, protecting stock gains with covered calls or stop loss orders that direct a broker to sell shares below a specific price, investing beyond U.S. shores in foreign securities, holding firm to a dollar cost averaging strategy, and focusing on the performance of an entire portfolio—not just specific investments.

3. Think long term. All too often, most recently in the summer and fall of 1998, investors panic at market downturns and buy high and sell low. This is a mistake. Instead, investment performance should be followed over time intervals of three to five years or more. If the annual rate of return on an investment is two to three times the inflation rate, an investor will make steady progress toward financial independence. To increase the potential for success, select low-cost investments and avoid unnecessary taxes (e.g., invest in a tax-deferred 401(k) or IRA).

4. Investor: know thyself. Investors should determine their goals and risk tolerance and be willing to do their homework to select securities, or find a qualified professional to assist them. Deciding to invest for future goals requires self-discipline: giving up something today in order to have financial security tomorrow.

5. Mix and match. It is wise to select stocks of companies that are affected differently by the same economic events. Cyclical stocks, like those of retailers, home builders, and auto manufacturers, are companies whose performance tracks current economic trends and should comprise only part of an investor's portfolio. Also needed are investments in companies that provide goods or services that people need or use on a daily basis, such as prescription drugs, food/beverages, laundry detergent, and health care.

10

Loanership Investments: Diversification and Fixed Income

*Investors tend to be lazy and lose money . . . I know
more people who spend more time smart-shopping
for paper towels, than for stocks and bonds.*

—Arthur Levitt, Chairman, U.S. Securities
and Exchange Commission

In previous chapters, it has been established that stocks are the highest returning asset class over the long term. Only during the depression of the 1930s did bond returns surpass stocks' in this century. If returns were all that investors were concerned with, they'd simply put all of their money in stocks and head for the beach. The problem is that with equity investing comes increased risk and volatility of stock prices. Fixed-income (aka loanership) assets mitigate that volatility and enable investors to feel more comfortable about having some of their money invested in the stock market.

Loanership investments include certificates of deposit (CDs), money market deposit accounts and mutual funds, mortgage-backed securities, Treasury securities, and bonds. An investor lends their money to a bank, corporation, or government entity in return for periodic interest and a promise to repay the principal.

Among the reasons for selecting loanership assets are: uncertainty about the stock market, the need for a stream of income (e.g., for retirement), the desire for a guaranteed rate of return (e.g., zero-coupon bonds), tax advantages (e.g., municipal bonds), and diversification. These investments are not without their risks, however. First, they have historically provided a lower rate of return compared to stocks. Bonds and similar investments also are subject to interest rate risk where their value fluctuates inversely with interest rates prior to maturity (e.g., when interest rates rise, bond prices fall). Another drawback is credit risk—the risk that the issuer of a particular loanership investment could default. On the other hand, in the event of liquidation of a company, bondholders have priority over other investors and will be paid before stockholders receive anything.

Generally, the more credit risk associated with an issuer, the higher the interest rate it must pay (as in the case of junk bonds) to attract investors to its securities. Investment grade bonds, which are considered the safest, are rated with one of the top four grades by a rating service such as Moody's (Baa and above) or Standard and Poor's (BBB and above). Fixed-income securities with longer maturities also typically pay a higher interest rate to compensate investors for years of additional exposure to interest rate risk and credit risk and the risk of loss of purchasing power due to inflation.

Bonds: The Foundation of Fixed-Income Investing

Bonds are debts, or IOUs, issued by government (federal, state, and local), corporations, or other entities (e.g., school districts and road and bridge authorities). They generally are purchased through brokers, who receive a commission on the sale, and even can be bought and sold again prior to maturity in the secondary (resale) market maintained by large financial institutions. Bond issuers agree to repay the face (aka par) value (e.g., $1,000) of the bond by a specified date and a fixed rate of interest, called a coupon, until maturity (e.g., an 8 percent coupon on a $1,000 bond pays $80 annually). The word *coupon* is a throwback to earlier times when investors detached actual coupons from bonds and turned them in to collect their interest.

Bonds generally provide investors with fixed interest payments twice a year. For example, the issuer of a ten-year, 6 percent, $1,000 bond would pay $60 of interest per year ($30 semiannually) for a decade and repay the $1,000 face value at maturity. Until then, the bond would fluctuate in value according to market conditions. If an investor had to sell the bond prior to maturity, he or she would likely incur a capital gain or loss, depending on whether interest rates have risen (loss) or fallen (gain) since the issue date. Only at maturity is an investor assured of receiving the full face value of a bond.

As an example, let's assume an investor has a $1,000 bond paying a coupon rate of 10 percent ($100) a year. Two years later, interest rates drop to 8 percent. The 10 percent bond will continue to pay $100 a year but it will be worth $1,250 if it were sold because $100 is 8 percent of $1,250. The investor could sell the bond and make a $250 capital gain (minus trading costs) or continue to hold the bond to maturity and collect $100 annually. On the flip side, the price of previously issued bonds drops when interest rates rise. If a $1,000 bond is purchased with a 6 percent coupon rate and rates rise to 8 percent, a 6 percent ($60 annually) return is less attractive and the price of the bond would fall to $750 ($750 × .08 = $60). Long-term bonds are affected by interest rate changes more than bonds with shorter maturities.

Another risk faced by bond investors is call risk. When interest rates decline, bond issuers often call bonds with high interest rates and reissue lower-rate debt to save money. If a bond is called, investors would get their principal back but would find it difficult to invest it at the previous high rate.

Despite the risks, bonds also offer investors several advantages:

- *Capital gains potential.* Bonds can be sold for more than their face value prior to maturity if interest rates decrease. These bonds are said to sell at a premium. Bonds selling for less than their face value sell at a discount.

- *Liquidity.* Most bonds can be sold at any time in secondary markets, although they are always subject to interest rate risk.

- *Low minimum investments.* Bonds are an excellent choice for shoestring investors. Most corporate bonds and all Treasury securities require $1,000 to make a purchase.

- *Safety.* Compared to stock, bonds held to maturity have less price volatility. In addition, federal obligations are backed by the U.S. government and are considered the safest way to invest.

- *Stable earnings.* The interest rate of bonds is set on the date of issuance and remains fixed. Thus, an investor knows up front the return he or she will receive for the duration of a bond.

- *Tax advantages.* U.S. bonds are exempt from state and local taxes and municipal bonds from federal tax as per the principle of reciprocal immunity.

Bonds are issued by a variety of sources including corporations, states and cities, and the federal government. Corporate bonds are debt instruments issued by public and private corporations to finance their operations and raise capital. They are typically issued in $1,000 increments and pay semiannual interest, which is subject to state and federal income tax. Corporate bonds typically pay the highest rates available on fixed-income securities because they engender higher risk than government bonds with comparable maturities. In order of increasing risk, corporate bonds can be classified as follows:

- *Mortgage bonds*—bonds backed by real estate, such as the company plant and property

- *Collateral trust bonds*—bonds backed by non–real estate company assets (e.g., securities)

- *Equipment trust bonds*—bonds backed by company equipment (e.g., airplanes and railroad cars)

- *Debenture bonds*—unsecured bonds backed only by a company's earnings and promise to repay

Generally speaking, the lower the priority claim on corporate assets a debt instrument has, the higher the rate of interest paid.

Corporate bond investors should pay particular attention to a bond's safety rating and whether a bond is callable by the issuer. Some corporate bond issues have "sinking fund provisions" that provide money taken from company earnings each year to redeem a certain percentage of bonds prior to maturity. Safety ratings are critical because they are an indication of a bond issuer's ability to make full and timely payment of principal. The investment grades in Figure 10.1 are used by the rating companies Standard and Poor's and Moody's to evaluate and report a bond issuer's creditworthiness.

Note that bonds that merit the top four grades (down through Baa/BBB) are considered safer investments. The medium-quality category is the borderline between financially sound corporate bond issues and those where speculative elements are evident. Substandard grade bonds are commonly known as junk or high-yield bonds and provide greater yields than investment grade securities to compensate for the increased risk of default.

Another type of corporate bond is the convertible bond. As the name suggests, convertibles (which can be bonds or preferred stock) can be exchanged for a specific amount of common stock of the issuer. As stock prices increase, convertible bond prices also increase because the option to convert becomes more valuable whether an investor chooses to convert or not. Convertible bonds provide the potential for appreciation in addition to regular income. They are a conservative way to invest in both the stock and bond markets and provide downside protection (a fixed return and repayment of principal at maturity) with upside potential (the opportunity to benefit from company earnings growth).

Figure 10.1   Standard and Poor's and Moody's Bond Ratings

Standard and Poor's Grade	Moody's Grade	Interpretation
Investment Grade Bonds		
AAA	Aaa	Highest quality bonds
AA	Aa	High-quality bonds
A	A	Upper-medium-quality bonds
BBB	Baa	Medium-quality bonds
Substandard Grade Bonds		
BB	Ba	Lower-medium-quality bonds
B	B	Uncertain/speculative bonds
CCC	Caa	Poor-quality bonds
CC	Ca	Very speculative bonds
C	C	No interest currently paid
DDD, DD, D	C	Bonds in default

Municipal bonds (aka munis) are debt instruments issued by state and local governments. As noted in Chapter 8, munis are sought after by investors in high marginal tax brackets because the interest earned is free from federal tax. In addition, states and cities provide an income tax exemption for interest earned on their own securities, and Puerto Rican bonds and those of other U.S. territories are double tax-exempt in all 50 states. As a result of their privileged tax status, municipal bonds generally pay a lower interest rate than taxable bonds and their attractiveness is measured by their tax-equivalent yield. Most munis are sold through brokerage firms in minimum denominations of $5,000 and pay semiannual interest. In the early 1990s, some localities also started issuing $500 and even $100 minibonds that provide tax-free income to small investors.

Municipal bonds come in two varieties: general obligation (GO) bonds that are backed by the taxing power of the state or local government that issues them, and revenue bonds that are backed by income (e.g., tolls, fares, or user fees) from the project they are sold to finance (e.g., bridges, roads, or sewers). Of the two, revenue bonds are considered riskier because governments are not obligated to bail out projects that fail with tax dollars. Thus, revenue bonds pay a higher rate of return than GO bonds to compensate for this extra risk.

Like corporate bonds, municipal bonds are subject to interest rate, credit, and call risk. Be sure to ask about call provisions and the credit rating of an issuer before investing. Another decision investors need to make is whether to purchase individual bonds or shares of a tax-exempt bond fund. An advantage of bond funds is that shares generally can be purchased for amounts less than the cost of an individual $5,000 municipal bond. There also is credit risk diversification because funds invest in many securities and there is a greater ability to hedge interest rate risk with a portfolio of bonds of varying maturities. Many financial advisers recommend investing in bond funds with less than $25,000 for these reasons.

The biggest disadvantage of bond funds is that there is no fixed maturity date as there is for individual municipal bonds. Thus, there is no point in time that investors can plan on getting back their full principal because the value of shares is constantly fluctuating. Investors who are concerned about the risk of loss of principal can select ultra short-term bond funds with average maturities of one year to reduce price volatility. Also advisable is the selection of bond funds with lower-than-average annual expenses (i.e., less than 1 percent of assets). Low expenses are especially important for bond fund investors because, unlike stock funds, there is limited growth potential to offset the drag (reduced return) caused by excessive fees.

Treasury securities are a third type of bond. They are interest-bearing bonds sold by the federal government. Treasury securities are marketable, meaning they can be bought or sold in secondary markets at prevailing rates, and provide regular payment of interest and repayment of principal guaranteed by "the full faith and credit" of the U.S. government.

As of August 1998, Treasury bills require a minimum investment of $1,000, with $1,000 multiples. They have the shortest term (3, 6, or 12 months) and least fluctuation in price with changes in interest rates of any Treasury security. Treasury bills are purchased at a discount with investors receiving an amount equal to the rate of interest determined by auction. An example is a one-year $10,000 Treasury bill selling at a 4 percent discount. An investor would receive $400 and, when the bill matures, their full $10,000. The $400 is their interest. In reality, the rate of return is 4.16 percent ($400 divided by $9,600) because the investor only paid $9,600 up front. Thus, the actual return, called the coupon yield, will always be slightly higher than the discount.

Treasury notes have a term from two to ten years and pay a fixed rate of interest semiannually until maturity, when investors get back their principal. For example, a $1,000, five-year Treasury note with an annual yield of 5.2 percent pays $26 every six months ($52 per year), with a return of $1,000 at the end of five years. Since August 1998, the minimum denomination for all currently available notes is $1,000 with increments in units of $1,000.

Treasury bonds are the longest-term debt obligation of the U.S. government. Currently, the only maturity offered is the 30-year bond. Treasury bonds are much more sensitive to interest rate changes than bills or notes. They are sold in units of $1,000 and, like Treasury notes, pay semiannual interest until maturity. Treasury bonds normally yield more than bills and notes because investors risk their money over a much longer time frame. Often, however, the additional return is scant for the risk of holding bonds 20 years longer, making notes a wiser choice.

Interest earned on Treasury bills is reported in the year in which they mature and semiannual interest on notes and bonds is reported annually. Laddering, that is, staggering purchases or buying Treasuries with different maturities, can be used to spread out the tax owed and receive income monthly instead of at six-month intervals. Over 50 mutual funds also invest in Treasury securities, including short-term (maturities of four years or less), intermediate-term (five- to ten-year maturities), and long-term (maturities over ten years) U.S. government bond funds. Advantages include a smaller initial deposit, professional management, and diversification. The major disadvantage is that, like municipal bond funds, there is no fixed maturity date.

A relatively new Treasury investment is the Treasury Inflation-Indexed Security (TIIS), available in 5-, 10-, and 30-year maturities. TIISs rise in par value along with overall price levels and the Treasury pays interest on the inflation-adjusted principal amount. For example, with 2 percent inflation and a 3.5 percent coupon, principal of $1,000 would increase to $1,020 ($1,000 × .02 = $20). The 3.5 percent interest rate would be applied to increasingly higher principal amounts with interest payments gradually increasing over time.

A fourth type of bond is the zero-coupon bond (aka zeros), which can be issued as a corporate, municipal, or Treasury debt instrument. The name zero-coupon comes from the fact that investors receive no (zero) periodic interest. Zero-coupon bonds are riskier than conventional bonds because they have the most volatility with changes in interest rates. They are purchased at a deep discount, with full face value paid at maturity, as indicated in Figure 10.2. The

Figure 10.2   Amount Needed to Purchase a $1,000 Zero-Coupon Bond

Years to Maturity	Yield to Maturity						
	6%	7%	8%	9%	10%	11%	12%
25	$228	$179	$141	$111	$ 87	$ 69	$ 54
15	412	356	308	267	231	201	174
13	464	409	361	318	281	249	220
11	522	469	422	380	342	308	277
9	587	538	494	453	416	381	350
7	661	618	577	540	505	473	442
5	744	709	676	644	614	585	558
3	837	814	790	763	746	725	705
1	943	934	924	916	907	898	890

further out the maturity date of a zero-coupon bond (e.g., 25 years versus 5 years) and the higher the interest rate paid (e.g., 10 percent versus 6 percent), the less an investor has to deposit up front to receive $1,000 later. A third factor that affects the interest earned on zero-coupon bonds, like all bonds, is the issuer's credit rating.

A big advantage of zeros is that they don't require as much money to invest as conventional bonds and their big disadvantage is that investors have to pay taxes on accrued interest (i.e., increases in principal) even though they don't see this money until a zero matures. For this reason, zero-coupon bonds are recommended for tax-deferred accounts such as IRAs or investors can select tax-free municipal zero-coupon bonds to avoid tax hassles.

Other Loanership Investments

Bonds and fixed annuities (see Chapter 8) are two common loanership investments. Below is a description of eight more.

Money Market Deposit Accounts and Mutual Funds

Money market deposit accounts (MMDAs) are federally insured (FDIC) bank accounts that pay a market-based interest rate that is generally higher than the rate available on passbook savings. MMDAs typically require a minimum deposit (e.g., $2,500) and charge fees if a depositor's balance falls below this amount. MMDAs also allow only six withdrawal transactions (three of which can be checks) per month and assess fees for additional check writing.

Money market mutual funds (MMMFs) are a professionally managed diversified portfolio of high-quality, short-term debt instruments with an average maturity of no more than 90 days. MMMFs are quick to respond to fluctuations in market interest rates and offer competitive variable yields. The interest earned on MMMFs is usually higher than MMDAs but there is no FDIC insurance. Each share of an MMMF is valued at $1, although it is possible to drop below $1 if a fund suffers a loss (a phenomenon called breaking the buck).

The minimum initial deposit (e.g., $1,000) for an MMMF is set by the sponsoring investment company and, like MMDAs, there is usually limited check writing with a minimum amount (e.g., $500) per check. There are several types of MMMFs, including funds that invest totally in Treasury bills (the safest of all money funds); U.S. government funds that invest in debt issued by federal government agencies as well as Treasury bills; and general purpose funds that invest in a broad array of high-grade securities. Also available are tax-free MMMFs that invest in short-term municipal debt instruments and thereby escape state and/or federal taxation.

Certificates of Deposit (CDs)

CDs (aka time deposits) are federally insured bank loanership assets that pay a fixed rate of interest for a specific period of time. Typical maturities are 7 to 31 days and 3, 6, 12, 18, 24, 36, 48, and 60 months. Generally, the longer the time until maturity and/or the more money deposited, the higher the rate of interest paid. A penalty (a specific number of days of lost interest) is assessed if funds are withdrawn from a CD prior to maturity and the minimum deposit (e.g., $500) is set by individual savings institutions.

Brokered CDs, available from most full-service investment firms, offer an attractive alternative to traditional CDs from banks. Available for as little as $1,000 each, they can be sold before maturity through any broker that maintains a secondary market. Maturities generally range from three months to ten years and there is no sales commission. Because brokers shop the country for the best yields, brokered CDs often pay a higher return than CDs available at banks. They are subject to interest rate risk like any other fixed-income security and brokers often charge a processing fee to sell them prior to maturity.

Guaranteed Investment Contracts (GICs)

GICs are fixed-income contracts, similar to CDs, typically issued by insurance companies as an investment option in 401(k) plans. They generally have three- to five-year maturities and pay a higher interest rate than other cash investments. GICs are backed by the issuing insurance company, not the federal government. In recent years, they have been criticized for offering low rates of return compared to alternative equity-based retirement investments. Unlike stocks and bonds, however, their value does not change with fluctuations in interest rates. Nevertheless, retirement is a long-term proposition for most 401(k) participants and, the longer their investment time horizon, the stronger the case for stocks.

Ginnie Maes

Ginnie Maes are issued by the Government National Mortgage Association (GNMA). Sometimes called a *pass through* security because mortgage principal and interest payments are distributed proportionately to investors, they are an investment in a pool of 30-year mortgages insured by the Federal Housing Authority (FHA) or guaranteed by the Veterans Administration (VA). As homeowners make monthly mortgage payments, their money is passed through to Ginnie Mae investors. Thus, part of each check is interest and part is a repayment of principal.

Ginnie Maes carry the full faith and credit backing of the federal government and require a minimum investment of $25,000. The interest earned on Ginnie Maes is about 1 percent higher than a 30-year Treasury bond. However, because the average life of a pool of 30-year mortgages in a Ginnie Mae is 10 to 12 years (because homeowners move and refinance), they behave more like intermediate-term debt. Ginnie Maes also can be purchased in smaller denominations through unit trusts ($1,000 minimum) and mutual funds, making them affordable for shoestring investors.

Other Federal Agency Debt

Two other federal government agency obligations that are not backed by the full faith and credit guarantee of the U.S. Treasury are Fannie Maes and Freddie Macs. Fannie Maes are mortgage securities sold by the Federal National Mortgage Association (FNMA). They include loans backed by the FHA and VA and other mortgages. Freddie Macs are pools of conventional mortgages issued by the Federal Home Loan Mortgage Corporation (FHLMC). Because both of these securities are not backed directly by the U.S. government, they typically yield ¼ to ½ of a percent more than Ginnie Maes to compensate for this extra risk.

Collateralized Mortgage Obligations (CMOs)

CMOs were developed in 1983 in response to mortgage security investors' unhappiness about getting their principal back in irregular amounts. CMOs divide a pool of Ginnie Mae, Freddie Mac, or Fannie Mae mortgages into 5 to 15 classes, called tranches, each with a different maturity date. These tranches provide investors with a choice of maturities to match financial goals and attempt to match the payback period of mortgages within the pool. Each tranche gets its principal back, in sequential order, when all the classes before it have been repaid. Tranches with a longer maturity receive a higher yield in return for accepting more interest rate risk.

Unit Investment Trusts (UITs)

Unlike mutual funds, which are continuously sold and redeemed, UITs buy and hold a fixed portfolio of similar securities—including corporate and municipal bonds and Ginnie Maes—with a set maturity. Increasingly, UITs also are being used to sell stocks, such as those that invest in the ten highest dividend stocks in the Dow Jones Industrial Average index. UITs are purchased for $1,000 per unit and provide diversification, professional selection, and periodic income. They also are highly marketable and may be redeemed at their current unit value, which reflects changes in market conditions. A trustee holds the securities, collects principal and interest, and distributes periodic payments to unitholders. The purchase price of a UIT includes a one-time sales charge, typically 3 to 5 percent of the amount invested. Occasionally, securities within a unit trust are sold or called prior to maturity and principal is returned prematurely. The assumption, however, is buy and hold and, after a stated period of time, a UIT terminates, sells its securities, and returns unitholders' original investment.

U.S. Savings Bonds

EE U.S. savings bonds provide a loanership vehicle for small investors and are available at banks in denominations ranging from $50 to $10,000. They are purchased for one-half of face value and the difference between the purchase price and value at redemption is the interest. EE bonds purchased after May 1997 earn 90 percent of the average yield on five-year Treasury notes for the preceding six months. Bonds cashed in before five years are subject to a three-month penalty. If a bond is cashed in after 18 months, for example, an investor would get 15 months' interest.

Savings bond rates are announced each May and November and apply for the next six-month earning period (e.g., November through April). EE bonds earn interest for 30 years that is exempt from state and local income taxes. There also are special tax benefits for education savings subject to income and other qualifications.

Series HH bonds can be purchased only through an exchange of at least $500 of EE bonds. They are issued at full face value and pay interest semiannually. HH bonds are sold in denominations of $500, $1,000, $5,000, and $10,000. They mature in 20 years and currently pay 4 percent. Investors can get HH bonds through banks, a Federal Reserve Bank, or The Bureau of the Public Debt, 200 Third Street, Parkersburg, WV 26106. An advantage of exchanging EE bonds for HH bonds is that investors continue to defer taxes on the increase in value (interest) on previously owned EE bonds until HHs reach their final maturity.

In September 1998, a new U.S. savings bond was unveiled: the inflation-indexed savings bond, or I-bond. Like traditional EE bonds, they are sold in denominations ranging from $50 to $10,000. Unlike EE bonds, however, I-bonds are sold at full face value (e.g., $50 instead of $25). They also include two interest rate components: a fixed rate that is set at the time of purchase, plus a variable rate that is adjusted every six months for inflation.

Five Tips for Loanership Investing

1. Beware of labels. Know what you're buying. Many fixed-income securities, such as UITs, MMMFs, and bond mutual funds, have reassuring words in their names such as "trust," "U.S.," "government," and "guaranty." They are not federally insured, however, nor is an investor's principal guaranteed. As the Securities and Exchange Commission chairman Arthur Levitt remarked in a 1994 speech, "I don't care if it's named 'The Rock Solid Honestly Safe U.S. Government Guaranty Trust Savings,' in any market investment you stand a chance of losing everything." This is true even for a portfolio of

Treasury securities guaranteed against default. Investors still can lose money if interest rates rise and they sell their securities for less than what they originally paid.

2. Limit your risk. Many investment pros recommend intermediate-term securities (e.g., ten-year UITs or two- to ten-year Treasury notes) instead of longer-term debt because investors often don't get paid much more to risk their money beyond ten years. Another way to reduce investment risk is to purchase a laddered portfolio consisting of bonds with staggered maturities. Laddering is a defensive strategy that exposes just a portion of an investor's portfolio to interest rate changes at any one time.

3. Beware of bond funds. While bond funds invest in fixed-income securities, they often behave as unpredictably as stock funds. Because bond funds don't mature, an investor's principal is always subject to interest rate risk. In addition, because bonds in a fund portfolio are constantly bought and sold, the income earned can change with market conditions. The simple truth is that bond funds are not bonds. If an investor wants to preserve their principal and earn a predictable stream of income for a specific period of time, they should probably select individual securities. On the other hand, bond funds also have their advantages such as low minimum deposits and the ability to reinvest cash distributions in additional shares. The important thing is to know what you're buying and not to panic if interest rates change.

4. Use bonds to hedge stock investments. You can have your cake and eat it too by combining Treasury zero-coupon bonds or corporate zeros with equity investments. The following example was provided by Celia Hayhoe, assistant professor at the University of Kentucky: Suppose an investor had about $5,500 to invest. They could purchase a zero-coupon bond that would guarantee the return of their principal and invest the difference. A $2,000 zero-coupon bond purchase, with a return of 6.95 percent, would mature to $5,480 in 15 years, which is the time frame set for a financial goal. Following is a table that indicates what the remaining $3,500 and the total investment would be worth after 15 years if invested at various rates of return:

Interest Rate	Investment Value	Zero-Coupon Value	Total Value
5%	$ 7,235	$5,480	$12,715
8	11,039	5,480	16,519
10	14,537	5,480	20,017
12	19,048	5,480	24,528

The beauty of using zero-coupon bonds to hedge equity investments is that an investor knows that he or she will get their principal back even if the equity portion goes belly up. This can provide the motivation to make an initial foray into the stock market. Because of the tax owed on the "phantom income" earned by zero-coupon bonds, however, this strategy is best implemented within a tax-deferred account such as an individual retirement account.

5. Remember the basics. TANSTAAFL is an acronym for the phrase "there ain't no such thing as a free lunch." Besides being a strange word, it is a reminder that all investments have some type of risk. There is no perfect investment—ownership or loanership—and there are always tradeoffs among risk, taxes, and return. This is certainly the case with bonds where, the more credit risk associated with an issuer, the higher the rate it must pay to sell its debt to investors. History tells us that time heals most wounds incurred in down markets and that holding different asset classes over the long term reduces investment risk.

11

Mutual Fund Basics

*As long as you are picking a fund,
you might as well pick a good one.*

—Peter Lynch

If ever there was a financial product designed for shoestring investors, mutual funds are it. Mutual funds pool money from many small investors and assemble a diversified portfolio of stocks, bonds, or other securities (e.g., Ginnie Maes). Investment companies manage mutual funds and buy or sell securities to achieve a stated objective (e.g., growth, income, etc.). A typical mutual fund might hold 100 to 150 securities and require a minimum initial investment of $500 or $1,000. Several hundred funds require $100 or less to get started, however, although some have high annual expenses. Minimum required investments also are typically reduced for individual retirement accounts (IRAs), childrens' custodial accounts, and automatic (e.g., $50 a month) investment plans.

Investment companies come in two varieties. The more popular and well-known open-end (mutual) funds issue an unlimited number of shares that are bought and sold continuously. The value of fund shares, which is called the net asset value (NAV), is determined by fluctuations in the value of portfolio assets. Closed-end funds, on the other hand, issue a fixed number of shares and trade on stock exchanges. Because there is a limited number of shares (supply and demand), closed-end funds generally trade at a discount below or at a premium above their actual value. They typically are purchased through brokerage firms with an up-front commission.

Compared to investing in individual stocks or bonds, mutual funds offer professional management and the ability to build a diversified portfolio for well under $10,000. They are especially well-suited for investors with small sums of money who don't have time (or don't want to make the time) to select investments (e.g., read annual reports and evaluate company performance). Individual securities usually require a lot more effort if you want to be successful. With mutual funds, yes, you have to select a fund initially but, after that, the manager does most of the work.

Advantages and Disadvantages of Mutual Funds

Mutual funds can be likened to a sports team. The team is the mutual fund and the players are the securities within the fund. The coach is the mutual fund manager and the spectators are the investors who buy shares in the fund. If one player doesn't do well on a particular day, the rest of the team is there to, hopefully, do better. As long as the team is doing well, spectators will continue to pay money to see it play (invest). Just like a winning team is attractive to sports fans, mutual funds offer investors the following advantages:

- *Automatic deposit option*—Shareholders can request a mutual fund to dollar cost average share purchases automatically by debiting their bank account monthly for a deposit (e.g., $100).

- *Automatic reinvestment option*—Shareholders can elect to have their dividends and capital gains reinvested in additional shares.

- *Automatic withdrawal plans*—Shareholders can elect to withdraw a specific amount (e.g., $300) automatically as a source of income (e.g., for retirees).

- *Instant diversification*—A mutual fund owns many different stocks and/or bonds, which reduces the impact of a poor selection.

- *Liquidity*—Mutual funds are required to buy back (redeem) shares at net asset value if an investor wants to sell. NAV is calculated by adding up the value of assets in a fund's portfolio, subtracting fund expenses, and dividing by the number of outstanding shares (e.g., $20 million of portfolio assets after expenses and 2 million shares equals an NAV of $10 per share). Investors should take note of required withdrawal procedures to avoid delays. Some funds allow check writing, wire transfers, or telephone redemptions while others require written requests with a signature guarantee from a commercial bank.

- *Low initial investment amount*—Even with dividend reinvestment plans (DRIPs) and direct purchase plans (DPPs), it could take $5,000 or more to assemble a diversified portfolio of stocks. Ditto for bonds. Many mutual funds require $1,000 or less and subsequent investments are even smaller, usually ranging from $100 to $250, depending on the policies of a particular fund.

- *Low up-front cost*—Mutual funds, especially low-cost index funds, often cost less than individual securities with commissions.

- *Professional management*—Most people don't have the time or skill to select and monitor individual securities. Once investors choose a mutual fund, the manager makes all portfolio decisions.

- *Regulation*—Mutual funds are regulated by the Securities and Exchange Commission (SEC), a federal agency established in 1934 to oversee investment firms. By law, funds must provide investors with a prospectus that describes their investment objectives, fees, and characteristics, and they must make periodic performance reports.

- *Simplification*—With professional management, instant diversification, and detailed statements and tax reporting information, mutual funds save investors a lot of time and effort.

- *Variety*—Mutual funds provide small investors with access to equity investments that offer a potential for high returns and to tax-free municipal bonds. There also are funds that invest in other countries or concentrate on particular industries. Choices exist for all types of investors: aggressive and conservative.

Mutual funds also have their disadvantages:

- *Higher risk*—Mutual funds are not as safe as federal debt or insured bank deposits and can be just as risky as stocks. Risks associated with mutual funds include credit, currency, interest rate, and market risk.

- *Lack of control over taxes*—Mutual funds are required to pay out 98 percent of their investment earnings each year and shareholders must pay taxes when distributions are made regardless of their tax situation. This is true whether investors take their distributions as cash or additional shares. If an investor purchased individual securities, on the other hand, they could control the timing of taxable income.

- *Losses due to poor timing or poor management*—Not every mutual fund is a winner and some, such as the Steadman funds, are perennial losers. This is why dollar cost averaging, to reduce the average cost per share, and selection of several mutual funds is advised.

- *Loss of flexibility*—Large popular funds can lose their ability to navigate nimbly in and out of financial markets and this can be a drag on performance. They are like battleships trying to set sail on a small lake. Because they own so many securities, they affect market prices when making a trade and have difficulty finding appropriate assets. Many funds that face this dilemma choose to close to new investors.

- *No free lunch*—All mutual funds, even no-load funds, charge a management fee, which lowers investment returns. Fund expense ratios also can include 12b-1 fees (for marketing and distribution costs), and other operating expenses. Some mutual fund families, such as Vanguard and TIAA-CREF, are known for low expense ratios while others charge more than average.

- *No guarantees*—There is no guaranteed rate of return on mutual funds as there is on bonds or unit investment trusts (UITs). In fact, most funds can't even match the performance of market indexes. According to Lipper Analytical Services, 86 percent of U.S. stock funds lagged the Standard and Poor's 500 stock index between 1988 and 1997.

Mutual Fund Selection Criteria

Three keys for selecting a mutual fund are its objective, historical performance, and expenses. Following is a brief description of the types of mutual funds by objective.

- *Aggressive growth (aka maximum capital gains) funds*—The riskiest of stock mutual funds, these funds generally provide the largest returns and heaviest losses. They typically concentrate on small companies, or new companies that may have good long-term prospects, and use risky investment techniques (e.g., derivative securities).

- *Asset allocation funds*—These are funds that include stock, bond, and cash investments—in varying proportions—in one mutual fund. The manager decides the percentage in each asset class, usually in response to economic conditions.

- *Balanced funds*—These are funds that hold bonds and/or preferred stock in varying proportions to common stock, for example, 60 percent stock, 40 percent fixed-income. They seek both current income and long-term growth of principal.

- *Bond funds*—These are funds whose objective is current income. They invest in corporate and municipal bonds and Treasury securities.

- *Clone funds*—These are funds that are designed to mirror the performance of a mutual fund that closes. This usually takes place after its predecessor grows too large and is unable to find attractive investment opportunities. Clones aren't carbon copies, however, and may have different management. Many have little in common with their predecessors except a similar name.

- *Concentrated (aka focus) funds*—These are funds that invest in a small number (i.e., 15 to 30) of securities. Examples are GCM Focus and the Janus Twenty Fund.

- *Emerging market funds*—These are funds that invest in developing countries, mostly in South America, Southeast Asia, and the Mideast.

- *Equity-income funds*—These are funds that pay above-average dividends by investing primarily in stocks, preferred stocks, and convertible bonds of companies with a good record of paying dividends. These funds have low volatility and are considered a relatively conservative ownership investment.

- *Fund of funds*—These are the more than 130 funds that invest in other mutual funds instead of stocks or bonds. An advantage is more diversification than a single fund and a disadvantage is two layers of fees: from the fund itself and the funds in which it invests. These expenses are lower, however, for funds that only buy funds from within their own family (e.g., Vanguard STAR).

- *Ginnie Mae funds*—These are funds that invest in mortgage securities issued by the Government National Mortgage Association (GNMA).

- *Global funds*—These are funds that invest in securities worldwide. They are permitted to have up to half of their portfolio in U.S. companies.

- *Gold (aka precious metal) funds*—These are funds that invest in gold mining companies, usually located in Canada and South Africa, and other securities associated with precious metals.

- *Growth funds*—These are funds that seek long-term capital gains on portfolio securities with income as a secondary objective. They are more conservative than aggressive growth funds because they invest in the stock of well-established companies.

- *Growth and income funds*—These are funds that seek to combine current income and long-term growth by investing in blue chip stocks that have a strong history of paying dividends.

- *Income funds*—These are funds that seek a high level of current income by investing in bonds and dividend-paying (e.g., utility) stock.

- *Index funds*—These are funds that attempt to match the investment performance of a specified stock or bond index, minus fund expenses. Managers invest in all or a cross section of securities that comprise an index, a strategy known as passive investing.

- *International funds*—These are funds that invest only in securities traded outside of the United States.

- *Junk (aka high-yield) bond funds*—These are funds that invest in debt obligations of issuers that are rated BB or lower.

- *Life-cycle funds*—These are a type of asset allocation fund marketed to investors with different portfolios based on age or risk tolerance. Some funds automatically become more conservative over time while others require investors to switch among portfolios.

- *Momentum funds*—These are very volatile (read: risky) funds that invest in fast-growing "hot" companies. They do well when prices are rising but suffer greatly during market (or company) downturns.

- *Money market funds*—These are funds that invest in short-term debt instruments such as Treasury bills, certificates of deposit (CDs), and commercial paper.

- *Municipal (aka tax-exempt) bond funds*—These are funds that invest in tax-exempt municipal bonds that are generally sought after by high tax bracket investors.

- *Option-income funds*—These are funds that attempt to increase their return by writing options (puts and calls) on securities.

- *Real estate funds*—These are funds that invest all or part of their assets in shares of real estate investment trusts (REITs). Examples are Cohen and Steers Realty Shares and CGM Realty.

- *Regional funds*—These are funds that invest in a small group of countries (e.g., Europe, Pacific Rim) instead of worldwide.

- *Sector (aka specialty) funds*—These are funds that limit investments to a specific industry, such as health care or biotechnology, or demographic group, such as baby boomers. Sector funds are riskier than growth funds because of reduced diversification. If a specific industry does poorly, share prices can plummet because the majority of stocks in a particular market sector move together.

- *Small cap funds*—These are funds that invest in companies with a median market capitalization of less than $1 billion.

- *Social conscience (aka socially responsible) funds*—These are funds that invest in stock of companies that management feels show "responsibility." Various screens are used to eliminate portfolio assets (e.g., companies involved with nuclear power, tobacco, alcohol, and gambling).

- *Value funds*—These are funds that take a contrarian approach and invest in out-of-favor stocks expected to turn around and make a profit.

Historical performance is the second screening factor for mutual funds. A key piece of information to look for is a fund's total return for the past three, five, and ten years or since its inception. Also check year-to-year changes as a measure of earnings stability. Total return includes income (e.g., dividends) received from a fund plus the gain or loss in the value of its shares. A fund's total return should then be compared to an appropriate index (as well as competing funds) as a measure of relative performance. For example, small company stock mutual funds would be compared to the Russell 2000, which is an index of small company stocks. An individual investor's total return can vary from a fund's, however, depending on the amount of deposits and withdrawals made during a year (see Chapter 6 for the formula).

There are a number of information sources about mutual fund performance including prospectuses issued by funds, periodic (e.g., quarterly) fund reports, rating services such as *Value Line* and *Morningstar*, performance reviews in personal finance magazines, and newspaper fund tables. To learn about fund performance in a newspaper, you must first know the headings:

- *Name*—Fund families are listed alphabetically, as are the names of funds within a family (e.g., Fidelity, Vanguard).
- *NAV*—This is the value of one share on the day being reported.
- *Change*—This is the net change (e.g., +.27) between a fund's NAV on the day being reported and the previous trading day. This figure can be positive (higher) or negative (lower) and is reported in cents (or dollars) per share.

To read a mutual fund table, simply locate a fund's name, find the NAV, and check the change in price. It is helpful to review newspaper fund listings at least once a week to identify trends.

Another source of information are the rating services *Morningstar Mutual Funds* and *Value Line Mutual Funds Survey*. One or both are available in most large public libraries. Both include historical performance data, a description of fund portfolio holdings, a brief profile, and information about fund expenses. *Morningstar* is known for its star rating system where the top 10 percent of funds earn five stars; the next 22.5 percent, four stars; the middle 35 percent, three stars; the next 22.5 percent, two stars; and the bottom 10 percent, one star. These ratings are based on risk-adjusted performance and are featured prominently in ads for top-ranked funds.

The third key factor in mutual fund selection is expenses. While a difference of a percentage point in fund expense ratios may not seem like a lot, it is. When it comes to investing, the one sure thing we know is that cost matters. Consider this example from the pension giant TIAA-CREF, which shows the impact of a 1 percent cost difference after 20 years. Two hypothetical funds were compared, each with identical portfolios and returns before expenses. The funds had expense ratios of 1.4 (high-fee) and .4 (low-fee) percent, respectively. If $100,000 was invested in each fund and averaged a 10.5 percent return, after 20 years, the high-fee fund would have earned $294,119 and the low-fee fund, $355,677, or about 21 percent more. Added to the initial $100,000 investment, these earnings also would translate into a higher annual income for the low-fee investor. If the two investors decided to withdraw their money over 20 years, the high-fee fund would pay out a $27,974 after-tax income compared to $35,898 for the low-fee fund. Once again, cost matters.

Listed below are costs associated with mutual fund investing.

Mandatory expenses.

- *Management (aka investment advisory) fee*—This is the fee charged to cover the cost of administering a mutual fund. This fee is usually one-half to three-quarters of 1 percent of fund assets. Anything over 1 percent is considered excessive.

- *Other (aka operating) expenses*—This is the fee charged to maintain shareholder records, furnish statements and reports, and provide other fund services, for example, legal and accounting fees.

Variable expenses.

- *Front-end load*—This is an up-front sales charge of up to 8.5 percent (but usually 2 to 5 percent) of the amount invested.

- *Back-end load (aka contingent deferred sales charge)*—This is a fee paid by investors when they redeem (sell) shares. Back-end loads are often a declining percentage (usually 1 to 6 percent) of the amount withdrawn that phases out after a specified (e.g., six) number of years. For example, investors may pay 6 percent if they sell in the first year, 5 percent in the second year, and nothing if they wait six years to redeem their shares.

- *12b-1 fee*—This is an ongoing fee charged annually to pay for the marketing and distribution of a mutual fund (e.g., sales commissions to brokers). 12b-1 fees are generally .25 to 1 percent of a fund's assets and are named for an SEC rule that permits this expense.

Information about a mutual fund's expenses can be found in its prospectus. Newspaper mutual fund tables also contain footnotes to explain a fund's fee structure. An "NL" or "n," for example, indicates a no-load mutual fund with no sales charge (load) to purchase or redeem shares. A "p" indicates a 12b-1 marketing fee and an "r" indicates that a redemption fee (back-end load) may apply. To make comparisons among funds, study the expense ratio, which includes three parts: the management fee, operating expenses, and a 12b-1 fee (if any) combined. Then compare a fund's expense ratio to the average for all funds of its type. The average expense ratio of diversified U.S. stock funds is 1.44 percent, for example. If a fund in this category charges 2.2 percent, its costs are way above average. Not surprisingly, funds with the extra third component, 12b-1 fees, tend to have higher expense ratios than those that don't.

Another feature to compare is share classes. Some mutual funds offer a choice of loads and have A, B, and C shares (of the same fund) to distinguish among cost options. Typically, class A shares charge a front-end load and are better for investors who plan to hold their shares for more than six or seven years (this is usually enough time to amortize the up-front cost). Class B shares charge a 12b-1 fee that never goes away, plus a back-end load, and class C shares charge a 12b-1 fee only. Needless to say, class B shares should be avoided by investors who plan to sell during the time that a back-end load is assessed and class C shares should be avoided by long-term investors.

How to Pick a Fund

Which mutual fund is right for you? It depends on both personal factors (e.g., timing of financial goals) and fund characteristics. Below are some key screening factors:

- *Expense ratio*—Compare a fund's expense ratio to the average of mutual funds within the same category. Avoid funds whose costs exceed the average.

- *Investment objective*—Primary fund objectives include preservation of principal, current income, capital appreciation, or a combination of income and growth. It is important to match personal goals with a fund's objective.

- *Investment policies*—These are the actions that a fund says it will or will not take. Examples include investing only in investment grade bonds or restricting the use of hedging techniques such as options.

- *Level of risk*—The risk level of mutual funds can vary from low (a portfolio of short-term Treasury bills) to high (sector funds or funds consisting of low-quality corporate junk bonds). As a general rule, if you wouldn't feel comfortable buying an investment as an individual security, don't buy it in a mutual fund.

- *Minimum required investment*—A fund obviously can't be selected if an investor can't afford the required initial deposit. It may be affordable for a custodial account or IRA, however.

- *Performance*—Check how a fund has performed each year for the last decade and whether the manager responsible for its past success is still in charge. Compare mutual funds to their peers as well as to a relevant market index.

- *Turnover*—This figure, found in prospectuses, indicates the frequency of buying and selling activity, that is, how often a fund portfolio changes or turns over. The higher the turnover figure, the more brokerage commissions a fund is likely paying and, if gains are realized, the higher an investor's tax bite.

For the past few years, *The Wall Street Journal* has published an annual article that narrows the universe of available stock mutual funds down to a manageable number (e.g., 65 in 1998) by eliminating alternatives such as sector funds (not enough diversification), global funds (too unpredictable), load funds and funds with above-average expense ratios (too expensive), newcomers (no track record), funds that require more than $5,000 initially (too expensive), and funds with poor performance (those that fail to outperform 60 percent of comparable funds over the past three and five years). The point of the articles is that, with just a few key screening criteria, investors can narrow their options to a manageable number from which to select. You, too, can do the same. Use Worksheet #11 to compare the key features of three mutual funds side by side. For a fair comparison, be sure to select mutual funds with the same objective (e.g., growth). All of the information needed can be obtained from a fund's prospectus, which is described in the next section, or sales literature, or by calling its toll-free number and speaking to a fund representative.

How to Read a Mutual Fund Prospectus

A prospectus is a standardized, formal document required by the SEC that contains information about a mutual fund's fees, past performance, management, and investment goals. The purpose of a prospectus is to disclose specific information about a mutual fund to investors. Many investment companies also enclose a recent financial report and application form when they mail a prospectus. Typically, a prospectus begins with a table of contents, the name of a fund, and its objective. A growth fund, for example, might state that its objective is long-term capital appreciation. Next, the fee table indicates the expense ratio of a fund, various expenses (e.g., a fee to transfer between funds in a mutual fund family) and loads that are charged to individual shareholders, and the amount that would be owed on a hypothetical $1,000 investment after one, three, five, and ten years. Performance data are found in other tables that indicate net asset value of a fund at the beginning and end of each year and its past annual returns. All mutual funds are required to provide financial data for ten years if they have been in existence that long.

WORKSHEET **11** *Mutual Fund Comparison Worksheet*

Fund Characteristic	#1	#2	#3
Name of mutual fund			
Back-end load (%)			
Expense ratio (%)			
Front-end load (%)			
Fund Expenses:			
After one year ($)			
After three years ($)			
After five years ($)			
After ten years ($)			
Manager tenure (years)			
Minimum initial deposit ($)			
Minimum subsequent deposit ($)			
Objective			
Services provided			
(e.g., telephone redemption)			
Telephone number (800 number)			
Total Return:			
One year (%)			
Three years (%)			
Five years (%)			
Ten years (%)			
Turnover rate (%)			
Type of fund (e.g., bond)			

Other key pieces of data in a mutual fund prospectus include the "How to Purchase Shares" and "How to Redeem Shares" sections. Here the minimum required amount and various loads are described, as well as requirements for the actual process of making a purchase or sale. Other sections explain a fund's investment policies and risks and the taxation of fund earnings.

In 1998, after a three-year experiment, the SEC gave its blessing to a streamlined *profile* prospectus that summarizes basic fund information succinctly, often on one double-sided page. Investors now are allowed to buy shares based on a profile prospectus alone, rather than a full-blown prospectus. Traditional comprehensive prospectuses will continue to be published and are required to be written in "plain English."

Five Tips for Mutual Fund Investing

1. Have a road map. Choose mutual funds based on financial goals and the expected time frame needed to achieve them. What financial objective do you want to set aside money for and how much do you need to invest? Make sure a fund's objectives coincide with your own and don't change investments or reduce the amount set aside unless you have a good reason. Once a fund is selected, invest for the long term. Short-term fluctuations will generally not affect long-term growth. Don't try to beat the market by timing your purchases and redemptions.

2. Build around a core. Especially with a shoestring budget, begin investing with a solid foundation of both stock and bond mutual funds. After selecting a core fund, for example, a large cap U.S. stock fund, you can later supplement it with other types of funds, such as small cap growth or international. If an investor has money for just one mutual fund, they should select a "total stock market" index fund that seeks to match the performance of the large and small company stocks that comprise the Wilshire 5000 index. As noted in Chapter 7, it is helpful to make asset allocation decisions in percentages and select mutual funds with minimum deposit amounts that match. An example of a model portfolio for equity funds is: 30 percent large company growth, 30 percent large company value, 10 percent small company growth, 10 percent small company value, and 20 percent international.

3. Don't overdo it. According to financial journalist Brenda Buttner, after automobiles, mutual funds are America's second favorite vehicle. Unlike auto purchases, however, many investors don't trade in their mutual funds but, instead, build an unwieldy, and often overlapping, collection. How many funds are too many? There's no exact consensus but 5 to 12 is probably enough for most people. After a dozen funds, the paperwork (e.g., statements, tax records) can become overwhelming and an investor runs the risk of becoming a "closet indexer." This means that they own enough mutual funds that, together, act like an index fund but have the disadvantage of the higher expenses of actively managed funds. It simply isn't true that the more mutual funds an investor owns the more diversified their portfolio. Some of their funds could be buying the same stocks or bonds which means duplication, not diversification. One way to tell if mutual funds are duplicating one another is to check a number known as R-squared (R^2), available in references such as *Morningstar*. With a maximum value of 100, R^2 tells how closely a mutual fund tracks a market index. If many of an investor's funds closely follow the same index (e.g., Standard and Poor's 500), they are not getting the risk-reducing benefits of owning a multi-fund portfolio.

4. Know when to sell. Times when a mutual fund redemption may be in order include: when financial goals change, when you're losing sleep over investment losses, when a fund has consistently lower returns than its peers for at least a year, when you can realize a loss and get a tax deduction, when fund policies or expenses change for the worse, when you have identified a better fund in a particular category (e.g., large cap value), when a fund has grown too rapidly, when a fund changes its investment style or doesn't stick to its stated objective, and when annual expenses are above average. Don't automatically dump a fund when its manager changes but watch subsequent performance figures carefully.

5. Remember risk and taxes. Evaluating a mutual fund's risk level is like looking under the hood of a car . . . it's important for a smooth ride but many people don't do it. Just remember to keep risk in perspective. While it is helpful to check a fund's record during down markets, and over the long term, it is even more important to remember that the greatest risk of all is being out of the stock market completely. As for taxes, consider tax-efficient or tax-managed mutual funds that often generate less than half the tax bill of average funds. Tax-efficient funds, such as some index funds, follow investment strategies (e.g., low turnover) that happen to result in lower taxes while tax-managed funds are designed especially with low taxes in mind. Dividend distributions, with the exception of municipal bond funds, are taxed as ordinary income, and capital gains at a rate that depends on the length of a fund's portfolio holdings. Most mutual funds make distributions during December so it is advisable to wait until the "date of record" before making a sizable investment.

12

Indexed
Investment Products

Most investors, both institutional and individual,
will find that the best way to own common stocks
is through an index fund that charges minimal fees.
Those following this path are sure to beat
the net results delivered by the great majority
of investment professionals.

—Warren Buffett

This chapter is about index mutual funds and other investments whose performance is tied to a market index. A market index, for example, the widely quoted Dow Jones Industrial Average, is an unmanaged group of securities whose overall performance is used as an indicator of economic trends. The first index was the Dow Jones Industrial Average, created by Charles Henry Dow in 1896. It originally consisted of 12 stocks (today it includes 30) and was developed to provide a simple way to follow market trends. Index funds invest in the stocks or bonds that comprise an index. They have been around since the first index fund was developed by the Vanguard Group in 1976. Stock index funds have been particularly popular in recent years. The second largest mutual fund, Vanguard's Index 500, had $69 billion of assets by December 1998, second only to Fidelity Magellan with about $76 billion.

Another term for indexed investing is *passive management*. As opposed to active management, where a mutual fund manager continuously buys and sells securities and changes the composition of a fund's portfolio according to company performance and economic events, passive investing is quite stable. With a passive investing style (indexing), a portfolio manager simply attempts to match the performance of a particular stock or bond market index by holding all of the securities contained within an index or a representative sample.

A good analogy for indexed investments is that they are like tasting a batch of homemade soup. If you want to know how salty the soup is, you taste a spoonful. Indexes provide a spoonful of the market and an indication of overall performance. Index mutual funds track various indexes, minus the cost of fund expenses, by investing in the companies that comprise them (e.g., the 500 large company stocks in the Standard and Poor's 500 index).

Stock index funds, especially those that track the Standard and Poor's (S&P) 500, are "hot" after four years (1995–98) of outstanding U.S. large company stock performance. In 1997, the S&P 500 index returned 33.4 percent and the average S&P 500 index fund earned 32.6 percent. Money has flowed into index funds at increasing rates as investors have come to realize that S&P 500 index funds beat a majority of actively managed stock funds most of the time. In 1997, for example, only one actively managed U.S. stock fund in ten outperformed the S&P 500 index.

A study by the Vanguard Group in 1996 found that, of 273 value and growth funds in operation throughout the ten years ending December 31, 1995, only 38 (14 percent) beat the S&P 500 index. Yet, ironically, less than 10 percent of all money invested in U.S. stock funds is indexed. There are several reasons for this: the appeal of "star" managers such as Peter Lynch and that actively managed funds offer hope and excitement instead of "boring" market-based returns. Just like a casino or lottery, there is always a chance of beating the odds in an actively managed mutual fund.

A third reason for the widespread use of actively managed funds is that many investors don't compare their returns to an index to see how they're doing. Thus, they miss a powerful incentive to change if they earn, say, 10 percent and think it is good because they don't realize they could have received more by tracking an index. Investors that hire commission-based advisers also tend to be steered toward actively managed funds, typically with a 12b-1 fee or front-end load.

Advantages and Disadvantages of Index Funds

Index funds are increasingly becoming the choice of new and experienced investors. Funds exist to track not only the S&P 500 large company stock index, but other market indexes for small and medium company stocks, international securities, real estate, and government bonds. Because an index fund is basically on automatic pilot, it underperforms an index only by the cost to manage it. Actively managed funds, on the other hand, have to work much harder to select a portfolio that can beat an index and overcome the drag of advisory fees, transaction costs, and operating expenses. Below are eight index fund advantages.

1. Broad diversification. Average equity mutual funds contain about 130 stocks. Index funds often have four or more times that number and are diversified like crazy if they invest in every security in their target index or a large representative sample. This means less volatility due to changes in the value of any individual security or industry sector. Funds that invest in the S&P 500 index, for example, include 500 companies in over 90 different industries. Broad diversification also means exposure to stocks that investors might not ordinarily buy (not every company within an index is a household name), some of which are out-of-favor value stocks that can appreciate handsomely.

2. Low expenses. Because index funds merely replicate a target index, their management and transaction costs are low. They do not require as much staff to analyze companies as actively managed funds, nor do they incur the brokerage fees associated with frequent trading. Index funds change portfolios only when an index changes. The average expense ratio for an S&P 500 index fund is .68 percent (compared to 1.44 percent for actively managed stock funds) and some funds charge much less (e.g., .20 percent).

3. Low turnover. There are two reasons why an index fund sells securities: to raise cash to meet redemption requests in a market downturn and to remove securities that have been dropped from an index and replace them with others. Index funds generally make a small number of trades, which means low brokerage commissions and small realized capital gains to pass on to investors at tax time. It is not uncommon for index funds to have turnover rates of 5 to 10 percent, that is, only 5 to 10 percent of their portfolio changes every year. Compare this to an average portfolio turnover rate of 76 percent for actively managed funds, according to Lipper Analytical Services (under 50 percent is considered relatively low and over 100 percent is high).

4. Management consistency. An index fund contains the same stocks or bonds whether its manager comes or goes so there is continuity with changes in management. Compare this to the anxiety that many investors feel when they learn that a traditional fund manager, especially a star, will leave or could leave. With index funds, the portfolio is preordained. This is not to say that index funds can be run by monkeys, as a caller to the Vanguard Group once suggested to Index 500 Fund manager Gus Sauter. It takes skill to maintain portfolio weightings and stay fully invested. However, the basket of securities to choose from rarely changes.

5. Performance consistency. Index fund investors receive the same gains or losses as an index, minus the expenses of running a fund. The manager doesn't second-guess the market by choosing different securities. In a bull market, stock index funds outperform a majority of funds with similar objectives because they are always fully invested in stock regardless of market outlook. Actively managed funds, on the other hand, typically maintain a cash reserve, which dilutes their performance, and change their stock and bond holdings in response to market conditions. In a bear market, however, index funds can suffer because they lack the ability to hold cash or fixed-income securities. They are more volatile than actively managed funds with a similar composition (e.g., large company stocks) because an all-stock portfolio is more volatile than a portfolio that combines asset classes. Nevertheless, some index funds still outperform actively managed funds, even in bear markets, as a result of their low taxes and expenses.

6. Simplicity. Once selected, index funds require virtually no investor management other than, perhaps, dollar cost averaging. This makes them an attractive choice for busy investors who don't want to take the time to oversee the performance of active managers who typically underperform an index. Indexing also passes the "four-year-old test" described in Chapter 3 because it is easy to understand and explain to others. It is simply matching the market, no better and no worse.

7. Stability. Index funds work well, despite market downturns, because they take the emotion out of investing. First, they ensure the purchase of a wide variety of securities, including unglamorous ones that investors would typically pass over. They also eliminate investors' (and active fund managers') tendency to try to catch market peaks and valleys. Index funds consist of stable portfolios that remain fully invested in the securities that comprise their target index, no matter what happens to financial markets. As long as an investor doesn't bail out and redeem their shares, an index fund will catch those elusive best trading days as described in Chapter 6. In other words, index funds reward investors who buy and hold for the long term. In fact, some charge a redemption fee for shares held a short time to reinforce the notion that they are not for short-term traders.

8. Tax-friendly. Index funds typically (but not always) realize and distribute modest capital gains—if any—to investors. This is especially true during bull markets when securities do not need to be sold to meet redemption requests. For this reason, many are said to be tax-efficient and are suggested for taxable accounts, especially at the 20 percent capital gains tax rate, while actively managed funds are recommended for tax-deferred accounts like IRAs. This is just a general guideline, however, and other factors like a fund's before- and after-tax return also need to be considered. It should be noted that not all index funds are tax-efficient. In addition to those that are forced to sell securities to meet redemption requests, there are some that track indexes that are subject to frequent change. The Russell 2000 (small company stock index), for example, is reconfigured twice a year and results in higher turnover (and taxes) than the S&P 500.

Index funds also have their disadvantages such as the five noted below.

1. "Double whammy" potential. Like all mutual funds, it is possible for index funds to provide investors with a double whammy: taxable capital gains and a negative return. While losing money and receiving a tax bill in the same year seem illogical, not to mention unfair, it is important to remember that the taxable gain is a prorated share of a mutual fund's capital gain, which is not realized until the manager sells securities within the portfolio. Index funds typically realize large capital gains in declining markets because they, otherwise, follow a buy and hold strategy. Thus, an index fund investor in a bear market could easily experience a double whammy. When a large number of shareholders exit a fund, those that are left get stuck with a higher percentage of the fund's gains . . . and a higher tax bill.

2. High cost of entry. The investment firm with the greatest number of index fund options, the Vanguard Group (two-thirds of all index fund assets are held by Vanguard), requires a minimum initial deposit of $3,000 to open an account. This can be a barrier for some shoestring investors. Vanguard also assesses a $10 annual fee on accounts of less than $10,000, which has the effect of raising their expense ratio for investors with small balances. IRAs and custodial accounts for minors require only a $1,000 minimum, however. Several other index fund sponsors, such as Dreyfus, Scudder, Strong, and Fidelity, charge $2,500 to open an index fund account and a few, such as Schwab, require $1,000. A review of index funds listed on the Web site www.indexfundsonline.com shows $1,000 to be the lowest minimum investment for regular index fund accounts, where minimums ranged from $1,000 to $50,000. A number of index fund sponsors, however, allow investors to establish a regular account for $500 or less with an automatic investment plan (required monthly deposits range from $50 to $500) or an IRA.

3. Indexing challenges. Index funds work best in efficient markets where information about companies is quickly reflected in the price of securities. Large company stocks that comprise the S&P 500 index are well-researched, making it difficult to beat the market with an actively managed fund. The same is true for the bond market, which also is efficient and difficult for fund managers to outperform. This isn't the case, however, with less efficient market sectors where research isn't as pervasive and active managers stand a better chance of outperforming a benchmark index. These sectors include small cap growth, international, emerging markets, and closed-end funds selling at a discount. In these sectors, index funds often provide relatively mediocre performance.

4. Lack of excitement. Investing in an index fund means that an investor will never outperform financial markets. Period. End of story. Many investors want more than this. They want excitement and drama and the possibility of a 10- or 20-bagger (i.e., a stock where you make 10 or 20 times your initial investment), as Peter Lynch would say. There also is a certain amount of star appeal when investing with a well-known fund manager. Investing in an actively managed fund makes for a much better story to tell around the water cooler than to brag about a boring index fund.

5. No downside protection. The share price of an index fund falls when prices of investments within an index drop. As noted previously, a stock index fund's ability to shine in bull markets by being fully invested in stocks provides scant downside protection in a bear market when share prices are declining. If a stock market index like the S&P 500 loses 20 percent of its value, an index fund could even lose a bit more because of trading and management expenses. Index fund investors need to accept this risk and stay invested for the long term. Unlike actively managed funds that can run for cover in other asset classes (e.g., cash) when stock indexes head south, stock index funds do likewise.

Types of Financial Indexes

Almost 200 index funds are available that replicate a variety of market indexes. All of the indexes that are tracked by index funds were developed by commercial firms, not the federal government. Industry leader Vanguard offers the greatest selection and among the lowest index fund expense ratios. Index funds also can be purchased through other industry behemoths such as Fidelity, Dreyfus, and Schwab. Below is a description of ten indexes commonly tracked by index mutual funds.

1. Dow Jones Industrial Average (aka DJIA or the Dow). The Dow is an average of the 30 largest U.S. companies chosen by the editors of *The Wall Street Journal* to represent the U.S. stock market. Although the Dow is the oldest and most widely quoted market index, it has not been widely used in index funds. One reason is problems associated with price weighting when stock splits. A higher priced stock can become a lower priced stock (or vice versa), which means a manager has to trade securities proportionate to the price changes associated with a split. Another reason is the narrowness of the index: only 30 stocks. The biggest reason, however, is that the Dow Jones company only recently began to license the DJIA name for use in index funds. The oldest fund that tracks the Dow is ASM Index 30.

2. Standard and Poor's 500 (aka S&P 500). The S&P 500 contains 500 large company stocks representing approximately 70 percent of the total value of the U.S. stock market. Unlike the Dow, the S&P 500 and most other market indexes are weighted by each stock's capitalization so that they are not affected by stock splits. The size of a company in the S&P 500—not the cost of a share of its stock—determines its relative weighting in the index. The S&P 500 is the most widely used index tracked by mutual funds and provides a broader representation of the U.S. stock market than the Dow. In July 1998, 77 investment firms offered S&P 500 index funds, most with the words "Index 500," "Equity 500," "500," or "S&P 500" in their title.

3. Wilshire 5000 Index. Trademarked by Wilshire Associates, this index includes all 500 stocks in the S&P 500. It is used to track the performance of the entire U.S. stock market and includes a sample of more than 7,300 small-, mid-, and large-sized company securities. Mutual funds that track this index often use the words "total stock market" or "total market" in their title.

4. Wilshire 4500 Index. This index consists of the Wilshire 5000 minus the S&P 500. In other words, more than 6,800 stocks, mostly from small and mid-cap companies. An investor might select a fund that tracks the Wilshire 4500 index if they have an S&P 500 fund in their 401(k) plan and want additional diversification. Mutual funds that track this index often use the words "extended stock market" or "extended market" in their title.

5. Schwab 1000. This is a proprietary index developed by the Charles Schwab Company that consists of the 1,000 largest U.S. stocks, including the 500 companies that comprise the S&P 500.

6. Russell 2000. This index, licensed by the Frank Russell Company, is the most commonly used benchmark of the performance of U.S. small company stocks. It consists of the smallest 2,000 companies within the Russell 3000, which is an index that tracks the 3,000 largest companies in the U.S. There also is a third index, the Russell 1000, that tracks the other (largest) stocks in the Russell 3000 index. Small company index funds that track the Russell 2000 often can be found with the words "small cap" or "small company" in their title.

7. S&P/BARRA Value Index. This index consists of half of the total value of the S&P 500 and includes companies with lower-than-average price-to-book ratios and above-average dividend yields. Index fund titles often include the words "index value."

8. S&P/BARRA Growth Index. This index consists of the other half of the value of the S&P 500 and includes companies with higher-than-average price-to-book ratios and below-average dividend yields. Index fund titles often include the words "index growth." If an investor places equal amounts in the S&P/BARRA growth index and value index, their return should approximate that of the S&P 500. Both of these indexes were created by the Standard and Poor's Corporation and BARRA Associates to enable investors to combine the benefits of indexing with growth or value-style investing.

9. Lehman Brothers Aggregate Bond Index. Trademarked by Lehman Brothers, this index is a composite of several smaller bond indexes and consists of almost 6,000 taxable, investment grade bonds representing Treasury, federal agency, and corporate issuers. The ratio of government to corporate bonds is about 2:1. Index funds that track this index often use the words "total bond market" in their name while those that track other bond indexes use words like "Treasury," "U.S. Treasury," "intermediate-term," or "corporate" to indicate the specific bond index being followed.

10. Morgan Stanley Capital International EAFE Index (aka MSCI EAFE). EAFE stands for Europe, Australia, and Far East. This index consists of about 1,100 large international stocks and is a market-weighted composite of indexes for 20 developed nations. The MSCI EAFE is widely used as a benchmark for the performance of international stock funds. MSCI also provides separate indexes for Europe, the Pacific, and selected emerging markets (developing countries). Index funds that track the EAFE index often use the words "total international" in their title.

Other Common Indexed Investments

With the increased popularity of index mutual funds, it is no surprise that other investments are featuring indexing also. One example is Treasury inflation-indexed securities, described earlier. Below is a brief description of three more indexed investments.

1. Indexed (aka equity-indexed) annuities. These are fixed annuities with a twist: the chance to benefit from increases in a stock market index. Indexed annuities are attractive to conservative investors who desire a guaranteed rate of return with the potential for stock market gains. Unfortunately, there are some flies in the ointment. First, investors generally receive only a portion of a stock index's gain because their return does not include dividends. Instead, most indexed annuities track the S&P 500's capital return (change in value), which may be only 60 to 70 percent of its total return.

Worse yet, many annuity sponsors cap an indexed annuity's growth rate at 10 percent annually. Thus, if the S&P 500 index soars past 30 percent, as it did in 1997, and, say, two-thirds of its growth, or 20 percent, is capital return, an annuity's actual growth rate could be capped at 10 percent. Many indexed annuities also charge penalties if contracts are surrendered prematurely. Despite all of these drawbacks, indexed annuities are selling well. They typically require a minimum of $5,000 and are sold by about 40 insurance companies.

2. Indexed (aka equity-linked) CDs. Like insurance companies with their annuities, banks and brokerage firms began linking certificates of deposit (CDs) to stock market indexes in the 1980s in an attempt to woo customers. Like indexed annuities, the earnings on these CDs, while based on the S&P 500, generally don't include reinvested dividends. Thus, investors only receive a portion of the S&P 500's total return. A minimum guaranteed rate (e.g., 3 percent) also may be promised (i.e., investors get the greater of 3 percent or a portion of the S&P's gain), although some indexed CDs offer no such protection.

Like all bank products, indexed CDs carry FDIC insurance so there is no risk to principal. Minimum deposit amounts vary among banks but can be as high as $10,000. Stiff penalties (higher than normal bank CDs) are assessed for withdrawal before a CD's maturity date, which is generally three or five years from the date of purchase.

3. Spiders, WEBS, and Diamonds (aka Basket Securities). All three trade like stocks on the American Stock Exchange and are similar to closed-end funds and unit investment trusts. Spider, or SPDR, is an acronym for Standard and Poor's Depository Receipts. They are units in a trust of stocks that make up the S&P 500 index. WEBS stands for World Equity Benchmark Shares and are single-country trusts that track market indexes of individual countries. Diamonds (Dow Jones Industrial Average Model New Depository Shares) track the 30 stocks that comprise the Dow. Advantages of basket securities include low annual expenses (similar to index funds) and the ability to buy or sell units during trading hours at a current market price. A disadvantage is the cost of brokerage commissions. Because they are relatively new, the jury is still out on basket securities. Further information can be found on the American Stock Exchange Web site at www.amex.com.

Five Tips for Indexed Investing

1. Beware "enhanced" index funds. Enhanced index funds appeal to investors who want to do more than settle for average results. Very simply, they are index funds that try to do better than their benchmark index. Many attempt this through the use of cash, bonds, and derivatives (e.g., index futures contracts), which can increase investment returns in bull markets and/or reduce losses in bear markets. Another common strategy is to weight certain companies in an index more highly than others. The tradeoff, of course, is more risk (i.e., a greater possibility of earning less than an index, or "tracking error" as the pros call it).

Enhanced index funds are, in reality, actively managed funds and, to date, their performance has been spotty. In addition, they tend to have higher expenses than plain-vanilla index funds and higher turn-over, which leads to higher taxes. Thus, even if an enhanced index fund does beat its benchmark index, much of the extra gain will likely be siphoned off. Enhanced index funds can be recognized by the words "equity plus," "index plus," "managed index," "value-added," or "stocks plus" in their title. A 1996 study by Ibbotson Associates found that most enhanced index funds provide little added value to investors. They concluded that the opportunity for higher returns was generally outweighed by additional risks and transaction costs.

2. Consider the Dogs. A popular index investing strategy is the *Dow Ten* (aka investing in *The Dogs of the Dow*). It involves buying equal amounts each year of the 10 highest yielding stocks of the 30 that comprise the Dow Jones Industrial Average. Each year, the portfolio of 10 stocks is held for the entire year and is readjusted the following January 1 to hold the 10 highest yielding stocks of the new year. High-yielding stocks are generally out-of-favor (read: cheap) stocks. Hence, the Dow Ten strategy uses a value investing approach, which means it selects cheap stocks that offer better bargains among the 30 in the Dow.

The Dow Ten takes the emotion out of investing and minimizes transaction costs because securities are traded only once a year. Often, only two or three of the ten stocks change. In addition, the total return can be higher than the Dow itself because the Dow Ten strategy doesn't rely on capital gains alone but also on superior dividend-paying ability. The Dogs of the Dow can be purchased in three ways, each with different dollar amounts:

1. The purchase of ten individual stocks, usually in round lots of 100 shares. This method requires the most amount of money.

2. Dow Ten unit investment trusts, packaged and sold through brokerage firms, usually in units of $1,000 each.

3. No-load mutual funds that employ the Dow Ten strategy.

The Dow Ten strategy produced an enviable record from 1973 to 1993, but it hasn't done quite as well since. Some attribute this to overvaluation of the blue chip stocks that comprise the Dogs or that the strategy has become more well known. Nevertheless, it is a disciplined investment method that combines value investing and in-dexing and should at least be considered.

3. Use index funds to craft a portfolio. Index funds can be used in several ways to build an investment portfolio. Some investors use them purely as a benchmark to measure the performance of a port-folio comprised entirely of actively managed mutual funds. Others do the exact opposite and construct a 100 percent indexed portfolio. They might purchase a total stock market fund for broad domestic stock exposure, a bond index fund for their fixed-income portion, and an international or regional index fund for additional diversifi-cation. Indexed portfolios, such as the one described above, can be bought and held for decades with the assurance that an investor will earn more than a majority of actively managed funds. A third option is to use index funds as the core of an investment portfolio, An in-vestor would then add additional actively managed funds, such as value or small cap funds, where they think they have a better chance of beating the market.

4. Index beyond the S&P 500. Because it was the first index to be tracked by a mutual fund (and, because of the U.S. stock market's long bull run), most of the money in index funds has gone into those that track the S&P 500. For additional diversification and downside protection, other index funds also should be explored. Examples are those that track the Lehman Brothers Aggregate Bond Index or the Russell 2000 small company stock index. The expenses of index funds in any market sector are usually low, making it easier for them to outperform similar funds that are actively managed. In addition, research has shown that using three or more asset classes in an indexed portfolio can provide higher returns with no change in the level of risk that an investor is willing to take. One study of investment returns from 1971 to 1996 found that increasing the num-ber of indexed asset classes from two to five increased annual returns by 1.25 to 2 percent with the same degree of risk.

5. Examine the cost. With the exception of international portfo-lios, which cost more to manage, it is best to stick with index funds with expense ratios below .5 percent and avoid those that charge a load. Otherwise, you're not benefiting from the low-cost advantage of indexing. Also take note of account maintenance fees for balances below a certain amount (e.g., $10,000). They may be waived if you have several low-balance accounts with one fund family that, together, exceed the minimum. Also beware of redemption fees and switching limitations and make sure that there is no conflict between these restrictions and your investment time frame.

13

Investing with
Small Dollar Amounts

*In the end, consistency of investing—making it a
real habit month after month—will make a much
bigger difference than how many funds you own
or even which ones you buy.*

—Brenda Buttner

Some people think that investing is just for the rich and that a
portfolio can only be assembled by people with last names like Buffett, Gates, and Trump. Not true. Investing is a means to help people
of all income levels achieve their financial goals. A portfolio can consist of $1,000 or $100,000 and is whatever an investor has accumulated at a particular point in time. In Parts Two and Three, you were
introduced to fundamental investment principles and available financial products such as corporate bonds and index funds. In Part
Four, you'll learn how to construct an investment portfolio with
small dollar amounts and how to make up for lost time if you're getting a late start.

You'll also be provided with a multitude of resources, including
Web sites, publications, and investor organizations, and factors to
consider when choosing professional financial advisers. The most
important thing to remember is that investing knows no income,

asset, or age boundaries. Even someone with $25 or $50 a month can get started. The sooner you start investing, the better, because compound interest is not retroactive. For every ten years an investor procrastinates and doesn't put money away for a future goal like retirement, they must invest three times as much in order to end up with the same nest egg at a future date.

So how does one become a shoestring investor? By first becoming a saver. Unless they are fortunate enough to inherit money or win a sweepstakes, people usually need to save first to accumulate money to invest. Consider the following strategy developed by Barbara Bristow, personal finance educator at Cornell University, which begins with weekly savings of $10. If someone puts $10 each week into a savings account earning 3.5 percent interest, compounded monthly, the total savings in their account at the end of one year would equal $529.12. They then purchase a three-year certificate of deposit (CD) paying 5.25 percent interest with the $529.12 and continue to save $10 weekly.

At the end of the second year, the saver purchases a two-year CD paying five percent with the second $529.12 saved and continues to set aside $10 weekly. At the end of the third year, they purchase a one-year CD (4.9 percent interest) with the $529.12 saved and continue saving $10 weekly. After four years, over $2,200 will have been accumulated to invest with:

Total in savings account at end of 4th year	$ 529.12
Value of three-year CD at end of 4th year	619.17
Value of two-year CD at end of 4th year	584.78
Value of one-year CD at the end of 4th year	555.68
Total accumulated in savings account and CDs	$2,288.75

Another way to find small amounts to invest is to practice voluntary simplicity (read: living below your means). Some people also find that their quality of life is improved through decreased consumption and work hours required to finance spending. Persons who downshift their lives often report reduced stress levels as a result of a less hectic lifestyle and more time for hobbies, friends, and family activities. Household expenses and debt levels also are reduced in the process. According to the Seattle-based New Road Map Foundation, items that were once considered luxuries often are deemed essentials today. Many people who supposedly "have it all" report that they are unhappy with their busy lifestyles. The foundation was started by Joe Dominguez and Vicki Robin, authors of the book *Your Money or Your Life*. A key principle in this book is that there comes a point in people's lives where more spending brings less fulfillment and happiness. Dominguez and Robin call this point "enough."

The bottom line is that there are only four known (legal) ways to accumulate wealth: inherit it, marry it, win a lottery/casino game/ magazine sweepstakes, or spend less than you earn. While the odds of the first two strategies happening are iffy and the third method overwhelmingly slim, spending decisions are within every investor's control. For example, over half of respondents to the 1998 Retirement Confidence Survey said they could save $20 a week if they put their mind to it, by eating out less or reducing entertainment expenses.

Shoestring Investing

Setting aside small amounts of money regularly and reducing household expenses to find money to invest are the keys to successful shoestring investing. It also doesn't take much to get started, despite popular misconceptions about the need to have lots of money. To accumulate $3,000 a year, for example, requires saving and/or reducing expenses by $250 a month, or $58.14 a week, or $8.30 a day. If an investor earns $10 an hour, it would only take about 50 minutes of work a day to "pay themselves first." Here's another example that illustrates the powerful combination of shoestring investing and compound interest: If an investor places $166 a month (about $5.50 a day) in an individual retirement account (IRA) and it earns a 14 percent average annual return (ambitious, but certainly possible with quality stocks or growth funds held long term), they would have almost $1.4 million in 35 years.

Of course, required minimum amounts to invest with can—and do—vary. Yet, there are many ways to invest with small sums. The first place to start, for all the advantages described in Chapter 8, is an employer-sponsored retirement plan. Some require only $10 or $20, or 1 percent of pay, as a minimum contribution. For someone earning $35,000 a year, that's just $350, and even less out of pocket after receiving a tax deduction. Does it really make a difference to invest such a small amount? Yes. Any amount of investing is better than none. Of course, the more you invest, the more money you'll accumulate, so, once enrolled, consider increasing the contribution by 1 or 2 percent each year or whenever you receive a raise. At the very least, plan to contribute enough (e.g., 6 percent of pay) to receive a full employer match because, otherwise, you are walking away from free money.

Another place to start investing with small dollar amounts is individual stocks available through a dividend reinvestment plan (DRIP) or direct purchase plan (DPP). As noted in Chapter 9, hundreds of companies allow investors to purchase as little as $10 or $50 worth of stock every month without brokerage commissions. This includes almost half of the stocks that comprise the Dow (e.g., Coca-Cola, Citicorp, and McDonald's). To enroll in a DRIP or DPP, simply contact the company that runs a plan and request an enrollment form. Then complete the application, enclose a check, and drop it in the mail.

A third strategy, tailor-made for shoestring investors, is an automatic investment program available through many mutual funds. Funds that require four- or five-figure sums to open an account often allow investors to deposit smaller amounts (e.g., $500) if they agree to have regular deposits (usually $50 or $100) deducted from their paycheck or a bank account each month or quarter. IRAs and custodial accounts for minors also may require $1,000 or less, plus there are a number of funds with low $250 or $500 minimums anytime and even lower (e.g., $25 or $50) subsequent deposits.

For investors with just a few hundred dollars, a broadly diversified no-load fund also may make sense. An example is T. Rowe Price's Spectrum Growth Fund, a fund of funds that invests in other (mostly stock) funds within the T. Rowe Price family. Investors who participate in the automatic investment program can open a Spectrum Growth account for just $50, versus a requirement of $2,500 for regular accounts. Another example of a broadly diversified all-in-one mutual fund is Vanguard STAR, which invests in ten different Vanguard stock and fixed-income funds. The STAR portfolio requires a $1,000 minimum initial investment and $100 subsequent deposits. Both T. Rowe Price and Vanguard offer these funds of funds without adding a layer of fees on top of the underlying fund portfolios, which keeps their expense ratios low.

An alternative strategy, depending on the amount of money required up front, is to build a starter portfolio using three or four different mutual funds: an S&P 500 index fund that serves as a core holding, a value fund that buys downtrodden stocks that nobody else wants, a fund that invests in U.S. small company stocks, and an international fund for foreign exposure. Automatic investment programs can be used to increase these accounts via dollar cost averaging. As the portfolio grows, other asset classes can be added according to an investor's overall asset allocation strategy. This way, funds are likely to perform differently in any type of market environment.

Places to Save or Invest $500 or Less

Most investors start small with just several hundred dollars of savings. Below are some rock-bottom saving and investment alternatives that can be purchased for $500 or less.

Bank passbook or statement savings accounts. Often, only $50 or $100 is needed to open a typical bank account, which is a good place for an investor's first $500 or so. After that, better yielding alternatives are available. Advantages include safety of principal and liquidity.

Certificates of deposit (CDs). Minimum denominations are often $250 or $500. CDs pay a fixed rate of interest for a fixed period of time, with higher interest paid for longer maturities. CDs purchased through a broker often pay a half percentage point more than those available at banks. Bank CDs are subject to penalties (foregone interest) for redemption prior to maturity and brokered CDs are subject to interest rate risk.

"Club" savings plans (e.g., holiday and vacation clubs). Banks pay little or no interest on club accounts and many stopped giving gifts years ago. Club plans still have their advantages, however, including reinforcement of systematic savings with weekly coupon books and the ability to save small amounts, for example, $5 to $50, weekly. Club plan proceeds can be used for any purpose, including accumulation of capital to invest.

EE U.S. savings bonds. EE bonds can be purchased at banks and through employer payroll deduction plans. They are purchased for one-half of their face value (e.g., $25 for a $50 bond) and come in denominations including $50, $75, $100, $200, $500, and $1,000. Interest is added to the value of the bonds every six months according to a formula based on the current yields available on Treasury securities.

Employer retirement plans. These include 401(k)s for corporations, 403(b)s for schools and nonprofit groups, and Section 457s for county and municipal government. Minimum savings amounts are determined by employers as either a dollar amount (e.g., $20) or a percentage (e.g., 1 percent) of pay.

Individual retirement accounts (IRAs). IRAs are a tax-deferred place to put assets, such as CDs and mutual funds, for retirement. All workers with earned income can contribute up to $2,000 annually, but it doesn't have to be invested all at once. Minimum investment amounts vary according to the investment selected but can be as little as $100.

Low-cost stocks. Over 1,500 publicly traded companies allow investors to buy stock directly through dividend reinvestment or direct purchase plans. Minimum investments are very affordable, often just $100. Another way to purchase stock inexpensively is through an investment club.

Minibonds. As noted in Chapter 10, traditional municipal bonds require $5,000. However, some municipalities offer small denomination minibonds in amounts of $500 or less. Some corporations also offer small-denomination bonds (aka baby bonds). Further information can be obtained through brokerage firms that sell fixed-income securities.

Places to Invest $1,000 or Less

Corporate bonds. These are corporate IOUs and typically sell for $1,000. Investors receive a fixed amount of interest at regular intervals, generally every six months, until the bond matures. Then they get back their principal. Conservative investors should select investment grade bonds.

Money market mutual funds (MMMFs). These are mutual funds that invest in short-term debt obligations. The minimum initial investment is often $1,000 or less and limited check writing (e.g., a minimum check of $250 or $500) may be available. Investors concerned about high taxes can purchase shares in a tax-free MMMF issued by their state of residence.

Mutual funds. Mutual fund shares provide ownership in stocks (growth funds), bonds (income funds), or other securities that comprise a fund portfolio. Many funds accept initial deposits of $1,000 or less and subsequent deposits are usually lower (e.g., $100). Funds that require more than $1,000 to open an account often take less (e.g., $500) for IRAs, custodial accounts, or automatic investment plans.

Treasury securities. Treasury bills maturing in a year or less require a $1,000 minimum investment, as do Treasury notes issued with two-, five-, and ten-year maturities. Treasury bonds are also issued in denominations of $1,000 for more than ten (currently 30) years. To avoid paying a commission to a bank or broker, request a tender form and instructions from a Federal Reserve bank and enroll via Treasury Direct.

Unit investment trusts (UITs). Sold by brokerage firms, UITs are a portfolio of securities (e.g., municipal bonds, Dow Ten stocks) that are sold to investors in small pieces called units. The cost of a unit is generally $1,000. Unlike mutual funds, however, UITs are not professionally managed. Instead, the securities in the portfolio are simply held to generate interest or dividends, which are distributed proportionately to investors.

Zero-coupon bonds. "Zeros" are bonds issued by governments or corporations that sell at a deep discount to face value (generally $1,000). Unlike other bonds that pay periodic interest, they don't pay anything until maturity, at which time an investor receives $1,000. Investors with a 15- to 20-year time horizon can purchase a $1,000 zero-coupon bond for about $200 to $300, depending on the maturity date and interest rate earned. Zeros are often sold with minimum values of $5,000 (i.e., five $1,000 bonds), however, so the up-front cost may be $1,000 or slightly higher.

Building Portfolios with $5,000 to $10,000

At the $5,000 to $10,000 level, an investor can diversify his or her portfolio by assembling a collection of non–highly correlated investments that do not move in tandem as economic conditions change. As always, it is important to know what you are investing for and to establish a financial base (e.g., adequate insurance and emergency reserves) first. Be sure also to consider investments together as a total package (e.g., tax-deferred employer plan assets and taxable assets) rather than as separate entities. That way, a lack of asset class representation in one portion of a portfolio can be sought somewhere else. An example is an investor with access to only U.S. index funds in a 403(b) plan selecting a fund that tracks the EAFE index (Europe, Australia, and the Far East; international investments) for a taxable account.

One way to invest $5,000 to $10,000 is to create a diversified portfolio of stocks, preferably in different industry sectors. If an investor purchases ten shares of stock in ten industries, using a DRIP or DPP, their portfolio might look as follows:

Airline Company	10 shares @ $ 51	$ 510
Entertainment Company	10 shares @ $ 64	640
Financial Services Company	10 shares @ $ 77	770
Food Product Company	10 shares @ $ 38	380
Health Care Company	10 shares @ $ 42	420
Oil Company	10 shares @ $ 56	560
Retail Company	10 shares @ $ 45	450
Technology Company	10 shares @ $ 73	730
Telecommunications Company	10 shares @ $ 33	330
Utility Company	10 shares @ $ 67	670
Total Stock Assets	100 shares	$5,460

Of course, there also will be fees charged by various company stock purchase plans (in lieu of brokerage commissions) so the actual up-front cost in this example will probably be closer to $6,000. Once a portfolio is established, additional shares can be purchased directly from the sponsoring companies, usually in increments of $50 or more. An investor simply decides how much to deposit and when and implements a dollar cost averaging strategy through their

DRIP or DPP. Dollar cost averaging takes the emotion out of investing by converting a set amount (e.g., $100) into stock shares on a regular basis (e.g., monthly). Over time, the results can be astounding. If an investor sets $50 per month aside in each of ten stocks ($500 total) for 20 years and the portfolio averages a 10 percent return, they'd have about $380,000 for future goals like retirement.

The same strategy can be followed with mutual funds; that is, select a variety of funds that fit investment goals and the amount available to invest that, together, provide portfolio diversification. An example is an investor with $10,000 who decides to spread their money equally across ten mutual funds ($1,000 per fund) in eight asset class categories. Each of the funds requires $1,000 or less initially. The investor's broad asset allocation mix is 60 percent equities and 40 percent fixed-income and their specific asset allocation is 10 percent real estate, 50 percent stock, 30 percent bonds, and 10 percent cash. From there, the investor selects specific mutual funds for each asset class as follows:

10%	Real estate fund
20%	U.S. large company stock funds (2)
20%	U.S. small company stock funds (2)
10%	International stock fund
10%	Intermediate-term U.S. government bond fund
10%	Short-term corporate bond fund
10%	International bond fund
10%	Tax-free money market fund

Like the DRIP or DPP stock example, additional shares can be purchased via dollar cost averaging to grow the portfolio over time. If the investor only has $5,000 initially, they could drop the real estate fund, select only one U.S. large and small company stock fund, and drop two of the bond funds and/or a bond fund and the money market fund. This way, they'd still maintain their broad 60/40 asset allocation with half the initial investment. How fast investments can be made, of course, depends on how much money has previously been saved. If there is only enough to purchase one or two mutual funds (or stocks) initially, that's okay. Simply use new money to complete the asset allocation strategy as it is earned. The important thing is to start investing right away with whatever amount of money is available.

For conservative investors or those with short-term goals, $5,000 to $10,000 also will purchase a laddered portfolio of Treasuries. Another option in this price range is a laddered portfolio of zero-coupon bonds with maturities timed to coincide with a future financial goal (e.g., a child's freshman through senior years of college). Zeros can be purchased individually through brokers, many of whom require a minimum investment of $5,000 of face value.

Another place to invest with a solid four-figure asset base is a specialty investment such as a real estate investment trust (REIT) or mutual fund that invests in REITs. Required minimums for realty funds vary from $1,000 to $2,500 for most funds to $10,000 for the largest REIT fund, Cohen and Steers Realty Shares. The cost of REITs themselves, of course, varies daily as they trade like stock on major exchanges. A second specialized strategy is to purchase one of the mutual funds that invest half of their assets in the Dow Ten or, depending on the cost, the ten individual Dogs (stocks) themselves. The Payden and Rygel Growth and Income Fund, for example, which places half of its assets in the Dow Ten, requires a minimum initial purchase of $5,000, or $2,000 for IRAs.

Convertible bonds or bond funds are a third specialty investment. A cross between a conventional bond and a high-dividend stock, convertibles allow investors to exchange a bond or preferred stock for a specific number of shares of common stock. With $10,000 or less, diversification is best achieved with a convertible bond mutual fund, most of which come with minimums of $500 to $5,000.

Automating Investment Purchases

As an investor accumulates wealth and increases their investment holdings from $1,000 to $5,000 to $10,000 or more, their next $1,000 should be used to increase existing asset class balances or reduce portfolio risk through diversification, for example, by adding new asset categories. Portfolio rebalancing also should be done periodically and new money used to keep target percentages on track. If rebalancing is not done, asset percentages will shift according to how financial markets have performed. The most important principle of shoestring investing is consistency (i.e., a plan to increase investment holdings on a regular basis by placing periodic deposits on automatic pilot). Seven systematic investment strategies include:

1. Authorize a paycheck deduction for a credit union, thrift plan, EE savings bond purchases, or retirement savings (e.g., 401(k)).

2. Authorize a mutual fund to debit a bank account for a specific amount to make a periodic purchase of fund shares (i.e., automated dollar cost averaging).

3. Authorize a mutual fund or stock purchase plan to reinvest dividends and capital gains into additional fund shares.

4. Authorize a bank to transfer funds periodically from a no- or low-interest checking account to a higher-yielding MMDA or CD.

5. Authorize employer to increase investment amounts by a specific percentage (e.g., 1 or 2 percent) per year by increasing payroll deduction.

6. Enroll in a mutual fund or brokerage firm automatic investment (aka sharebuilder) plan to purchase mutual fund shares or stock with small dollar amounts.

7. Save loose change in a jar as a daily habit and/or use a weekly club savings plan to accumulate money to invest.

Don't wait until tomorrow to start investing. Do it today, and automate your investing so you don't even have to think about it. Use Worksheet #12 to outline a personal investment action plan that includes planned investments and their dollar amounts.

WORKSHEET **12** *My Personal Investment Plan*

Complete the following questions with the names of specific investments and their dollar amounts. An example is provided for each question.

1. **I plan to make the following investments:**

Name of Investment	Amount of Annual Deposit
XYZ Growth Fund	$1,200

2. **I plan to dollar cost average by making the following periodic deposits to investments:**

Name of Investment	Frequency/Amount of Deposit
XYZ Growth Fund	$100 per month

3. **I plan to implement these automatic investment strategies:**

Get XYZ Growth Fund to debit checking account for $100 monthly.

4. **Other actions I plan to take are:**

Start an IRA with a $40 per week Christmas club.

14

Investing to Make Up
for Lost Time

One always has time enough,
if one will apply it well.

—Johann Wolfgang von Goethe

Time is truly a magical gift, especially when combined with systematic investing (e.g., automatic mutual fund purchases). This chapter is designed for people who could have started investing sooner but didn't. It is time to stop beating yourself up over what you should have done decades ago and start investing something—anything—today. The good news is that time is still on your side. Even at age 45 or 50, accumulating a substantial nest egg for retirement is possible. The tradeoff is that procrastinators may need to do more than simply invest money in order to enjoy a comfortable retirement. Other catch-up strategies that often also need to be implemented include moving to a less expensive home or area, working part time in retirement, and/or delaying retirement.

Financial security in retirement is especially of concern to the 76 million baby boomers born between 1946 and 1964. It is estimated that a baby boomer will turn 50 every eight seconds throughout the next decade. To respond to boomers' increased concern about retirement, Fidelity Investments recently ran an advertising campaign with 1960s rock music blaring and the words "It's about time." The federal government also has gotten into the act with a 1998 summit on retirement savings. To date, it appears that many baby boomers are unprepared for the financial impact of a long retirement. In 1900, the average life expectancy of an American was 47. Most people didn't age, they died. Today, a 60-year-old's life expectancy is 27 years, and a 75-year-old's life expectancy is 15 years. These numbers are expected to increase further in future years with additional medical advances.

Facing Demographic Realities

Baby boomers face several unique challenges. No generation has ever had such poor timing due to its size. Sandwiched in between two smaller generations, supply and demand has been, and continues to be, the name of the game. The widely used "pig in the python" metaphor provides a visual image (i.e., a slowly moving bulge) of the effects of this large population group on American society as they move through successive stages of the life cycle. The pig remains indigestible while the python (i.e., society) gets stretched out of shape and never returns exactly to its original form as baby boomers pass through. Four competing issues affect the finances of many baby boomers: the adequacy of retirement savings, childrens' education expenses, the financial needs of aging parents, and uncertainty about job security. What can be done to address these concerns? Consider the following:

- *Save for college and retirement simultaneously, especially if children were born after age 35.* Money placed in a tax-deferred plan like an individual retirement account (IRA) is not included in calculations for college financial aid. If it comes down to a choice between the two competing goals, fund retirement investments first. After all, there are loans and financial aid for college but no one gives scholarships for retirement.

- *Avoid job complacency.* Be a team player and seek out opportunities to develop knowledge and skills that are transferable to a variety of employers. Economists call this "general human capital." Entrepreneurship through a sideline business also should be explored, both for an additional source of income now and as a possible transition to semi-retirement later.

- *Don't count on an inheritance or making a killing in the real estate market to make up for years of not investing.* Although there's been a lot of press about baby boomers inheriting massive amounts of wealth as an entire generation, the typical individual inheritance is expected to be modest . . . less than $20,000. As far as real estate goes, baby boomers will be selling to a smaller generation so the forces of supply and demand are against them.

- *Downscale your lifestyle.* Many boomers have more than enough "stuff" by their late 40s or 50s and easily can reduce spending. Identify expenses that can be pared and use this money to invest.

- *Keep Social Security in perspective.* When baby boomers start retiring, there will be fewer workers paying into the system to support a large number of beneficiaries. This ratio is predicted to be 2:1 by 2040. A number of proposals have been made to bring the Social Security system into balance. Experts differ on a remedy but all agree that something must be done soon. While Social Security will most likely not be eliminated, boomers and younger generations can expect a significant reduction and/or postponement of benefits.

So How Much Do You Really Need to Retire?

Financial planning for retirement has often been compared to target shooting while blindfolded. It is difficult to take aim at a goal that's far away and hard to see. In addition, there are many unknowns in the planning process like inflation rates, life expectancy, and possible changes in Social Security, pensions, and tax laws. The further you are from retirement age, the more likely it is that conditions will change. Nevertheless, it is possible—and necessary—to develop specific plans. One resource, found in Chapter 2, is *Ballpark Estimate,* a worksheet that determines the amount needed to invest annually for retirement. Other guidelines also exist, such as 60 to 80 percent of preretirement income to maintain one's lifestyle, and insurance company life expectancy data to gauge how long funds need to last.

Perhaps the most important assumption needed—for planning purposes—is an investor's retirement date. People who plan to retire early (at ages 50 to 62) usually must rely heavily on personal savings because income from other sources may not be immediately available. They also need to invest more than later retirees because there is less time to put money aside and a longer retirement period over which funds must stretch. Some people, on the other hand, choose to work beyond age 65 and, for them, bonuses are available from Social Security. For each year of delayed retirement—up to age 70—benefits are increased from 4 to 8 percent, depending on date of birth.

To estimate financial needs in retirement, make a list of current household expenses and estimate which ones will increase (e.g., health care), decrease (e.g., transportation), or remain the same (e.g., gifts). This will help determine the percentage of income that needs to be replaced. It also is advisable to estimate household expenses, not only at the date of retirement, but 10 or 20 years later. Evidence exists from the government Consumer Expenditure Survey (CES) that spending voluntarily declines as retirees get older. By age 75, spending is reduced by approximately 20 percent of spending levels at age 65. Thus, if an initial replacement ratio is set at 80 percent of preretirement income, the age 75 replacement ratio would be 64 percent [80 minus $(80 \times .20)$]. Not to account for this phenomenon risks overstating the amount needed to invest.

One simple way to account for changed spending patterns during retirement is to use a blended replacement ratio, based on CES data, as indicated in Figure 14.1. For example, a retiree who assumes an

Figure 14.1   Blended Income Replacement Ratios

Life Expectancy after Retirement	Original Replacement Ratios			
	80%	75%	70%	65%
10 years	.800	.750	.700	.650
15 years	.750	.700	.654	.610
20 years	.720	.675	.630	.585
25 years	.704	.660	.616	.572
30 years	.693	.652	.608	.565

initial replacement ratio of 75 percent and a life expectancy of 25 years after retirement would use a blended rate of 66 percent (.660).

Once an investor knows how much income they need to replace, they can complete their plans by answering these questions:

- How much income will be available from Social Security and/ or an employer pension?

- How long will retirement last (i.e., an assumed life expectancy)?

- How much money is needed to fund the gap between planned retirement income and expected benefits over an investor's lifetime?

- How much money must be invested annually to close the gap?

The *Ballpark Estimate* and other retirement planning worksheets or Internet and software financial calculators can be used to answer these questions and calculate a required annual investment amount. Just remember the old adage, garbage in, garbage out. The more accurate the answers to the questions listed above, the more reliable a calculation will be.

Generic estimates of required savings amounts also are helpful. The chart in Figure 14.2 assumes a 10 percent tax-deferred yield and shows what investors of various ages would need to set aside in order to accumulate $1 million by age 65. Why $1 million? This is a hypothetical amount used to illustrate that it takes a large nest egg to live off investment income for 30 or 40 years. At age 40, an individual would need to deposit a lump sum of $92,296 or make monthly investments of $754 to accumulate $1 million. At age 50, the required lump

Figure 14.2 Amounts Required for a $1 Million Retirement Fund

Age	Lump-Sum Amount	Monthly Investment Amount
25	$ 22,095	$ 159
30	35,584	264
35	57,309	443
40	92,296	754
45	148,644	1,317
50	239,392	2,413
55	385,543	4,882

sum jumps substantially to $239,392 and monthly investments to $2,413.

Of course, many investors are not starting totally from scratch. You may need to make up for lost time but have managed to invest somewhere, like an IRA or 401(k). The chart in Figure 14.3 shows how far toward the $1 million mark you have already come. Simply multiply the amount of current assets by the number that corresponds to years remaining until retirement. For example, if you plan to retire in 20 years and have $10,000 already invested, multiply this amount by 6.73 to see what it will be worth in two decades ($10,000 × 6.73 = $67,300). The future value of current assets then can be subtracted from the nest egg needed to generate retirement income.

Is Catch-Up Investing Possible?

Catch-up investing is not only possible, but necessary (for many people), and can be practiced successfully by virtually every middle-income investor with a desire to do so. As President Harry S. Truman once said: "A pessimist is one who makes difficulties of his opportunities, and an optimist is one who makes opportunities of his difficulties." Even people in their 50s with little or nothing invested have an opportunity to make up for lost time. After all, they will most likely live 30 or 35 years and can use at least 20 of those years to build assets. In addition, baby boomers in their late 40s and 50s are approaching their peak earning years and are poised to earn higher incomes than ever before, some of which can be invested. Listed below are ten catch-up investment strategies for financial late bloomers or ways to reduce retirement living costs so that less money is required to invest.

Figure 14.3   Multipliers for Future Value of Current Retirement Assets*

Years Until Retirement							
5	10	15	20	25	30	35	40
1.61	2.59	4.18	6.73	10.83	17.45	28.10	45.26

*Assumes a 10 percent investment yield and 4 percent inflation

1. Kick it up a notch. No, this doesn't mean that Chef Emeril Lagasse is adding more spice to a recipe. It simply means ratcheting up the amount currently invested in retirement plans such as 401(k)s. For workers eligible for 403(b) plans, it also means making catch-up contributions above and beyond the normal limits to make up for years when no investments were made. At the very least, contribute enough to qualify for full employer matching. If this isn't possible, or you're already getting a full employer match, then kick it up 1 percent more, especially after receiving a raise. The results can be awesome.

According to the *401(k) Booster Calculator*, produced by Advantage Publications (800-323-6809), 1 percent of a $35,000 salary, for example, is $350. For a 40-year-old, an extra $350 in a 401(k) would translate into $39,474 of additional retirement savings at age 65, assuming an 8 percent average annual return and 4 percent average annual pay increases.

2. Slash expenses. When household expenses, like child care or college tuition, end, invest this money for retirement. Ditto for a mortgage and other debts, like a car loan or credit card bills, and money spent to raise children or purchase losing state lottery tickets. Another place to reduce spending is entertainment and leisure expenses. Look for discounts on airline travel, meals, and lodging or simply just spend less. Middle age is also a good time to reevaluate life insurance coverage. If a mortgage is nearly repaid and children are no longer financially dependent, a term policy could be dropped or whole life insurance converted into a paid-up policy. Further expense reduction will, of course, also be possible after retirement, including amounts spent for clothing, transportation, taxes, and retirement investing.

3. Trade down. One of the first questions future retirees need to ask themselves is "Where am I going to live?" The answer to this question may, in fact, have a greater impact on retirement well-being than any investment decision. If you're willing to downsize into a smaller home, you probably will be able to live on (read: and, therefore, have to invest) less. Trading down to a smaller home can free up equity and reduce the cost of maintenance, insurance, utilities, and property taxes. For example, if an investor owns a $200,000 home free and clear, a substantial portion of their net worth is probably tied up in the house. If they were to sell it and buy a $90,000 home, they'd have about $100,000 after expenses to invest. With an 8 percent average annual rate of return, trading down could provide an additional $8,000 per year of income, plus the savings from reduced household expenses. The 1997 tax law allows investors to earn up to $500,000 in capital gains, tax-free, without any age restriction. Downsizing a home has, therefore, become an attractive option for catch-up investors. Another way to tap equity in a home is to use a reverse mortgage, which is a loan against the value of a home that can be structured to provide monthly income. The loan is repaid when a homeowner sells the house or when it is sold by their estate following their death.

4. Geographic arbitrage. In investing, arbitrage is the profit earned when a security trades at different prices in different financial markets. Geographic arbitrage refers to the value of the same home (e.g., a 2,000-square-foot ranch) in different locations. An article in the April 1998 issue of *Worth* noted that "changes in geography and shelter are great surrogates for a lifetime of investing." In other words, moving to a smaller home in a less expensive area can substantially reduce the percentage of preretirement income that needs to be replaced and, hence, the amount required to invest for retirement. While it could take years—even decades—to accumulate a six-figure sum, an investor can get the same effect by moving from a high-cost state to a lower-cost state. A good source of information about the cost of living in various locations and city-to-city comparisons is the Homefair Web site at www.homefair.com/homefair/ cmr/salcalc.html.

5. Start moonlighting. Many people have job skills that are portable and in demand by a second employer or as a self-employed consultant. Moonlighting provides an opportunity to earn additional income for catch-up investing and provides a bridge to postretirement employment. Self-employment income also entitles an investor to additional tax-deferred opportunities such as a SIMPLE plan, Keogh, or simplified employee pension. Approximately eight million Americans worked second jobs in 1995 and millions more had small sideline businesses. If job skills have become a bit rusty, consider taking courses to increase your marketability.

6. Retire later. Increasing the age at which you retire provides two benefits: more time to invest for retirement and to allow assets to grow and fewer years in retirement during which money is spent. In addition, pension benefits also can increase substantially by staying on the job a few more years. Someone with 25 years of service might receive $15,000 a year, for example, at age 55 and, maybe $20,000 at age 60 or $25,000 at age 65. Specific amounts, of course, will depend on a worker's income and pension plan regulations. Social Security benefits also are higher for persons who wait longer to collect benefits.

The amount of money needed to retire at age 55 versus 65 is substantial. Working later—even just a few years—can make a big difference in one's lifestyle. For example, by waiting three years and factoring in compound interest on assets that are not depleted, an investor's nest egg might be able to last another seven to ten years, depending on the rates of return and withdrawal.

7. Earn a higher return. The higher the rate of return earned on investments, the less that needs to be invested. Period. Therefore, earning even an extra percentage or two per year both before and after retirement can have a tremendous impact on the amount of assets that are accumulated. An investor who wants to make up for lost time basically has four choices: work longer, invest a higher percentage (say 20 or 25 percent) of income, downscale retirement lifestyle expectations (e.g., a smaller home), and/or invest aggressively (read: 60 or 70 percent of a portfolio in stock).

Between 1995 and 1998, investors who chose option four were incredibly lucky and saw the bull market compensate them handsomely for years of foregone investing. While 20 percent returns certainly can't be counted on in future years, we know that the greater the percentage of stock in an investor's portfolio the greater its return over time. Furthermore, some futurists are calling for continued upward pressure on stock prices for at least another decade as the baby boom generation affects financial markets (i.e., supply and demand) like it previously impacted real estate, employment, and education.

8. Maximize tax deferral. After taking full advantage of tax-deductible contributions to an employer plan, invest in an IRA. There are no age limits for contributing to a Roth IRA so contributions can be made by anyone with earned income and an adjusted gross income that qualifies. Even 50-year-olds with a 20-year investment horizon will see their investment grow handsomely. A couple that remains employed and contributes $4,000 annually, for example, with an 8 percent annual return will have about $183,000 at age 70, which can later be withdrawn tax-free. When investors need to tap their retirement nest egg, it is advisable to draw down taxable accounts first and let retirement plans like 401(k)s enjoy tax-deferred growth until mandatory withdrawals are required. This, too, will result in a higher accumulation and require less money up front to invest.

9. Make the most of an inheritance. Let's make one thing clear: Inheritances are not a given and usually can't be counted on as a source of retirement income. There are just too many unknowns, like parents' longevity and nursing home costs, to count on inheriting a nest egg that would, otherwise, result from investing. Having said that, however, it also would be foolish not to acknowledge that the possibility exists or to make the most of an inheritance, should one occur. A widely quoted 1994 study by two Cornell professors, Robert Avery and Michael Rendall, indicated that the baby boom generation is poised to inherit $10.4 trillion, or a little over $90,000 apiece. This number is overstated for many boomers, however, because inheritances are based on parental assets and those from affluent families will naturally inherit more.

Two key points about inheritances are this: First, don't use the possibility of an inheritance as an excuse not to invest. Second, if an inheritance should be received, follow all the rules of prudent investing discussed earlier (e.g., diversification and asset allocation) and take the time to make informed decisions.

Communication among family members about the size of an estate can provide a realistic frame of reference about an inheritance, although many people understandably find this difficult because it means talking about the death of a loved one or appearing to sound greedy. Another course of action that some elderly persons (or their adult children) are taking is to purchase a long-term care insurance policy that covers the cost of a nursing home or in-home health care. This way, an inheritance will not be depleted by these expenses and can be viewed by heirs more as a probability than a possibility.

10. Just do it! Make catch-up investing a priority and don't play the "as soon as" game (e.g., "as soon as . . . we get a new car, the children graduate from college . . . etc.") any longer. Consider combining several of the strategies listed above. For example, retire at age 65, instead of 62, and move to a smaller house in a cheaper locale. Or start a home-based business and work until you're 70 and increase the stock percentage of your portfolio. The most important thing is that you do something to catch up and get started today. Use Worksheet #13 to list your personal financial catch-up strategies. As Secretary of Labor Alexis Herman remarked at the 1998 National Summit on Retirement Savings, "There may be a lot of people who want to simply hit the snooze button on this issue but, if you snooze, you lose."

WORKSHEET **13** *My Personal Financial Catch-Up Plan*

List below the strategies you plan to follow in order to make up for lost time. (For example, increase 401(k) plan contribution from 4 percent to 6 percent of salary.)

1. _____

2. _____

3. _____

4. _____

5. _____

6. _____

7. _____

8. _____

9. _____

10. _____

15

Choosing Professional Financial Advisers

The illiterate of the 21st century
will not be those who cannot read and write,
but those who cannot learn, unlearn, and relearn.

—Alvin Toffler

Financial planning is an ongoing process that requires constant continuing education. Virtually every year, something changes that affects investment decisions, such as tax laws or Treasury Department policies related to the purchase of government securities, or personal circumstances, such as a job change or birth of a child. There's just one problem . . . many people have a day job or other major responsibilities and lack the time required to research investments or develop and monitor a diversified portfolio. Investors need to honestly assess what they are prepared to do (e.g., calculate net worth, screen mutual fund prospectuses) and consider hiring professional advisers for areas where they lack the necessary time or expertise. Many people feel that financial advisers are only for the wealthy and that their income or assets are not high enough. Nonsense. Anyone with a moderate income and a desire to take action to achieve financial goals may be able to benefit from professional advice.

Another concern that many people have about financial advisers is the cost. Yes, professionals such as lawyers, accountants, and financial planners are basically selling their time so hourly rates can range from $100 to $250. But if a consultation results in decreased income or estate taxes or an increase of a few percentage points of investment yield (which can translate into tens of thousands of dollars at retirement), few people would argue that the fee was not money well spent (e.g., spending $500 to make or save $5,000). Not only that, but investors who hire professional advisers can spend more time with their families or doing what they do best instead of managing their finances.

Professional advisers also are helpful for people who lack the discipline or confidence required to invest. Suddenly, there is someone to be accountable to and/or to hold your hand through personal crises or market downturns. If paying a fee to a professional adviser forces an investor to stay the course and not panic or abandon their investment strategy, then the cost also is well worth it.

Who Needs a Financial Adviser?

Probably you do. After all, it's a rare person who enjoys doing investment research *and* has the time *and* expertise to make wise decisions without some professional guidance. This is especially true as an investor's financial and/or personal situation becomes more complex (e.g., increased income and assets, change in marital status) or a triggering event, such as a job change, occurs. Review the situations listed below and check those that apply to you and your family. The more items you check, the more likely you'll benefit from professional advice:

☐ Annual household income over $50,000

☐ Change in employment or employer-sponsored retirement plans

☐ Change in marital status (e.g., marriage, widowhood)

☐ Concern about reducing income and/or estate taxes

☐ Desire to assess adequacy of retirement or college savings

☐ Desire to assess overall financial status

☐ Desire to change spending habits and increase savings

☐ Desire to develop a diversified investment portfolio

☐ Federal income tax over $5,000 a year

☐ Gross estate over $650,000 or $1.3 million for a couple (1999 figure that will be adjusted annually for inflation)

☐ Have certificates of deposit (CDs) or bonds worth $10,000 or more coming due

☐ Household assets (exclusive of home) in excess of $100,000

☐ Lack the time and/or expertise to make major investment decisions

☐ Need help understanding insurance policies and/or employee benefit programs

☐ Need to save money for retirement or a child's college education

☐ Procrastination or analysis paralysis

☐ Receipt of a major windfall, such as an inheritance, lump-sum pension distribution, or gambling winnings

☐ Sale of a major asset such as a business or highly appreciated property

☐ Significant lifestyle change such as a promotion, early retirement, birth of a child, or purchase of a home

☐ Time-specific financial decisions (e.g., 30 day early retirement buyout offer)

Choosing Financial Advisers

There are many types of financial advisers, each with a specific function and area of expertise. Over 250,000 professionals call themselves financial planners. Some advisers provide comprehensive financial planning advice or a specialized service (e.g., asset management, tax preparation), while others hold securities or insurance licenses that allow them to buy and sell financial products (e.g., annuities) for which they earn a commission. When choosing a financial adviser, don't be afraid to interview several candidates and ask about their services and how they are compensated. Once an adviser is selected, delegate—but don't abdicate—responsibility for financial decision making because you (not the adviser) must live with the results.

When choosing a financial adviser, focus on the "Three Cs" as criteria for selection: competence, credentials, and compensation.

Competence

Look for an experienced professional who specializes in providing the service (e.g., portfolio management) being sought and has worked with clients in situations similar to yours in both bull and bear markets. This is no less important than selecting a doctor. If someone needed heart surgery, they most likely would bypass an inexperienced surgeon and look for a seasoned professional. One indication of an adviser's competence is positive comments or referrals from knowledgeable family and friends who have had previous experience with financial advisers. Better still, ask another financial adviser, for instance, an accountant or attorney, to recommend a financial planner because their own professional credibility is on the line when they reply.

Look for advisers who take the time to learn about investors' financial goals and attitudes and avoid those who immediately start recommending investment products. Another way to assess an adviser's competence is to call the North American Securities Administrators Association (NASAA) at 202-737-0900 or 1-888-84-NASAA, or a state securities regulatory agency (whose number you can get from NASAA) to check on the registration status and disciplinary history (e.g., lawsuits, complaints, fines) of securities industry professionals. All of these agencies can access the Central Registration Depository (CRD), which contains licensing and disciplinary information about financial advisers nationwide. Of course, it goes without saying that any adviser who is not properly licensed or has serious infractions in their past, for example, making unsuitable or unauthorized investments, should be eliminated from consideration. End of story. When there is smoke, there is usually fire.

Credentials

There are letters after financial professionals' names that indicate something about their educational background and there are those that don't. Know the difference. Letters that indicate completion of various programs of study include:

- *CFP (certified financial planner)*—The Denver-based Certified Financial Planner Board of Standards, Inc. (CFP Board) owns the CFP certification mark and licenses qualified individuals to use it. A CFP licensee must take six college-level courses, pass a ten-hour examination, have three years of financial planning-related experience, fulfill a biennial continuing education requirement, and adhere to the CFP Board's code of ethics.

- *CPA/PFS (certified public accountant/personal financial specialist)*—This designation is awarded by the American Institute of Certified Public Accountants in New York to approximately 8,500 CPAs with a specialization in financial planning. CPA/PFSs must pass a special examination and meet certain additional requirements such as participation in continuing education courses and a practice that includes at least 750 hours of personal financial planning during a three-year period. As CPAs, they also must pass a rigorous tax and accounting exam and meet state licensing requirements.

- *ChFC (chartered financial consultant)*—The American College in Bryn Mawr, Pennsylvania, awards the ChFC designation primarily to insurance industry professionals on completion of a ten-part course of study. Like CFPs, ChFCs must have three years of professional experience and participate in continuing education courses to maintain this credential. The ChFC is usually coupled with Chartered Life Underwriter (CLU), a designation indicating training in life insurance, and is held by over 30,000 financial advisers across the United States.

- *JD (juris doctor)*—These letters indicate that someone is an attorney. Often JDs doing work in personal financial planning also will hold a designation such as CFP. This indicates that they have expertise in both legal and financial matters.

As for letters that don't indicate anything about an individual's educational background, try RIA (Registered Investment Adviser). Unlike professions such as dietetics and nursing, where the word "registered" indicates successful completion of a course of study, registered investment advisers have simply complied with a legal requirement to register with the Securities and Exchange Commission (SEC) or a state securities agency and are licensed to sell securities. Thus, RIA is a mandatory legal obligation, not an educational credential.

Since 1997, financial advisers with more than $25 million of assets under management are required to register with the SEC, and smaller firms with state regulators. Of course, investors should always look for financial professionals who are RIAs. This means that an adviser is in compliance with the law by registering with the appropriate state or federal regulatory agency. Unregistered advisers are in violation of the law and should be avoided. A second key point is to not confuse RIA with other three-letter credentials like CFP. For one, advisers pay a fee to the SEC; for the other they must study, pass exams, and continue taking courses. That's a big difference.

Compensation

If you thought the alphabet soup of financial planning credentials was hard to follow, try the following terms used to describe commonly used methods of adviser compensation.

Fee-only. This is where compensation comes entirely from fees charged for an individual consultation, development of a financial plan, or portfolio management. Fees can be charged per hour, per project (e.g., preparation of a college savings plan), or as a percentage (e.g., 1 percent) of assets under management. The last has been an industry trend throughout the 1990s.

Commission-only. Common among professionals at insurance and brokerage firms, an adviser charges little or nothing for a consultation or preparation of a financial plan but receives commissions from the sale of financial products such as stock. A potential conflict of interest exists between advisers' need to both generate an income and recommend suitable (and, hopefully, low-cost) products to clients. Not surprisingly, some advisers may give biased advice. For this reason, caution should be taken before the purchase of securities and questions asked about an adviser's compensation.

Salary. Some financial advisers earn a salary by working at a financial services institution such as a bank or credit union. While investors don't contribute to advisers' compensation directly, they may do so indirectly through fees or service charges that are assessed to maintain their account.

Fee and commission (aka fee-based). A combination of the fee-only and commission-only methods of compensation, a fee is charged for a consultation or development of a financial plan. Fees are assessed on an hourly, per-project, or percentage of assets basis. Then, if a client chooses to implement their plan with an adviser, the adviser also receives a commission for selling recommended products (e.g., mutual funds).

Fee-offset. This is another fee and commission hybrid method where an adviser's commission income is used to offset all or part of the fees charged for financial planning services. For example, if a financial planning engagement costs $1,500 and an adviser earns $1,000 from product sales, the fee portion would cost only $500.

Financial media and consumer watchdog groups routinely suggest that the fee-only compensation method is preferable because it reduces potential conflicts of interest. On the other hand, the cost of fee-only advice may be prohibitive for persons with, say, $50,000 or less to invest. Thus, there are no hard and fast rules to follow. The best course of action is to inquire about costs and conflicts of interest at the beginning of a professional engagement. Sometimes a commission-only adviser seems inexpensive until expenses (e.g., mutual fund 12(b)1 fees and front-end loads) are tallied, while a fee-only adviser that charges more up front may earn their fee several times over in superior investment performance and/or tax savings. Not surprisingly, the issue of which compensation method is superior has been debated in financial planning circles for decades and probably will continue to be discussed for years to come. The most important outcome for individual investors, however, is to find a competent and experienced adviser who provides sound recommendations based on individual goals and constraints (e.g., risk tolerance) at an affordable cost.

Questions to Ask Financial Advisers

When selecting a financial adviser, ask plenty of questions. After all, it's your money at stake and, therefore, no question is too dumb.

Below are 20 questions that can help determine an adviser's education, experience, compensation method(s), and business practices.

1. What is your area of expertise (e.g., retirement planning) or specialization (e.g., small business owners)?

2. What services do you provide (e.g., asset management)?

3. How are you compensated for your services (e.g., fee only)?

4. What education and training do you have (e.g., CPA, CFP)?

5. How do you keep up to date on financial planning topics (e.g., professional association meetings)?

6. How long have you been in business?

7. What did you do before becoming a financial adviser?

8. Are you registered with state or federal securities regulators?

9. What are the typical commissions charged for financial products?

10. How much will it cost initially and per year to become a client?

11. Describe your typical client (e.g., age, income, assets).

12. Can you show me a sample financial plan?

13. Can you provide me with references, such as current or previous clients or other financial professionals?

14. What is your investment philosophy (e.g., active management versus indexing, value versus growth)?

15. How do you research the investment products that you recommend?

16. How often will my portfolio (or financial plan) be reviewed?

17. How often will I receive portfolio statements and other follow-up information?

18. Do you have a working relationship with other professionals who provide related services (e.g., attorney, accountant)?

19. Who will work with me: the adviser or associates?

20. Will you provide a written letter of engagement?

Some financial advisers provide a brief introductory consultation at no cost. Use this time to ask questions and assess an adviser's personal style. Look for an adviser who listens attentively and asks questions about investment attitudes and financial goals. Also ask an investment adviser to provide a copy of the SEC form ADV or its state equivalent. This form, or a brochure that contains the same information, describes how an adviser conducts business (e.g., compensation methods, potential conflicts of interest). File the ADV form with other important financial documents for future reference.

Financial advisers help clients clarify their present situation by assessing financial data, such as net worth. They also consider "the big picture," that is, how financial decisions work together, and select investments that match financial goals. Want to get the most value from the fees paid to a financial adviser and build a solid relationship? Consider the following advice from the Financial Literacy Center in Kalamazoo, Michigan:

- *Be accessible.* Give an adviser your fax number or E-mail address so you can be contacted quickly, if necessary.

- *Be considerate.* Don't call an adviser every time the stock market takes a nosedive. Remember, you're investing for the long term.

- *Be honest.* About risk tolerance and investment preferences. Don't try to appear more aggressive (or conservative) than you are.

- *Be receptive.* If an adviser suggests a specific course of action (e.g., preparing a will, buying disability insurance), do it.

- *Be open.* Tell an adviser what you want to accomplish and why and include important details about your financial situation.

- *Be prepared.* Organize financial records and calculate net worth and cash flow. The less time an adviser has to spend deciphering financial data, the less you'll have to pay.

- *Be proactive.* Contact an adviser before taking action (e.g., change of employment) that can affect your finances.

- *Be reasonable.* Don't expect an adviser to produce a 20 percent return every year. Expectations should be based on the historical performance of asset classes.

- *Be responsible.* Keep an eye on financial statements and changes in portfolio value and ask questions as warranted.

- *Be smart.* Slow and steady wins the race. Trying to time the market or buying today's hot investment will thwart any adviser's carefully crafted plan.

How to Find a Financial Adviser

Want to find a financial adviser in your area? Several organizations provide the names and contact information. These include:

American Institute of Certified Public Accountants (AICPA)
1211 Avenue of the Americas
New York, NY 10036
Phone: 888-999-9256 or 800-862-4272
Web site: www.cpapfs.org
The names of certified public accountants who hold the personal financial specialist (PFS) accreditation can be obtained by calling one of the toll-free numbers listed above or visiting the CPA/PFS Web site. Online, consumers can view a list of practitioners in an entire state or by zip code or area code.

American Society of CLU and ChFC (American Society)
P.O. Box 59
Bryn Mawr, PA 19010-0059
Phone: 888-ChFC-CLU (888-243-2258) or 800-927-2427
Web site: www.agents-online.com
Consumers can call one of the American Society's toll-free numbers or visit its Web site to obtain the names of up to five society members in their area who hold the Chartered Life Underwriter (CLU) and/or Chartered Financial Consultant (ChFC) designation. Information also is available about financial planning topics.

Certified Financial Planner Board of Standards (CFP Board)
1700 Broadway, Suite 2100
Denver, CO 80290-2101
Phone: 888-CFP-MARK (888-237-6275)
Web site: www.cfb-board.org

The CFP Board is a nonprofit regulatory organization that protects the public by establishing and enforcing the requirements necessary to hold the certified financial planner (CFP) designation. Consumers can call or visit the CFP Board's Web site to obtain publications, check the licensing status of individual practitioners, or obtain the names of CFPs (listed by state) who have been subject to disciplinary action.

Institute of Certified Financial Planners (ICFP)
3801 East Florida Avenue, Suite 708
Denver, CO 80210
Phone: 800-282-PLAN (800-282-7526)
Web site: www.icfp.org
The ICFP is a professional association consisting of over 11,000 certified financial planners or persons working toward the CFP designation. Consumers can call the ICFP's toll-free number or visit its Web site to obtain the names of local CFP practitioners.

International Association for Financial Planning (IAFP)
5775 Glenridge Drive, NE, Suite B-300
Atlanta, GA 30328
Phone: 888-806-PLAN (888-806-7526) or 800-945-4237
Web site: www.iafp.org
The IAFP consists of over 13,000 financial services professionals representing a variety of educational credentials and compensation methods. Consumers can get a list of financial advisers in their area and free publications on financial planning topics by calling one of the IAFP's toll-free numbers or visiting their Web site.

National Association of Personal Financial Advisors (NAPFA)
355 West Dundee Road, Suite 200
Buffalo Grove, IL 66089
Phone: 888-FEE-ONLY (888-333-6659)
Web site: www.napfa.org
NAPFA consists of almost 650 members who are fee-only financial planners compensated solely by fees paid by their clients. Consumers can call NAPFA's toll-free number or visit its Web site to obtain a list of fee-only advisers in their area. If a request is made via the Internet, the list is sent quickly by E-mail.

Other helpful organizations that provide information to check the disciplinary history of a financial adviser include:

National Association of Insurance Commissioners (NAIC)
816-842-3600 or www.naic.org

National Association of Securities Dealers (NASD)
800-289-9999 or www.nasdr.com

North American Securities Administrators Association (NASAA)
888-84-NASAA or 888-846-2722 or www.nasaa.org

U.S. Securities and Exchange Commission (SEC)
800-SEC-0330 or 800-732-0330 or www.sec.gov

Think twice about hiring a financial adviser who employs any of the following "red flags" associated with investment fraud:

- Assurances that an investment is risk-free and you can't lose your money
- Claims of inside or confidential information
- Excessive reliance on testimonials instead of actual investment performance data
- Lack of written information about an investment
- Limited-time offers that require immediate action
- Promises of spectacular profits or guaranteed returns
- Urgency to invest assets without first discussing financial goals and risk tolerance

Never allow a financial adviser to make decisions or purchase investments for you without prior approval. In addition, when recommendations *feel* wrong and you don't understand them or feel comfortable with the risk involved, take a pass. When in doubt, get a second opinion.

·············· Inexpensive ··············
Investment Resources

An investment in knowledge
always pays the best interest.

—Benjamin Franklin

The best way to get something done is to begin. This is true for most things in life, including investing. Fortunately, there are many public and private resources available to assist both new and experienced investors, including books, periodicals, television programs, investor organizations, library references, government agencies, software, industry associations, and Web sites.

Books

A Random Walk Down Wall Street by Burton G. Malkiel

Beating the Street by Peter Lynch and John Rothchild

Bogle on Mutual Funds by John C. Bogle

Buying Stocks without a Broker by Charles C. Carlson

Consumer Reports Money Book (3rd Edition) by Consumers Union

Die Broke by Stephen M. Pollan and Mark Levine

Downsize Your Debt by Andrew Feinberg

Everyone's Money Book by Jordan E. Goodman

Four Easy Steps to Successful Investing by Jonathan D. Pond

Get a Financial Life by Beth Kobliner

Get a Life: You Don't Need a Million to Retire Well by Ralph E. Warner

Investing for Dummies by Eric Tyson

Investment Clubs: A Team Approach to the Stock Market by Kathryn Shaw

Investment Gurus: A Road Map to Wealth from the World's Best Money Managers by Peter J. Tanous

Live Long & Profit: Wealthbuilding Strategies for Every Stage of Your Life by Kay R. Shirley

Making the Most of Your Money by Jane Bryant Quinn

Mutual Funds for Dummies by Eric Tyson

No-Load Stocks by Charles B. Carlson

One Up on Wall Street by Peter Lynch and John Rothchild

Retire Rich: The Baby Boomer's Guide to a Secure Future by Bambi Holzer

Saving on a Shoestring by Barbara O'Neill

Stocks for the Long Run by Jeremy J. Siegel

The Baby Boomer Financial Wake-Up Call by Kay R. Shirley

The Beardstown Ladies' Common Sense Investment Guide by the Beardstown Ladies Investment Club

The Beardstown Ladies Stitch-in-Time Guide to Growing Your Nest Egg by the Beardstown Ladies Investment Club

The Complete Idiot's Guide to 401(k) Plans by Wayne Bogosian and Dee Lee

The Millionaire Next Door: The Surprising Secrets of America's Wealthy by Tom Stanley and Bill Danko

The Money Answers Dictionary of Finance and Investment Terms by John Downes and Jordan E. Goodman

The Money Book of Personal Finance by Richard Eisenberg

The Money Diet by Ginger Applegarth

The Motley Fool Investment Guide: How the Fool Beats Wall Street's Wise Men and How You Can Too by David and Tom Gardner

The 100 Best Mutual Funds to Own in America by Gene Walden

The Only Investment Guide You'll Ever Need by Andrew Tobias

The Prudent Investor's Guide to Beating the Market by Carl H. Reinhardt, Alan B. Werba, and John J. Bowen

The Richest Man in Babylon by George S. Clason

The Way to Save and the Way to Invest by Ginita Wall

The Wealthy Barber by David Chilton

25 Myths You've Got to Avoid If You Want to Manage Your Money Right by Jonathan Clements

You Have More Than You Think: The Motley Fool Guide to Investing What You Have by David and Tom Gardner

Your Guide to Understanding Investing by The Securities Industry Association

Government Agencies

*Board of Governors of the Federal
Reserve System*
20th and C Streets, NW
Marriner S. Eccles Federal Reserve
Board Building
Washington, DC 20551
Web site: www.federalreserve.gov

Federal Trade Commission
6th Street & Pennsylvania Avenue, NW
Washington, DC 20580
Phone: 202-326-2000
Web site: www.ftc.gov

Social Security Administration
6401 Security Boulevard
Baltimore, MD 21235
Phone: 800-772-1213
Web site: www.ssa.gov

*U.S. Department of Agriculture Cooper-
ative State Research, Education, and
Extension Service (CSREES)*
1400 Independence Avenue, SW
Washington, DC 20250-0900
Web site: www.reeusda.gov

*U.S. Department of Labor, Pension, and
Welfare Benefits Administration*
200 Constitution Avenue, NW
Washington, DC 20210
Phone: 800-998-7542
Web site: www.dol.gov/dol/pwba

*U.S. Department of the Treasury, Bureau
of the Public Debt*
999 E Street, NW
Suite 553
Washington, DC 20239-0001
Phone: 202-874-4000
Web site: www.publicdebt.treas.gov

*U.S. Securities and Exchange
Commission*
Office of Investor Education and
Assistance
450 5th Street, NW
Washington, DC 20549
Phone: 800-SEC-0330 or 800-732-0330
Web site: www.sec.gov

Industry Associations

The Bond Market Association
40 Broad Street
New York, NY 10004-2373
Phone: 212-440-9400
Web site: www.psa.com

Investment Company Institute
1401 H Street, NW
Suite 1200
Washington, DC 20005
Phone: 202-326-5800
Web site: www.ici.org

*National Association of Securities
Dealers, Inc. (NASD)*
1735 K Street, NW
Washington, DC 20006-1500
Phone: 800-289-9999
Web site: www.investor.nasd.com

Options Clearing Corporation
440 South LaSalle Street
Suite 2400
Chicago, IL 60605
Phone: 800-OPTIONS or 800-566-9642
Web site: www.optionscentral.com

Securities Industry Association
120 Broadway
New York, NY 10271
Phone: 212-618-1500
Web site: www.sia.com

Investor Organizations

American Association of Individual
    Investors (AAII)
625 North Michigan Avenue
Suite 1900
Chicago, IL 60611-3110
Phone: 312-280-0170
Web site: www.aaii.com

The Investors Alliance, Inc.
219 Commercial Boulevard
Fort Lauderdale, FL 33308-4440
Phone: 888-683-1181
Web site: www.freequote.com

National Association of Investors
    Corporation (NAIC)
P.O. Box 220
Royal Oak, MI 48068
Phone: 248-583-NAIC or 248-583-6242
Web site: www.better-investing.org

Library References

Morningstar Mutual Funds
225 West Wacker Drive
Chicago, IL 60606
Phone: 800-876-5005 or 800-735-0700
Web site: www.morningstar.net

Value Line Investment Survey and
    Value Line Mutual Fund Survey
220 East 42nd Street
New York, NY 10017-5891
Phone: 800-535-9648
Web site: www.valueline.com

Magazines

Consumer Reports
P.O. Box 53017
Boulder, CO 80321-3017
Web site: www.consumerreports.com

Kiplinger's Personal Finance Magazine
P.O. Box 3293
Harlan, IA 51593-2473
Web site: www.kiplinger.com

Money
P.O. Box 61790
Tampa, FL 33661-1790
Web site: www.money.com

Smart Money
P.O. Box 7536
Red Oak, IA 51591-2536
Web site: www.smartmoney.com

Mutual Funds
2200 SW 10th Street
Deerfield Beach, FL 33442-9948
Web site: www.mfmag.com

Worth
P.O. Box 55424
Boulder, CO 80323-5424
Web site: www.worth.com

Newsletters

A. Investing/Stock/Mutual Fund Newsletters

Dow Theory Letters	619-454-0481
DRIP Investor	219-931-6480
Fidelity Insight	617-369-2500
Fidelity Monitor	800-397-3094
Funds Net Insight	800-444-6342
Hulbert Financial Digest	888-485-2378
Moneyletter	800-433-1528
Morningstar Investor	800-876-5005
No-Load Fund Analyst	800-776-9555
No-Load Fund Investor	800-252-2042
The Money Paper	914-381-5400

B. Newsletters with Money-Saving Tips

Cheapskate Monthly	310-630-8845
Living Cheap News	816-523-3161
Skinflint News	813-785-7759
The Banker's Secret Bulletin	914-758-1400
The Penny Pincher	516-724-1868 or 800-417-3669

Most investment newsletters charge between $100 and $225 for an annual subscription. Newsletters that promote thrift and frugal living generally charge between $10 and $20. Trial subscriptions and/or free sample issues are often available. Some investment newsletters claim to provide market-timing advice but a 1997 study found no statistically significant relationship between newsletter forecasts and subsequent market performance.

Newspapers

Barron's (published weekly on Monday)
Dow Jones and Company, Inc.
200 Burnett Road
Chicopee, MA 01020
Web site: www.barrons.com

The Wall Street Journal (published
daily)
200 Burnett Road
Chicopee, MA 01020
Web site: www.wsj.com

Investor's Business Daily (published
daily)
12655 Beatrice Street
Los Angeles, CA 90066
Web site: www.investors.com

Nonprofit Organizations

Alliance for Investor Education
The Alliance is a coalition of government agencies, consumer organizations, and investment industry
groups.
Web site: www.investoreducation.org

*American Association of Retired Persons
(AARP)*
601 E Street, NW
Washington, DC 20049
Web site: www.aarp.org

*American Savings Education Council
(ASEC)*
2121 K Street, NW
Suite 600
Washington, DC 20037-1896
Phone: 202-775-9130
Web site: www.asec.org

Consumer Federation of America
1424 16th Street, NW
Suite 604
Washington, DC 20036
Phone: 202-387-6121

*Employee Benefit Research Institute
(EBRI)*
2121 K Street, NW
Suite 600
Washington, DC 20037-1896
Phone: 202-659-0670
Web site: www.ebri.org

*National Foundation for Consumer
Credit*
8611 Second Avenue
Suite 100
Silver Spring, MD 20910
Phone: 301-589-5600
Web site: www.nfcc.org

*North American Securities
Administrators Association
(NASAA)*
10 G Street, NE
Washington, DC 20001
Phone: 888-84-NASAA or 888-846-
2722
Web site: www.nasaa.org

Software

Fidelity Retirement Planning Thinkware	800-544-8888
Kiplinger's Simply Money	800-773-5445
Kiplinger's Tax Cut	800-235-4060
Managing Your Money (MECA)	800-537-9993
Microsoft Money	800-326-0401
PowerPay Debt Reduction Software	800-797-2251
Prosper (Ernst & Young)	800-225-5945
Quicken Deluxe (Intuit)	800-446-8848
Strong Funds Roth IRA Analyzer	800-368-8644
T. Rowe Price IRA Analyzer	800-541-8353
T. Rowe Price Retirement Planning Kit	800-331-7244
TurboTax (Intuit)	800-446-8848
Vanguard Retirement Planner	800-876-1840

Stock Purchasing Services

First Share
103 South 2nd Street
P.O. Box 222
Westcliffe, CO 81252
Phone: 800-683-0743

The Money Paper
1010 Mamaroneck Avenue
Mamaroneck, NY 10543
Phone: 914-381-5400 or 800-388-9993
Web site: www.moneypaper.com

*National Association of Investors
Corporation (NAIC)*
P.O. Box 220
Royal Oak, MI 48068
Phone: 248-583-6242
Web site: www.better-investing.org

Television Shows

CNBC
Web Site: www.cnbc.com

Headquartered in Fort Lee, New Jersey, CNBC provides up-to-the-minute business news and analysis of financial topics and market trends. Weekday financial programming begins with "This Morning's Business" at 4:30 AM and includes "Market Wrap" at 4 PM and "Business Center" at 7 PM.

CNN Financial Network
Web Site: www.cnnfn.com
Part of the Atlanta-based Cable News Network (CNN), CNN Financial Network includes business and financial news (e.g., market trends) throughout the day. "The MoneyLine News Hour" with host Lou Dobbs airs Monday through Friday at 6:30 PM and 11:30 PM.

Nightly Business Report and *Wall $treet Week (PBS)*
Both shows air on Public Broadcasting Stations (PBS) nationwide. Wall $treet Week, hosted by Louis Rukeyser, is broadcast on PBS networks Friday evening and/or Saturday morning. The program includes one or more guests and regular contributors, called elves, who analyze the stock market's performance and attempt to forecast future trends.

Web Sites

Credit Information

Bankrate Monitor
www.bankrate.com

Credit Reporting Agencies
www.experian.com (Experian)
www.equifax.com (Equifax)
www.tuc.com (Trans Union)

Federal Reserve Board Credit Survey
www.bog.frb.fed.us/pubs/shop/

National Foundation for Consumer Credit
www.nfcc.org

*National Institute for Consumer
Education (NICE)*
www.emich.edu/public/coe/nice/

RAM Research
www.ramresearch.com or
www.cardtrak.com

Ratenet
www.rate.net

Fraud Prevention

Better Business Bureau (BBB) Online
www.bbbonline.org

Internet Fraud Watch
www.fraud.org

Scambusters
www.scambusters.org

General Personal Finance Information

American Express
www.americanexpress.com/advisors

FinanCenter (financial calculators)
www.financenter.com

Financial Literacy Center
www.financialliteracy.com

First Source (financial calculators)
www.1stsource.com

Insurance News Network
www.insure.com

Intuit, Inc.
www.intuit.com

Investorguide
www.investorguide.com

Money Magazine Roth IRA Calculator
www.money.com/rothira

Microsoft Money Insider
www.moneyinsider.msn.com

MoneyMinded
www.moneyminded.com

Money Pages
www.moneypages.com

National Center for Financial Education (NCFE)
www.ncfe.org

Quicken Financial Network
www.qfn.com

Roth IRA Web site
www.rothira.com

Trader's Haven
www.tradershaven.com

U.S.A. Today Money Section
www.usatoday.com/money/mfront.htm

Government Agencies

Consumer Information Center
www.pueblo.gsa.gov

Federal Trade Commission
www.ftc.gov

Internal Revenue Service (IRS)
www.ustreas.gov/treasury/bureaus/irs

National Summit on Retirement Savings
www.saversummit.org

Social Security
www.ssa.gov

U.S. Bureau of the Treasury
www.publicdebt.treas.gov

U.S. Securities and Exchange Commission
www.sec.gov

Housing Information

CNNfn's Mortgage Calculator
www.cnnfn.com/yourmoney/mortcalc

Freddie Mac
www.freddiemac.com

Homefair Salary Calculator (relocation analysis)
www.homefair.com/homefair/cmr/salcalc.html

HSH Associates
www.hsh.com

Improvenet (home contractors)
www.improvenet.com

National Association of REALTORS®
www.realtor.com

National Center for Home Equity Conversion (reverse mortgages)
www.reverse.org

Investment Information

Alliance for Investor Education
www.investoreducation.org

Big Charts
www.bigcharts.com

Bloomberg
www.bloomberg.com

Good Money (socially conscious investing)
www.goodmoney.com

Index Funds Online
www.indexfundsonline.com

Index Investor
www.indexinvestor.com

Investment FAQ (frequently asked questions)
www.invest-faq.com

Investorama
www.investorama.com

Morningstar
www.morningstar.net

Motley Fool
www.fool.com

Mutual Fund Companies Online
www.investorlinks.com/mfcomp.html

Mutual Fund Education Alliance
www.mfea.com

Mutual Funds Interactive
www.brill.com

The Street.Com
www.thestreet.com

Wall Street City
www.wallstreetcity.com

Yahoo Finance
www.quote.yahoo.com

Zacks
www.zacks.com

Public Company Information

DRIP Central
www.dripcentral.com

Hoovers OnLine
www.hoovers.com

NetStock Direct (direct purchase stocks)
www.netstockdirect.com

Society for Direct Investing
www.sdinews.org

Index

232 Index

U
U.S. savings bonds, 145–46, 183–84
U.S. Treasury securities, 140–41, 185
  mutual funds of, 153
  risk, 48
  Treasury Inflation Indexed Security
    (TIIS), 141
Unit investment trusts (UITs), 145,
    152, 185
Unsystematic risk, 47–48
Utility expenses, reducing, 60–61

V
Vacation clubs, 183
Value averaging, 49
Value funds, 156, 182. *See also* Mutual
    fund(s)
Value Line, 156

Vanguard fund family, 152, 154
  Asset Allocation, 104
  index funds, 165, 170
  Life Strategy Funds, 104
  STAR, 182
Variable annuities, 121–22
Voluntary simplicity, 180

W–Z
WEBS, 175
Widowhood, 40
Wilshire 5000 Index, 163, 172
Wilshire 4500 Index, 172
Windfalls, 40, 86–88, 90
World Equity Benchmark Shares, 175
Your Money or Your Life, 181
Zero-coupon bonds, 141–42, 185